Afghanistan:
Crossroads and Kingdoms

My 1970s Peace Corps Service and Recent
Afghan History

Guy Toby Marion

A PEACE CORPS WRITERS BOOK

Afghanistan: Crossroads and Kingdoms
My 1970s Peace Corps Service and Recent Afghan History

A Peace Corps Writers Book — an imprint of
Peace Corps Worldwide

Printed in the United States of America
by Peace Corps Writers of Oakland, California.

For more information, contact peacecorpsworldwide@gmail.com.

Peace Corps Writers and the Peace Corps Writers colophon
are trademarks of PeaceCorpsWorldwide.org.

Editing, layout and design: Robyn J. Harrison

Front cover: Preparing for the hunt. Second from front left is
Abdullah, then Toby, Ashraf and Shah Wali. Behind is the *mirgun*,
his two aides, and on right Sharaf and Ashraf's son.
Photo courtesy Juris Zagarins

ISBN-13: 978-1-950444-69-4
Library of Congress Control Number: 2024900055

First Peace Corps Writers Edition, January 2024

In memory of my parents Jane and Charles,
for love, spirit and support

For my wife Eileen,
and children, Guy and Louisa

Remember, you are just an extra in everyone else's play.
--Franklin Delano Roosevelt

Afghanistan: Crossroads and Kingdoms
My 1970s Peace Corps Service and
Recent Afghan History

Preface   11
Introduction   12

I. PRIST and Peace Corps Training, 1971
  1. PRIST in Denver   15
  2. Arrival in Afghanistan   18
  3. Peace Corps Offices and Training   23
  4. Pashtuns, Afghans and Afghanistan   29
  5. The National Science Center   33
  6. Trips to Jalalabad, Istalif and Kapisa 34
  7. Life in Kabul and Developing Friendships 39
  8. Foreign Agencies and Missions in Afghanistan 47
  9. Trip to Tashkurgan   48
  10. End of Training   55

II. Science Supervisor Year One in Kapisa, 1972
  11. Kapisa and Home in Baku Kham   60
  12. Science Teacher Training   66
  13. Teaching at Local Schools   68
  14. The First Anglo Afghan War   76
  15. Life at Home and Bringing Movies to Kapisa 78
  16. Teaching at Distant Schools   84
  17. Kabul Visits   90
  18. More Teaching at Distant Schools   96
  19. Language, Religion and Women   100
  20. Afghan History from Antiquity to Zahir Shah 111
  21. Year End 1972   116

III. Year Two in Kapisa, 1973
  22. January Trip to Iran   122
  23. NSC Winter Seminar   125
  24. February Trip to India   125

25. Back in Kapisa Teaching with New Confidence 132
26. Possible Job Transfer 138
27. Tragedy at Lycée Mirmasjadi 140
28. Culture—Sex and Humor 142
29. Baku Kham Bazaar 147
30. Visiting Kabul and Logar 150
31. History from King Zahir Shah to Prince Daoud's
1973 Coup d'Etat and the Republic of Afghanistan 153
32. Visits of Senator Chuck Percy and My Parents 156
33. Friends Moving On 163
34. Finishing as Science Supervisor 166

IV. Reupping for a Third Year of Service, Teaching at Kabul University in Faculty of Engineering, 1973–75

35. Move to Kabul and the Faculty of Engineering, Fall
of 1973 171
36. Home Leave 175
37. At the Faculty and Life in Kabul 180
38. Tragedy in the Panjshir River 185
39. Volunteer Living Allowance Study 187
40. Studying Persian Literature 189
41. Hike across Central Afghanistan from Samangan to
Bamiyan 191
42. Keeping the Fast, Ramadan, 1974 222
43. Final Term at the Faculty 224
44. Visit of Secretary of State Henry Kissinger,
November 1, 1974 226
45. Finishing up in Kabul and Heading Home, 1975 234

V. Modern History—Crossroads Again

46. President Daoud to the Soviet-Inspired Coups of
1978–79 and the Democratic Republic of
Afghanistan 241
47. Resistance to the Communist Democratic Republic
of Afghanistan to the Fall of Najibullah in 1992 244

48. Civil War to the Islamic Emirate of Afghanistan
    and 911   246
49. Overthrow of the Taliban in 2001, US and NATO
    and the Islamic Republic of Afghanistan to the
    Return of the Taliban and the Islamic Emirate
    in 2021   249
50. What Happened and Where Afghanistan
    Stands Today   258
51. Looking Forward   262

Afterword   264
Acknowledgments   272
Glossary   274
Bibliography   277
About the Author   279

Afghanistan: Crossroads and Kingdoms

My 1970s Peace Corps Service and Recent Afghan History

Guy Toby Marion

Preface

About twenty years ago I decided to write these memoirs because I wanted to share my experience of being a Peace Corps volunteer in Afghanistan with my children and family. Source material included my letters home that my mother had kept, notebooks and diaries from the time, and more than a thousand negatives, slides, and photographs.

My approach was to weave together the reasons for joining the Peace Corps, the training received, and service work done, the experience of learning another language and adapting to a new culture, and the history and changes in Afghanistan that I saw.

As the new century developed, Afghanistan's recent tragic history continued to unfold, culminating with the withdrawal of American forces in 2021. As my writing continued, I realized that I needed to know much more to understand this bewildering era. And I decided to share this because our longest war had seen so much sacrifice by Americans and suffering by Afghans.

I believe that this memoir adds to the collective knowledge of recent Afghanistan history from the viewpoint of a volunteer who became intimately involved in the culture while working at the grass roots in the Afghan educational system. I hope that readers will take from this an increased understanding of both Afghanistan and America's difficult and tragic efforts to build a modern democracy and modernize Afghanistan.

Introduction

Toward the end of my Peace Corps service in the summer of 1974, I took an almost month-long hike with three friends across central Afghanistan to the high *Hazarajat* mountains.

On day 21 in the early morning, we headed west up from the marshy village of Ajar and met a man who told us that the trail ahead was regularly used by shepherds and *koochis* (nomads), and we had only to follow the path and that there were no turnoffs to be taken. He said that if we walked all day, by evening we would come to a spring.

It was hot and cloudless, dusty, and the air was thin. On dry and treeless rolling hills at 12,000 feet elevation, it felt like we were literally on top of the world, with mountains looming high in the far distance. Up until this day we had been following rivers and creeks, climbing through canyons and huge mountains, and we were never far from water. For the first time I felt fear should we fail to find the spring…

This memoir is about my Peace Corps service in Afghanistan from late 1971 to January 1975, a time of learning, hard work, and fun. It is also about 50 years of pivotal Afghan and American history.

I hope to provide the reader with insights into Afghanistan and America's role in its recent history, and how I served both countries as a volunteer. I also describe many experiences that were fascinating to me.

The reader will learn about the multi-ethnic Afghan culture as well as the disastrous conflicts of the past 50 years. I also attempt to describe Afghanistan's Islamic culture and viewpoint, and its role as a key crossroads of many kingdoms. Some call it the "cockpit of Asia", alluding to its violent past.

I wrote this for my family and to distill what I believe has happened in Afghanistan in the current era. I learned by living and working with the people, then observing Afghanistan over five decades, by reading excellent recent histories and memoirs, and from the perspectives and advice from Afghan and foreign friends.

I learned the Farsi language (Persian, officially called Dari in Afghanistan) fluently and lived in an under-developed province for two years followed by a year-and-a-half teaching at Kabul University. The meanings of words appearing in italics in the text can be found in the glossary at the end of this book.

My joining the Peace Corps was largely a result of coming of age during the turbulent 1960s and graduating from college in 1970. We had seen our national cultural chaos stemming from the Vietnam War, the civil rights movement, the pill, women's lib and drugs. At graduation I had a high draft lottery number and shortly afterwards became exempt from the military draft. After getting a Master's degree in 1971 just before turning 22, I found that I was not yet willing to join the mainstream of American industry and business.

My brother was a Peace Corps volunteer in Guatemala at the time, and I was taken with seeing the world, learning another language, experiencing another culture, and I believed in the obligation to serve the country. The Peace Corps offered me a job as a science teacher supervisor in Afghanistan, and after some reading and advice from mentors, I quickly became intrigued by Afghan and Central Asian history.

The journey began with accepting the offer and being invited to a PRIST in Denver, in late October, 1971.

I

PRIST and Peace Corps Training

1971

1. PRIST in Denver

The first step to becoming a Peace Corps volunteer is vetting. My neighbors in New York told my parents that an FBI agent had been around door-to-door asking questions about me and my family. Soon after this, I was invited to a Pre-Invitational Staging, or PRIST, to be held in Denver, a required step before being invited to join in-country training. When my mother, along with a close high school friend, put me on the airplane at La Guardia, I was surprised that when hugging goodbye, I had a lump in my throat.

Our PRIST began on October 27, 1971. There were lectures and events where we were taught about the Peace Corps experience and Afghanistan. We were also tested and observed, with private interviews by the Trainee Development Officer, a psychologist, to determine if we were suitable for the service ahead.

The first cycle of Peace Corps volunteers to be sent to Afghanistan was Group 1 in 1962. My group of seven Science Teacher Supervisors was part of Cycle 11, in 1971. We were 11A, along with several dozen English teachers in 11B and Food for Work volunteers in 11C.

We in the Science Teacher Supervisor program quickly developed a sense of camaraderie as we had all studied science or engineering and had similar academic backgrounds and temperaments. Our group comprised Charlie Ferrell from Cornell, Dan Kugler from Rochester, Tom Schillinger from Pittsburgh, Juris Zagarins from Massachusetts, Joe Griffin from Virginia, Larry Bennett from the Midwest and Alan Gold from New York.

We were advised that we would get more respect as teachers if we cut our hair short and wore suits which could be cheaply bought used, imported from Germany. We shared hotel rooms. I recognized Charlie Ferrell from winter training in Barton Hall at Cornell where we were both students. Charlie was in track, I played for the tennis team. He ran circles around me on the track. Dan Kugler had come from Hawaii where he'd spent a couple of years surfing and had shoulder length blond hair, straight and beautiful like a Breck girl.

That day after lunch he returned to our conference room with very short hair parted on one side and looking like a high school kid. We all roared with laughter.

We saw a movie showing wheat-colored people dressed in baggy pantaloons, knee-length shirts and turbans, mud houses, streets filled with donkeys, oxen, cars, and buses, and ancient work methods for producing goods and building houses. These images were set against the stark desolation of a brown treeless terrain surrounded by massive mountains. And there were almost no women. It was fascinating, and we looked forward to seeing the mosques, Buzkashi games and large Buddhas. The fruits and bazaars looked incredible. We met our Cross-Cultural Coordinator, Marty Kumorek, who had been in Afghanistan for about five years. Larry Wonderling, the Trainee Development Officer (TDO), told us that Marty was a world authority on Afghanistan.

We also saw a Peace Corps India movie showing volunteers helping Indian women equip a kitchen. The women were squatting on their haunches on the floor cutting up vegetables, stirring big pots, kneading dough for *naan* (bread). The volunteers proudly brought in a table and set up everything on top of it. In the next scene the women were squatting on the table, two-and-a-half feet off the ground, working exactly as they had been before. We all laughed, having had no idea that for them squatting on their haunches was the comfortable way to sit and cook.

A neighbor and high school girl friend of mine sent me the names of two women in Denver that she'd been in college with. Charlie and I gave them a call and we had a couple of evenings of alcohol-infused fun in local pubs. We also went to several art museums, enjoying western masterpieces before the coming dearth of art in Afghanistan.

Another session was on the full-length veil, called *chadri*. This was one of our few sessions with the larger group, which was inspiring, including women and people of more varied backgrounds. A woman wearing *chadri* entered the room of 30 of us and silently sat down. Shortly we started to explore. One volunteer said, "This is strange."

She said, "Not at all." Another asked if it was hot underneath. She answered, "No, it's cool, because the material is light."

Another said that he felt unsure of himself, being seen but unable to see who he was talking to. "When do you wear the *chadri*?"

"When I go outside."

"Where can you go?"

"Anywhere I like, to the bazaar, school, government offices."

"What happens when you go to the bazaar?"

"Men get out of my way."

"Is it okay for men to talk to you?"

"Yes, of course."

"Can I walk with you?"

"Sure, but you mustn't invade my space."

Unbeknownst to us, this session touched on much of what we would learn during our service.

At the end of PRIST, after the TDO had passed us as suitable to take the next step of training in Afghanistan to be Peace Corps volunteers (PCVs), we went to the Veterans Administration hospital in Denver for six immunizations. This was sobering. The corridors and waiting rooms were filled with veterans, mostly our age or younger, returning from Vietnam. Many were missing limbs, on crutches or bandaged. Most of us were opposed to the war but coming face to face with those who had suffered so much appalled us, and we had profound sympathy for them. I recall feeling somewhat unsteady seeing such devastation and the looks from injured servicemen as they waited in line for attention.

The PRIST was a helpful transition that eased us into the coming culture shock of life in Afghanistan. I was filled with curiosity and apprehension for what was to come, but already certain this was going to be a great experience. We were also told that either during the PRIST or during training it was acceptable to decide to drop out and not go forward, and that we should only commit to becoming Peace Corps volunteers when we believed we could complete our two years of service.

From Denver we flew to Dulles Airport in DC for a flight to Rome. At Dulles we were transported between gates in new, huge mobile lounges that seemed like something from the future. Decades later I was to realize they never caught on.

We had a 28-hour stopover in Rome. Passing over the Alps in the early morning was breathtaking, not at all like the "goddamned crater on the moon" that Marty described of his first flight into Afghanistan. We walked off the plane in Rome into sunshine and fresh air, happy to be in Italy. In the center of the old city the roads were jammed with tiny Fiats. All along the road were scores of parked cars with one huge car in the distance towering over all others. When we got close, we saw to our surprise that it was a VW Beetle. We weren't in Kansas anymore.

Our hotel was the Validier, a classic stone and marble structure a block off the Piazza del Popolo. Joe and I hung together and soon met two young American women, UCLA students, whose company we enjoyed, again fearing the dearth that was approaching us. We spent time sightseeing: the Trevi Fountain, cathedrals, Michelangelo's Moses at San Pietro, the Coliseum, the Temple of Saturnus, of Romulus, of Caesar.

From here we flew to beautiful Beirut, Lebanon, covered with green vegetation, gardens and multi-story apartment buildings. The airport roof was lined with hundreds of people. They were waiting to see the first Boeing 747 on a round-the-world flight – landing in Beirut, Tehran, New Delhi. Soon we were on our way to a night landing in Tehran, Iran. The city was flat, orderly, and with strings of lights seeming like Christmas time at home. In the small airport, we sat at the bar drinking rum and Coke, waiting for our early morning flight to Afghanistan, laughing at occasional bursts of the popular song "I want to go home."

2. Arrival in Afghanistan

During the one-and-a-half-hour flight from Tehran to Kabul we saw only sand, brown mountains and massive dust storms, some rising to our 37,000 ft elevation. We expected a change in the terrain and to see trees and vegetation as we flew across the desert and began to rise into the mountains, but no such change occurred and soon mountains were to our right and left as we descended into Kabul. I was in awe of the terrain, but not filled with apprehension, as we had expected this. As we taxied to the airport building in the Iran Airlines Boeing 737, we passed soldiers, ancient trucks and tanks, and AAF (Afghan Airlines) prop planes, including a biplane.

We arrived in Kabul to a royal reception—not for us, but for the brother of the Shah, the King of Iran. There was a gallery of several hundred atop the airport, two small formations of soldiers at attention including a marching band, and from the plane's front exit was a long red carpet leading to a black and polished 1968 Cadillac, 1955 Cadillac, 1955 Buick and several '62 and '63 Chevys. We exited thru the rear of the plane. The band began a cacophonous rendering of Iran's national anthem. Inside the airport, waiting to carry bags, were Afghan porters with dark brown skin and deeply lined faces, wearing turbans and baggy pants and shirts or western suits that didn't fit and were saturated with dust.

We were rushed through customs and headed into town piled into Peace Corps trucks with drivers dressed in western clothing and wearing *karakul* caps. We passed heavily laden burros and camels. We saw carts made from a truck axle with tires and a wooden platform laden with goods pushed and pulled by two men. Cows, turkeys, chickens, donkeys, camels and sheep were on the road

Bala Hissar, the ancient Kabul fortress

and roadsides, tended by their owners. The road narrowed as we got into the city, where the dusty streets were lined with trees. The architecture was mostly mud houses painted white, dotted with western style buildings.

Although sleepless for a day and a half, we were hustled into the training center, divided into classes and sent upstairs for an hour of language training. This irked us, as we were tired and hungry. Following class, we were back downstairs in the conference room for introductions and explanations, then driven to our training house several blocks away. We met our cook named Omar who served us a fine meal of rice, meat, vegetables and *naan*. We remembered nothing of the morning's language lesson and commented somewhat resentfully how ill-timed it had been. Juris and I took a walk after lunch, then returned "home" to collapse on the wooden frame *charpoi* ("four feet") beds, made with crisscrossed straw ropes supporting stuffed cotton mattresses in otherwise empty bedrooms. Awaking at 2:00 a.m., to our surprise we could repeat every phrase of the language lesson.

A camel driver with loaded camels was a common sight.

After early tea we took another walk from 3:00 to 5:00 a.m. It was bitterly cold. Men were up and about, and donkeys were braying. It was *jeshun* (the holy month of Ramadan and daytime fasting), and people were up for the early morning meals before daybreak. We saw a number of policemen on patrol, and they made me nervous because overseas travel and the uncertainty of foreign police were new to me and made me fearful at that time. I was to learn that police normally acted in deference to the tiny, educated classes and respectable foreigners, a typical third world situation.

My most interesting observations? The dust, the hazy distant mountains, the women in veils (maybe three-quarters in Kabul) who looked like ghosts ephemerally fleeing down the streets, and the apparent pride and purposefulness of the people, evoking no pity from us westerners. Beggars were rare, and carpenters, wood choppers, craftsmen, shopkeepers abounded, working with the same tools and methods as their forefathers. The city was dirty and, by our standards, the people seemed to know little of cleanliness, but we were told that those who survived the 60% infant mortality rate were strong.

Horse drawn *gawdi* used for transport throughout Afghanistan

Map 1: Kabul 1967

1. Share Naw
2. Royal Palace
3. Prime Ministry
4. U.S. Embassy
5. British Embassy
6. Faculty of Engineering
7. Kabul University
8. Deh Mazang
9. Kabul Stadium
10. Bala Hisar Fort
11. Tapa-I-Bibimahro
12. Qalai Fatullah
13. Share Naw Park
14. Kabul Hotel
15. Khyber Restaurant
16. Sor Bazaar
17. Jada-I-Maywand Avenue
18. Kabul River
19. Kote Sangi
20. Kohe Aliabad
21. Road to Kohistan
22. Polytechnic Institute
23. Bagh-I-Bala Café
24. Karte Char

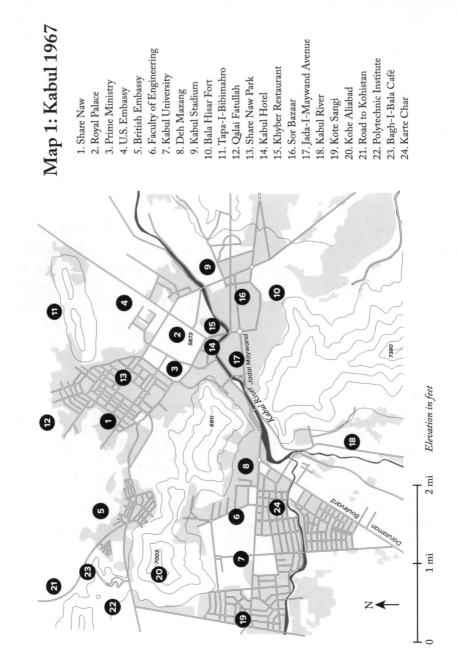

Elevation in feet

N

0   1 mi   2 mi

3. Peace Corps Offices and Training

Peace Corps had a large compound on the main drag of Share Naw—New City—in the northern half of Kabul, just up the main road from Chicken Street, where live chickens were sold and slaughtered. In this area were many small hotels, hostels and bars frequented by World Travelers (WTs), otherwise known as hippies.

The Peace Corps compound was a three-story training center on the back street, a central parking area and the two-story administration building on the front main street. PC had a number of International Harvester trucks that entered through a large entrance gap in the training building. These vehicles were excellent pickup trucks with two rows of seats for six or more.

Our Peace Corps Country Director was Lou Mitchell, a charismatic and outgoing advocate for both the PC and Afghanistan. He was supported by a staff including Don Croll, Language Director; Marty Kumorek, Cross Culture; Dave Chamberlain, Accounting & Admin; Abdul Matin, Programs; Dr. Rollins, heading the Medical Department; and Carl Johnston, the psychologist. There was a large group of language teachers, clerks, drivers, and janitors. There was

Kabul Shah Dushamshire Mosque on the banks of the Kabul River

a sense of excitement and camaraderie amongst everyone, and we quickly got to know most of the staff and benefited from their help and advice.

Abdul Matin looked after all work programs and volunteers, and UCLA grad Mohamed Yassin was one of the key people for programs and assignments, and we all quickly identified with him. He told us of his first breakfast at a UCLA cafeteria where he chose corn flakes and proceeded to eat them dry from a bowl, wondering how Americans could eat this for breakfast. Soon he found out that milk plus fruit or sugar was the way to eat cereal. He also once stayed at the home of an American friend, and arriving before the host, had been told to help himself to whatever was in the cupboards. He was aghast the next day to learn that he'd eaten a can of dog food.

The staff regularly turned over, with Dr. Rollins being replaced by Dr. Dean Johnson, assisted by an able local nurse named Sajia. John Guyer, the brother-in-law of Senator Chuck Percy, replaced Country Director Lou Mitchell, who returned to Washington to stay active in international affairs. There was also a psychologist

Kabul in spring looking east along Jadai Maywand. Shah Dushamshire Mosque is central left, the Kabul Friday Mosque minaret is distant left.

whose responsibility it was to assess our fitness and help us adjust to Afghanistan. From time to time, trainees and volunteers would wash out or quit.

There were frequent all-hands meetings for volunteers and staff, as well as parties and socializing. All in all, we were well looked after and believed we were part of a good program.

Five of us—Juris, Tom, Dan, Joe and I—were assigned to a training house a few blocks from the PC training center and the Share Naw Park. It was a cement structure with a living room and dining room, kitchen with servants' quarters behind it, three bedrooms, and a bathroom with a western toilet. It was sparsely furnished, so we got accustomed to sitting on the floor or our beds. The site was in the front of our landlord's large home and garden, accessed thru a metal gate to the side. Our landlord was a respected medical doctor and an astute political cartoonist for a local newspaper. He spoke English and was welcoming and friendly, and he had three little girls who would climb up from their driveway and sit on the windowsill in the living room and talk with us. They were lively and cute, and made us feel at home. They also had some international knowledge and liked to talk about movies and their favorite stars, like "guriguri peck," Gregory Peck. They spoke Farsi to us slowly and carefully, helping us to improve our language.

Training was Monday to Friday, nine to five. As we would be going to Farsi speaking provinces, we had Farsi language training every day for most of the day. As teacher trainers, our communication skills were critical and so our training was expanded to four months long, more than the one to two for other volunteers. Farsi is written in the Arabic script with 26 letters, written from right to left. We were surprised that it was easy to learn the alphabet, probably because we scientists and engineers in college had learned the Greek alphabet used for equations and laws.

We were taught about the renowned hospitality of the locals. Tawab Assifi described them like this:

> Afghans are known for their hospitality. If anyone comes
> to an Afghan home and seeks refuge, he or she will be

accepted as a guest and taken care of until the time comes when he or she chooses to leave. Afghans, no matter how poor they are, will share whatever they have with anyone in need who comes to their house. Afghans will fight for the rights of property, dignity, and the honor of any member of their family, clan, or tribe, even if it requires personal sacrifice." (Assifi, p. 289)

An interesting aside to this was the common good-natured bantering that hosts would give you when you were the guest, saying that coming had been up to you, but leaving was up to them. They'd laugh and say you mustn't have enjoyed yourself or liked the food, please eat more, please share more time with us. All in good fun.

We also found out that, as in many Asian cultures, it's quite okay to ask another person his salary and how much she paid for something. Such info is openly shared, and they think us strange that we hide this kind of info. We would also later learn such customs as walking and reading at the same time is dangerous, the lid of a cooking pot should always be set upside down so that what faces the food cannot get dirty, and that one shouldn't eat the blackened part of bread because it causes cancer.

We met with our employer the National Science Center (NSC) and Americans from other official missions to Afghanistan. We participated in cross-cultural lectures, safety and security discussions, administrative briefings, regular quarterly immunizations, and training trips. New trainee cycles continued to arrive, assigned to programs: most commonly English teachers, healthcare workers, agricultural extension agents and sometimes unique assignments like journalism. All jobs were based on requests from the Afghan government.

Early on we met with US Ambassador Robert G. Neumann, who was born in Vienna and emigrated to America, eventually becoming a political scientist and professor at UCLA. A moderate Republican, he was appointed Ambassador by Lyndon Johnson. He addressed about 50 of us. The theme of his presentation was that the fundamental difference between Afghanistan, a backward country with over 90%

illiteracy, and the USA was America's democratic government and the rule of law, which had allowed for our stability and development. As a chemical engineer, I was skeptical, thinking that technology was a big reason for our success. Later in life I came to appreciate that how a country functions is deeply tied to its political and educational structure and the bedrock of the rule of law.

Another important lecture was with our first PC doctor, nearing completion of his tour of duty. He told us never to drink the local water without boiling or putting in iodine tablets, to soak all vegetables and fruit in iodine treated water, and that raw lettuce and fruits like strawberries cannot be cleaned. He warned of the prevalence of amoebic dysentery from unclean water, which would make us sick with sometimes violent diarrhea and would require treatment with tetracycline, a strong antibiotic. He also warned of other dangers such as hepatitis and infections from wounds. In general, most volunteers were careful about the eating instructions,

Welcome party at Dr. Johnson's house. Seated from right are Mark Svendsen, Tom Schillinger, Dr. Johnson. Bottom left is Dr. Rollins. Charlie Ferrell is half hidden behind navy sweater on left.

although many if not most nonetheless would get amoebic dysentery because of the difficulty of following all the rules. Afghan hospitality had a role here, as it was tough to turn away fresh melons and mulberries and many other foods in season.

He warned against smoking hashish, saying that Afghan hash was incredibly powerful and described an incident where a local man smoked it and, in his delirium, cut off his penis. This advice we received with polite silence. During the turbulent 1960s, most of us had taken part in war protests and learned to smoke marijuana in college. However, it was PC policy that smoking hash was grounds for immediate termination. So, for better or worse, we adapted to this the same way that we adapted to New York Governor Rockefeller's recent law of 25-year prison sentences for possession of marijuana: with great care. This was an "us vs. them" issue also related to the Vietnam War. So, while not right, we lost no sleep over sneaking around and occasionally smoking dope.

One of the best parts of training was cultural trips, with busloads of trainees and staff visiting rural areas, historical sites and future

A karachi pulled by two men transporting carpets

28

workplaces. The trips were like school outings, and we learned not to be surprised when the bus stopped at night and everyone jumped out to pee, with men and women on opposite sides of the road.

We also brought the teachers home to our training houses and shared meals with them, learned to play card games, board games like checkers, chess and carroms played with the hands. There was a cultural awakening one evening when a Pashto teacher cheated at cards, and when caught he laughed good naturedly, demonstrating that "all's fair in games." Over the years I learned an Asian platitude that "one peek is worth a thousand finesses."

We also learned about bargaining from day one. Afghans bargain for nearly everything. Taxi rides were first up because there were no taxi meters at that time in Afghanistan. The method was to hail a taxi and tell him your destination and he'd call out a price. It cost Afs 30 (about 33 US cents) to go across the city, but drivers would offer 50 to foreigners, then you'd reply no, too expensive, it should be 30. He'd say, "but you are three people," which was irrelevant. After haggling back and forth, you'd eventually get your fair price. Similarly, buying chicken from the chicken bazaar: you'd watch the head being chopped off and the feathers plucked before you agreed on a price and took your bird home wrapped in newspaper. We had to learn that this was normal and a game, and your weapon was to take it or leave it.

4. Pashtuns, Afghans and Afghanistan

Afghanistan in 1971 was desperately poor but had an ancient Islamic culture and a Pashtun monarchy. The population was about half Pashtun with the balance Farsi-speaking minorities descended from ancient Central Asian empires. The largest minority groups were Tajik, Uzbek, Turkoman and Hazara. The structure of their society was long established, and people respected authority and knew their roles. Learning about the culture, religion and history of the Afghan people was essential to being able to function in our jobs and get along with local folks.

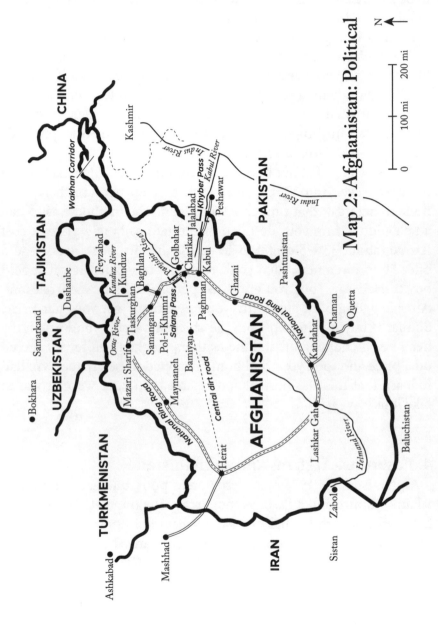

Map 2: Afghanistan: Political

One of the first things we learned was that one meaning of "Afghan" was "Pashtun", the ethnic tribes in the south and east of Afghanistan. They are also known as Pakhtoons or Pathans (pronounced Pattán), the word the British used for this fiercely independent people living along the Northwest Frontier of British India. Pakistan also had about twice the number of Pashtuns as Afghanistan. If a Tajik is asked if he is an Afghan, he might say yes, meaning an Afghan citizen. If asked if he is Afghan, he might say no, I'm a Tajik.

The question arose: why were Kabul citizens and the educated elite Farsi speaking if the leaders and the largest population were Pashtun? From the spread of Islam to Central Asia in the 7th to 10th centuries, Dari, or Farsi, was created from the mixing of ancient Pahlavi (old Persian) and Arabic and became the dominant language for centuries of different empires and regimes, today including Iran, Afghanistan and Tajikistan. Kabul was in the center of this geography, and Farsi had become its main language since early times.

Thus modern generations of Pashtuns in Kabul learned to speak Farsi as their first language, and it was a challenge for them to learn Pashtu. Few managed it as Pashtu is notoriously difficult. An often-told story was that you could always tell a young ethnic Pashtun who is a Farsi speaker by asking him to say in Pashtu, "the dog bit me." Farsi speakers mangle this, ending up saying, "I bit the dog," to great laughter.

Pashtuns are dominant in the south and east, as well as in northwest Pakistan. They also make up most of the *koochis*, the nomads who travel back and forth from the lowlands to the highlands in Central Afghanistan. The next two largest ethnic groups are Tajik in the northeast and Uzbek in north central. Hazara are in the very central mountains while pockets of Turkoman live along the norther border. Nearly all are Sunni Muslims except for Hazara and the people near Herat and bordering Iran on the west, who are Shia.

The Pashtun larger population and the strength and ferocity of their tribes have meant that the Pashtuns have always led Afghanistan. Even larger numbers of Pashtuns in Pakistan complicate this.

Pashtuns are united by an ancient culture and language and since the 18th century have not been colonized or conquered, making them both proud and unabashed. Nonetheless from ancient times Afghanistan has been an historical crossroads, seeing many wars and changes of empire, thus being dubbed by some as the "cockpit of Asia," meaning where battles are fought for the control of Central Asia.

Pashtun tribes are independent by nature but come together in times of need, and share an Islamic tradition, literature, and civilized heritage of thousands of years. The tribes are governed by *Loya Jirga,* large meetings of elders ("white beards") who together discuss and decide policies by consensus, often taking days. This is their form of democracy. To us it is impressive, bringing to mind George Washington's view that decried parties in favor of political unity. The Pashtuns have a saying for family strength and security: "Against my enemies give me cousins, against my cousins give me brothers and against my brothers give me sons." And for revenge, they say, "If you take your revenge in a hundred years, you are being hasty."

Pashtun tribes make up the southern and eastern provinces, each with a reputation. For example, the Laghmanis, east of Kapisa, are

Pashtun *koochis*, nomads, in front of their campsite by the roadside. These are the most downtrodden of the Afghans.

said to be clever, able to trick the devil. The story goes that the Laghmani and the devil were on a long walk and agreed that each would carry the other for as long as the rider could sing a song. The devil rode first and sang a very long song, but eventually finished and had to carry the Laghmani, who climbed on the devil's shoulders and started "na na na, na na na, na na na na na na…", a tune with no ending.

5. The National Science Center

As science teacher trainers, we seven PCVs worked for The National Science Center which was established by the Ministry of Education with support from UNESCO, and headed by Dr. Ghaznowi, who had a doctorate in education from Columbia University in New York. He was a serious person who always looked formal and well dressed in a dark blue suit.

One of the NSC's key missions was to bring science education to high school students by training their teachers to perform their school textbook experiments for the first time. Afghanistan's high schools were patterned after the French system, and hence called lycées, where the students studied biology, chemistry, and physics every year, with two or three classes per subject per week. There were no laboratories or equipment, hence no lab work. Students simply needed to memorize the words of the textbooks and repeat them on tests to receive high grades. This also fit culturally, as learning from time immemorial was largely memorizing poetry and the Qran.

The NSC built science kits that were packed into wooden boxes the size of large suitcases. The kits contained all the equipment needed for the textbook science experiments. In addition, we would be using commercial kits used in education in the west and called Oddo Carini Physics and Singer Discovery. We were to be assigned to local provinces to work alongside NSC local counterparts. Together we would distribute these kits, books and teaching guides (to be developed by us) to middle and high school math and science teachers and instruct them in their use. The goal was to raise the standard of education at the grass roots level. We would be required to travel continuously throughout our assigned province to numerous local schools.

Our local counterparts were graduates of Kabul University (*Pohontoon*-i-Kabul), Kabul Polytechnic and several teacher training colleges. Kabul University had been established by the western nations, who provided faculty and facilities and trained local faculty. The faculty of engineering was from the USA, medicine from France, arts and sciences from the UK and architecture from Germany. Another tertiary college, the Polytechnic, was an engineering and technical college supported by the USSR.

We had several meetings at the NSC to meet our counterparts and to prepare us for the upcoming work. We also wrote practice lessons and made presentations to the other trainees and teachers for critiques to improve our work.

6. Trips to Jalalabad, Istalif and Kapisa

Trips to see the country and experience the culture were an important part of training. We went to Jalalabad in eastern Afghanistan in early December, just after the start of the Indo-Pakistan War of 1971. It was a four-hour bus ride for us and our teachers on a two-lane paved road following the Kabul River running east from Kabul through the Tangi Gharu, a spectacular pass of winding switchbacks dropping vertically 4,000 feet. The road was protected by low, cemented stone walls overlooking the precipitous drop off. At the bottom, the land spread out and was dotted with mud houses, cultivated land and palm trees. The temperature rose from the frigid winter weather in Kabul at 5,000 feet elevation to a balmy mid 70°F in the valley.

Our hotel in Jalalabad was filled with Americans, most from the US Embassy and the USAID Mission in Pakistan, who had been evacuated through the Khyber Pass to be safe from the war. We spent several days sightseeing and learning about this easternmost part of Afghanistan close to the Pakistan border. We visited the Gandara Museum, which housed exquisite foot-high stone sculptures from the Buddhist era prior to the advent of Islam.

Even as Pakistan and India were waging war, we had practically no news. It appeared to be going badly for Pakistan. There were rumors that Afghanistan might join in to help its Muslim brother, later understood to be wildly inaccurate speculation given the long-term antagonism between the two countries. The war lasted from December 3 to 16, when Pakistan capitulated, losing East Pakistan which soon became Bangladesh.

The next provincial trip was to the town of Golbahar in Kapisa Province, several hours northeast of Kabul. We were three trainees, our language teacher and her servant, and a Panjshiri teacher from the National Science Center. Just south of the town was the Golbahar Textile Factory, a German aid project and a somewhat modern presence. We stayed in the factory hotel, which had electricity and running water. The rooms were furnished with army barracks type metal beds and electric heaters. Guests brought their own towels, toilet paper, and hangers. Our teacher was the prime minister's niece, and hence we were met by the

Ancient Buddhist 12-inch high sculptures from the 7th century at the base of a shrine in Ghandara

commandant (chief of police) and the provincial mudir sahib (director of education) and were later invited to the governor's house.

The purpose of this trip was to visit two boys' and one girls' lycées and determine their suitability for a Peace Corps volunteer to work there. We were to find out about the availability of science equipment, its utilization, and the education level of the teachers. However, it wasn't too revealing as they had prepared a good show in the classes we attended. The seniors who observed the chemical neutralization of hydrochloric acid with sodium hydroxide knew all the answers. The job looked to be interesting with some frustrations.

We enjoyed galivanting after the work was finished. We hired a jeep and drove up the dirt road into the mountains to villages along the Panjshir River Valley. The scenery was massive, dusty, jagged rock mountains reaching up into a clear blue cloudless sky. The high brown-gray snow color scheme was regularly broken along the river by terraced green farmland surrounding small villages of mud houses.

That day we also experienced culture shock. We had with us two tins of corned beef and prawns and a box of Coca Cola for lunch. We

The Panjshir River and cultivated valley in the Hindu Kush Mountains, looking downriver with flat topped adobe houses in the distance

stopped at a small village cut into the mountains, causing a flurry of activity. A young man about my age promptly peeled and broke a hardboiled egg in two, giving me half. We were hustled to the second floor of a home, where we sat on straw mats leaning against poplar support poles. We were facing the open air, seeing the bright sun, blue sky, and many children on the street garbed in blues, purples, reds, greens. Shortly, many plates of food were brought to us: fried eggs in mutton oil, naan, tea, hot peppers, grapes. We feasted on this and the corned beef, egg and prawn sandwiches, washed down with Coke and tea. Then came a monstrous dish of qabuli pilau—rice laced with sliced carrots and raisins, which we ate with our hands. Attendants sat on their haunches serving us, pouring water on our oily hands to cleanse them, and bringing more tea and food.

After the meal we took pictures and were shown wooden toys. We left satiated, happy and having paid 150 Afghanis (about two dollars) for the lunch.

After crossing several shaky wooden bridges over the rushing rapids and a few jaunts into the hills, we headed home. For a second time we had to stop to let a shepherd with hundreds of sheep clear the road. We dropped off the Panjshiri teacher, later to be one of

Our trainee house guard's family, third from right in front of their qala (family compound) with grandfather, father, uncle, cousins and children

37

my counterparts. He climbed far down to the river, took off his suit pants and forded the now lazy river, and climbed to his village home on the other side.

On another trip, Juris and I joined our house guard on a venture to his home 15 miles north of Kabul. We spent a fabulous 40 hours, straight out of the Middle Ages. The guard's extended family lived in a large mud castle complex. We met his uncles and brothers, and many children including two young cousins who had been betrothed to each other at ages two and three. There was no electricity nor machines of any sort. The families lived an entirely agricultural existence.

We saw a flour mill, called an asia, driven by water turning a wooden propeller connected to a millstone in the mill. They had no English, so we could only try to communicate in Farsi, our language training still at the beginning.

I also tried neswar, Afghan snuff, for the first time, a green mixture of tobacco and white lime tucked under the tongue. It makes the user dizzy, a buzz somewhat like that from tobacco. Though a dirty and uncouth habit, I would occasionally use it over the following years,

Inside an "asia" (pronounced ossiyah): a water powered flour mill with two hoppers on the right gravity feeding millstones and miller tying off a burlap sack of flour

part of experiencing what the locals do. Where it is used there are dark green patches on the mud floors and spittoons in teahouses. We also learned that, when necessary, clay pebbles are used in place of toilet paper.

7. Life in Kabul and Developing Friendships

In addition to language lessons, lectures, trips, and parties during training, we also developed bonds and friendships that were to last for years.

One of the first people I got to know was Marty Kumorek, the Cross-Cultural Consultant on the Peace Corps Staff, whom we met in Denver. He had been a volunteer in Afghanistan teaching English at the college level and had learned Farsi well. His abilities and interest in the country led him to stay for years. By the time we arrived he was an icon, sharing his learning earnestly with all and a man about town, well known to diplomatic, education, and aid people in Kabul. He lived in a large, well-appointed house in Share Naw, managed by his excellent cook and the cook's son. Marty was

Istalif in winter looking in the direction of the Hindu Kush Mountains and the Salang Pass

very generous and frequently invited volunteers and other guests to his soirées and dinners, with delicious food and flowing liquor. This began an enduring friendship as well as mentorship.

Another person I got to know was Heidar Nowrouz, the Cultural Director in Peace Corps, who was five years older than I. Heidar's father was named Nowrouz Khan because he was born on *nowrouz*, New Year's Day in the solar Hijri or Persian calendar, the first day of spring. His father was a brilliant student and became the personal secretary of the Pashtun king, Zahir Shah. It was said that Nowrouz Khan had memorized the Qran by the time he was a teenager, as well as the works of many of the famous poets. He was Pashtun from Logar Province, southwest of Kabul and had two wives and 13 sons and four daughters. Heidar was son of the younger wife, known by the nickname of Shirin Jan ("sweet dear"), who had eight sons and two daughters. Heidar was the fourth son, after Hussein, Feroz, and Rahman, and before Akbar and Asghar, twins, and Daoud.

Afghans do not share the names of their women with outsiders, considering this dishonorable. We were told the story of the Afghan

Marty Kumorek (right), Director of Culture in Peace Corps, with a visiting professor from a Buffalo university

40

and the Frenchman who were arguing and about to fight. The Afghan asked what the Frenchman's mother's name was. Perplexed, he replied "Marie." The Afghan scoffed and walked away saying he couldn't be bothered to fight with a man who had no honor.

The two halves of the Nowrouz family lived on a large compound in Guzargah in northwest Kabul, beyond the narrow passage between the mountains running east and west through the city. The compound was on the banks of the Kabul River and had a wall down the middle, separating the two wives' homes. According to Muslim law, the wives were equally cared for in every respect: size of house, area of compound, money, etc. Heidar was previously in the military and trained in America, and sadly, his father passed during that time.

Heidar and family often had large parties in their large two-story home made of adobe with very thick external walls. The large living and formal dining rooms were L-shaped. Tables in the center would be piled high with Afghan dishes: *qabuli pilau* (fried rice infused with raisins and carrot strips), lamb kebab, roast chicken, yogurt and cucumbers, *naan*, purple onions, fruit and melons of all types, and sweets, like baklava. The men often drank liquor, sometimes

Mark Svendsen and Heidar Nowrouz

41

surreptitiously, sometimes openly, depending on who the guests were. Juris also became a good friend of Heidar, and we often attended these parties together.

Heidar and I started hanging out regularly and shared our experiences in America and in Afghanistan. Later, he would sometimes visit me in Kapisa, and I would stay in his home in Kabul after we had been to a party, dinner, movie or poker night. He drank with us and sometimes got high with us, the only staff member whom we trusted. His teaching and insights in poetry, history and philosophy were eye opening, and he never let us Americans get away with lazy thinking about our two cultures. This was not simply self-protective; he was quick to recognize and point out insincerity or hypocrisy. For example, when Americans would criticize Muslims for drinking alcohol, forbidden by Islam, he would point out that Christians had pre-marital sex, though this also was forbidden by religion. Another example was our preaching peace while we made war in Vietnam. Or that we, too, told lies as a social salve, such as saying that a dinner was delicious when it wasn't. A Persian poem says that "the lie that spreads peace is better than the truth which causes anger."

Learning about the culture and how it differed from our own was never ending. Heidar told me of how surprised he had been when he first heard of a death certificate. Why would anyone need that? He laughed at why the Democrats would have the donkey as a mascot, *khar* (donkey) being the most common Afghan insult for a fool. I explained that it came from teamsters, working the donkeys for transport long before cars and trucks.

Our language director was Don Croll, from Poughkeepsie, New York, who came to Kabul on a short-term contract before going to Iran on a Fulbright Scholarship to work on a PhD in Farsi studies. Don had been a volunteer in Iran, and spoke the language brilliantly, obviously with an Iranian accent. This comparison with Afghan Farsi might be similar to Oxford English vs. American country speech. Don's wife Marcia and daughter Nora were with him. He was full of life, always ready for a challenge and had many funny and interesting stories from his time in Iran. He told of the young Peace Corps volunteer architect given the job of designing a rural town hall. He decided to make the windows at the top of the walls shaped like the letter U. But in Iran such windows would always be shaped as arches, round at the top, not the bottom. When finished, the Iranians would all chuckle good naturedly that the building had been designed by a young American who mistakenly built the windows upside down.

Juris and I also became buddies and often hung out together. We later traveled to Iran and India together. Our Massachusetts and MIT background, as well as love of camping and the outdoors were shared experiences. He was older than I and sometimes interestingly outspoken and made good friends with the Afghans and his work mates.

I also got to know and enjoy the company of Mark and Robin Luce, who along with Juris, were based in Ghazni. Years later Robin married Juris and went back to her maiden name, Robin Varnum. Recently she wrote an excellent memoir of her time in Peace Corps. Bill Barlak was another interesting guy, a Ukrainian American volunteer based in Kabul who hung with Juris, Mark and Robin and was an entertaining conversationalist.

Other close friends from Peace Corps included John and Denise Blake who joined me in Kapisa during my first year there. They had been in Peace Corps in South America, and when he washed out and returned to the States, they reapplied and were assigned to Afghanistan, marrying in the interim. He was from Texas and she from Pennsylvania, and they were devoted to one another while being very idealistic and at the same time clear headed about the world.

Juris Zagarins with his cat named Peshak (means cat in Farsi) in our training house

I also got to know Mark Svendsen, a second time PCV who worked on the Food for Work Program launched to address the current drought and famine and who was my roommate in Kapisa during my first year. His knowledge of the country and how Peace Corps and Afghanistan worked were a big help, and he became a close friend.

My class in Farsi training was taught by Zarghuna Qaderi. She was the niece of the Prime Minister and part of a large and distinguished Pashtun family originally from Laghman, a province east of Kabul. She was an excellent teacher, and I learned much from her, including poetry and stories. We also socialized and did things together. One of my PCV friends correctly called this bold, and we had to be very careful. We would meet at parties and sometimes go for a ride with some of her older friends who had a car. The culture of Kabul was, to a degree, liberated amongst the upper and educated classes. There were girls' high schools and many women Kabul University students, who never wore the *chadri*. I knew, and saw from Heidar and his friends and family, that young people dated and partied, usually surreptitiously.

At Christmas and American New Year, we joined other volunteers and met Embassy and USAID folk to party and share our rich experiences in this exotic land. We felt we were starting to get our feet on the ground. The sights and sounds were still startling, such as donkeys braying at 3 a.m. to start the day, the incessant sound of horns honking in Share Naw, the modern part of the city, and the delicious smell of lamb kebab barbecuing over charcoal beds laid in 10-inch diameter iron pipes cut in half on the sidewalks in front of restaurants.

One day Dan Kugler came home to our training house and said, "I did it!"

"What?" we asked.

He had stopped into one of the kebab restaurants and eaten kebab. We had all been afraid of this because, while it smelled great, the hygiene looked fearful. But he said it was delicious, with the rich brown wheat naan, spices of ground dried grapes and pepper, and sweet tea. After this, the dam was broken, and we all began to eat all types of local foods.

I soon began to understand that our American diet at that time was quite parochial. My Indian flat mate in grad school had told me that in India they were traditionally vegetarian, describing cauliflower as a favorite. I was amazed and wondered how that could be interesting. He told me there were scores of ways to cook cauliflower, and now I was starting to learn this. In the 1960s, we didn't know how to eat spaghetti, by twirling it on a spoon, and thought raw fish, a Japanese specialty, was disgusting. I developed a taste for many foods in Afghanistan, with the simple purple onion a quintessentially common vegetable that I learned to love.

The summer before I joined Peace Corps, a Chinese fellow at Union Carbide told me that Afghanistan was like the Middle Ages, and I should have believed him. For every car, bus, and truck, mostly old, there was a donkey, a cow, a chicken, and a shop at least several times over, and this was modern Kabul. Mud houses, turbans, *karakul* hats, and baggy pants and shirts far outnumbered western dress and modern looking (but quite basic) apartments. We learned that in Afghanistan recycling was not a catch phrase but a way of life, as everything was used and reused. And poverty was not as simple as lack of a tuition stipend.

The terrain was best described as a crater on the moon: the dust unimaginable, and the jagged mountains that cut straight through Kabul were treeless and brown. Dust storms were called *khak bod*, and when they blew, people stayed indoors or wrapped themselves with a shroud or turban covering all but a slit for the eyes.

Afghanistan was in its second year of long-term drought and facing famine. Nonetheless, the bazaars were filled with fruits and vegetables, and buying was an interesting game for those of us with limited language and bargaining skills. The open-air butcher shops were not like our supermarkets. Lamb carcasses hung from hooks, and the butcher cut off a few pounds and handed it to us dripping blood, unless we asked him to wrap it in newspaper.

The general population in Afghanistan, while poor, were spirited. Beggars were rare, and everywhere people worked hard using the same methods handed down by their fathers, as carpenters, metalworkers, wood sellers, food merchants, house builders. People worked six or more days a week living on a daily diet of naan, water, onion, some vegetables, a few pieces of meat, and tea. Rice and chicken were only for special days.

One evening Dan and Tom invited to dinner two British guests from the Volunteers in Service Overseas (VSO), the UK equivalent of Peace Corps. They enjoyed the meal and liked our training house. We found out that they had much lower salaries than us, and very little institutional support: no head office, training center or health and admin staff looking after them. They were also hard-core working class. Trying to make small talk, we mentioned how highly regarded Winston Churchill was in the US. They jumped on this, vehemently criticizing him as an upper-class imperialist and told how, when miners went on strike during the second World War, he called out the army and forced them back down into the mines like rats. When we asked what they liked from American literature, they rather arrogantly asked, was there such a thing? The evening was illuminating but not so enjoyable.

Ladies in *chadri* entering the Shrine of Hazrat Ali in Mazar-i-Sharif, the site of huge New Year's Celebrations every first day of spring

8. Foreign Agencies and Missions in Afghanistan

The US Government had a well-established presence in Afghanistan, which included the United States Embassy, the US Information Service (USIS), the US Agency for International Development (USAID), the American School in Kabul, the Asia Foundation and a number of NGOs. During my first year, our Ambassador Robert Neumann was replaced by Ambassador Theodore (Ted) Eliot from Massachusetts. USAID was headed by Bart Harvey. The Embassy was staffed by officers and administrators responsible for consular, economic, and political affairs, military affairs and intelligence, and a contingent of Marine Guards for security.

Peace Corps volunteers were sometimes wryly referred to as the "soft underbelly of the capitalist system." Simply, we were the bottom of the American totem pole, with the lowest salaries and the most basic jobs and housing. But we were nonetheless protected by the American Government, and as time went on, it became ever more obvious that this advantage was no small benefit.

Many other countries also had embassies and aid missions. The United Nations was represented by UNESCO and UNICEF, staffed with many different nationalities. I got to know folks from Canada, the UK, Yugoslavia, Germany, and India, among others. The USSR was also an important foreign community, with many aid and development projects, but we had almost no contact with them as they kept apart from us. I once briefly visited a natural gas producing field developed by the USSR in the far north. I was taken by my Afghan hosts to see it but during the visit had minimal conversation with the Soviets working there. The feeling of the Cold War was palpable. In Kabul and occasionally elsewhere we would see Soviet Tajiks in kebab shops, and they dressed and looked more like us but at the same time looked like locals who were thoroughly comfortable with the local environment, speaking Farsi as their native tongue.

There was a real sense of shared experience and camaraderie amongst foreigners working in Afghanistan. Westerners were genuinely friendly to one another and there was a lot of socializing and generosity. Whenever we'd meet, say, a German, there would be genuine interest in one another about where we were from, where we lived and what we were doing. This mostly did not include the WT's (World Traveler, a euphemism for hippie). This came from being so far away from home in such a remote culture and economy and gave me a very positive feeling about working overseas. In my later experience, I learned that this was largely unique to Afghanistan, not often seen in other foreign countries.

9. Trip to Tashkurgan

Toward the end of training, we were sent on a final training trip to experience the country alone. I chose to go to Tashkurgan, in ancient times a flourishing Buddhist city called Khulm, in the far north about 250 miles from Kabul. To get there I had to cross the *Hindu Kush* mountains and go through the famous Soviet-built Salang Pass. In the 1950s and '60s a national ring road was built by USSR in the north and the US in the south, part of the Cold War competition for influence.

From my journal:

> January 4, 1972: I am writing from Tashkurgan, a town in the far north of Afghanistan, about an hour from Mazar-I-Sharif. This is my second training field trip and is completely unstructured. We were given 900 Afs travel money (about 10 dollars) and are free to go where we please for four days.

Juris and I traveled together, arriving at the Karte Parwan open air depot at 8 a.m., where many *kilinars* (cleaners, the assistants to drivers) were shouting their destinations. We listened for "*Yeke* bureem ta Mazar" ("We're going to Mazar"). We paid 100 Afs and climbed aboard a bus jammed with turbaned men and one woman in chadri and headed north for the scenic trip. The now-familiar *Kohi Daman* (skirt of the mountains) valley was a beautiful prelude to the historic Salang pass. We passed Charikar and Istalif, taking in the many-colored mountains, the desert-like valley studded with leafless trees, and then endless orchards and farms enclosed by mud and stone walls filling the valley.

The road soon became steeper, as we joined the daily attack made by countless trucks and buses on the Hindu Kush. After much climbing we stopped at the last *chai khanah* (teahouse) for a mid-morning snack. All along the road we had seen mud and stone houses clinging precariously to the steep and jagged mountains, and now we were in a typical compound filled with hot burning wood stoves to greet the traveler. The snow was several feet deep.

At this point we put on every stitch of clothing we could manage and climbed atop the bus to sit in the luggage rack and enjoy the scenery. The sun was warm and the sky as blue as I have ever seen it. Completed in 1964, the Soviet-built Salang Pass is the world's highest tunnel, boring through the Hindu Kush at 12,000 feet elevation, and a length of almost 9,000 feet. Just before entering the tunnel, looking south, we could see vast mountain ranges looming in the distance. The snow was brilliantly white in every direction except for the jagged solid-black rock peaks high overhead.

When we came out of the tunnel, we began a rapid descent, and were delighted to see Asian conifer trees, as trees are rare here. We began to feel the cold and could only lie against the tarpaulin-covered baggage looking backwards. Soon the mountains were brown and beautiful against the white background of the Hindu Kush.

An hour later we stopped at Khinjan for naanichaste (lunch). Turbaned faces greeted us as we climbed down a bit shakily from the bus, and they asked us, grinning from ear to ear, "*khanook khordi?*", which literally means, "Did you eat cold?" They laughed thinking we were a couple of *dewana khoriji*, or crazy foreigners. Throughout the trip Afghans talked to us in a friendly way, asking questions and telling us things that we mostly couldn't understand. An hour earlier I had removed my boots and covered my feet with my gloves, trying to get the circulation going. At each stopping point along the road, people were surprised to see a couple of nutty foreigners on top of a bus in the freezing dead of winter, one with hands for feet.

We grabbed a quick *khorak* (serving) of kebab and a pot of tea, and found ourselves shivering inside the warm, large, buzzing "truck stop diner." Kebab here is delicious. A khorak is eight skewers, each with some chunks of lamb meat and fat. Sheep here are fat-tailed sheep, with tails that are flat, thick and wide, tapering at the end. The fat is very tasty. A favorite kebab specialty is *karoi*. At first sight, you think you'll never eat it, but it is delicious. It's cooked in a small, blackened frying pan with an egg, kebab, chopped onions, spices, tomato chunks, and boiling oil. The pan probably has never seen soap or a scouring pad. But constant reuse and cleaning with boiling water keep it sanitary.

We hit the road going north and soon passed through the towns of Doshi, Puhli Khumri, and Samangan, where the bus picked up a mail bag. The glacial terraces of smaller and smoother mountains along the plains soon gave way to a last range of towering mountains before the flat northern plains adjoining the USSR. There we passed through the staggering Tangi Khulm (Khulm narrows) pass just after sunset. This pass along the river flowing north cuts through a thousand-foot-high mountain range and is only about 50 feet wide at the ground level and several hundred yards long.

Winter traffic on road to the Salang Pass tunnel, at 12,732 feet elevation the highest in the world, completed in 1964 by the USSR

Once through, we drove for half an hour before stopping at the turnoff road to Tashkurgan. It was very cold and windy, and I bid Juris and the other passengers goodbye and stepped out into the night and a small bazaar and teahouse. The bus chugged off and I walked into the teahouse with feelings mixed between fear and delight. There wasn't an English speaker to be found.

I saw a dozen Afghan faces surprised to see a *khoriji* at this time of night, 6 p.m., black outside and in a very rural location. It was a typical rural teahouse, with mud walls and wooden beams covered with straw mats overhead. Inside were a dozen eight-foot-square dais, two feet off the ground and covered with inexpensive rugs and *kilims*. One sits cross-legged with shoes removed on these platforms, with food put on a cloth over the carpet. I ordered a black tea and a plate of pilau, took off several layers of clothing and shortly began a delicious meal. Food in teahouses is brought within minutes, there's no waiting. There was a hubbub about my need for *kashook* and *panjah* (spoon and fork), but I ate Afghan style—with my hands. This can be done neatly by making a conelike clump of rice with your right hand (left hand is not used for eating) and then pushing the clump into your mouth with your thumb. We were trained by our Kabul cook who normally ate with us. Unlike us, he rarely left a grain of rice on the mat before him. One night a bigwig came to dinner, and he used a fork. When we finished, the place before him looked like it had rained rice.

After the meal I enjoyed another pot of tea and talked to a few others for a time. My Farsi was rated as 2 on a scale of 5 from the Princeton Testing Service, which had four certified testers in Afghanistan. Regular testing is part of the Peace Corps training process. Level 2 is a useable basic knowledge, with limited vocabulary and grammar. Though it was only 7 p.m., I decided that writing a letter and sleep were most important for me—so I paid my bill and said *bamani khoda* (God keep you, goodbye) and left with a *gawdi* (horse drawn buggy) driver. We walked out and I climbed aboard and leaned back to see the black sky studded with brilliant stars. It was breathtaking. We trotted down the bumpy road in the starlight and the only sounds

Farmlands surrounding Khulm with ancient ruins mounds and looking back in direction of the Tangi Khulm, the narrows through the mountains to Central Asia

were of the horse's footsteps, jangling bells on the buggy that warn pedestrians, and the soft rustle of the wind.

We soon arrived at the small single-story government hotel, and I was shown to a nice, if sparse, room. The old *tawildar* (clerk), the only employee at the hotel, greeted me happily—his only lodger. It was terribly cold, and he lit the wood stove for me and let me know that he lacked a good winter coat. Later that year in March, I returned on a trip to the Nowroz (new year) festival in Mazar-i-Sharif and present him with a large wool coat from the used clothes bazaar. Though he seemed not to remember me, he was delighted.

Tashkurgan was famous for its covered bazaars and excellent handicraft work. The ancient city of Khulm was just north a few miles, and we had learned during training that it was a great center of learning and culture. The Chinese scholar Hsuen Tsung (Xuanzong) wrote of 10 temples and 500 monks here in 7th century CE. Unfortunately, an Afghan Khan razed the city in the 1700s so now only ruins remain.

Tashkurgan was filled with friendly Tajiks and Uzbeks. The Tajiks generally have angular faces and the Uzbeks rounder faces and lighter skin color. I spent my days walking through the bazaars covered with wooden arches, seeing iron workers making tools and utensils by heating iron on hot coals to red hot and then hammering it into various purposes, carpenters making furniture, tailors making clothing, jewelers making jewelry. There were also many shops selling textiles, foodstuffs, household items, artwork, trinkets and more. I befriended a young Uzbek man who spent a day taking me around town, and we struggled to try to understand one another.

The next afternoon a long caravan of camels arrived from the northern plains and entered a large caravanserai, an enclosed terminus with 15-foot high mud walls and a huge gate with a massive pair of wooden doors. The caravan leaders rode big chestnut and black horses and looked Mongol, with dark brown leathery skin and deeply wrinkled faces. They wore leather chaps and took off holsters holding huge six shooters and two bandoliers slung around their shoulders, crisscrossing their chests. They had come from

Tashkurgan caravan leaders unpacking after crossing Central Asia

Central Asia—possibly from Tajik SSR or Xinjiang in China—on the same paths as the old silk road starting in Xian, China, reputedly the largest city in the world in the 1400s. The caravan was 40 or 50 camels long, each loaded with four or five large burlap sacks filled with dried oriental olives. This was a staggering sight, straight from the Middle Ages. I ate some of the dried olives. The taste and feel started almost like powder inside a dried skin and surrounding a pit, becoming a rich and unusual flavor. They could be like peanuts: once you start eating them, it's hard to stop.

On my last day, I played my first game of *buzkashi*, the national sport of Afghanistan. The game is similar to polo and is usually played by two teams of up to 15 players mounted on horses in a huge oval field. The dried carcass of a headless goat is used as the "ball", with the four legs used as handles by the players wrestling for control. The goat is dropped in the center of the field, and the players try to grab the goat, ride with it to their own end of the field and drop it inside a circle for a score or goal.

My game was actually *khar* (donkey) *buzkashi*, but a shadow of the real thing. I'd gone to the plain outside of town to watch, and a fellow came up to me and insisted I take his donkey, so I handed him my camera, tightened my one-day-old turban, jumped on the donkey, and took off for the other players and the goat. It was like being in the middle of a rugby scrum. I managed a few pulls of the goat, galloped around like a fool, delighted the spectators, and fell off on my behind (it hurt!) once in the middle of a gallop toward the goal line. A couple of times other players poked me with their sticks used to make the donkeys run faster. The sticks had nails sticking out the ends. This was disrespectful of course, but I suppose to be expected as I was acting like a local villager.

Juris showed up after the game, and we caught a bus on to Pohl-e-Khomri and Kunduz, two northern cities, for one night. Standing by the roadside waiting for any form of transport was the standard way to travel on the open road.

This whole trip was a great time to let off steam and explore, and we acted like tourists, though not WTs. Our lives ahead were to be highly regimented and both respectable and respected. We had short hair, wore used suits, and minded our Ps and Qs.

The WT hippy trail was fueled by westerners who rode buses that ran daily between Paris and Delhi, with passengers free to get off or on in any country from France to India. Afghanistan was a favorite stop because it was so cheap to live there. Most WTs had long hair and straggly clothes, used drugs, drank alcohol, and often behaved promiscuously. Some even ended up begging or prostituting themselves, which we PCVs saw as terribly wrong for those from a rich country to do in a poor country.

After the long bus ride south, we arrived back in Kabul, refreshed after some amazing new sights and experiences.

10. End of training

Our PCV cycle of science teacher trainers initially had 11 people scheduled for training, all graduates in science or engineering. That eventually dwindled to seven. At the end of training, we had to be approved by the staff, including the psychologist, were required to commit for two school years of service, had to choose our work locations and to take the oath:

> I do solemnly swear that I will support and defend the Constitution of the United States against all enemies, foreign and domestic; that I will bear true faith and allegiance to the same; that I take this obligation freely, without any mental reservation …

With this we became Peace Corps volunteers.

I had shared a training house with Juris, Dan, Tom, and Joe. We naturally became allies and good friends. At the end of training, our assignments were: Juris to Ghazni, south of Kabul; Dan to Maimana in the remote northwest; Tom and Charlie to Baghlan, north of the *Hindu Kush*; Larry Bennett to Charikar just north of Kabul; Alan Gold to Baraki Barak in Logar Province; and me to Kapisa, in Kohistan at the base of the *Hindu Kush* and the Panjshir Valley.

Joe decided it wasn't for him and returned to grad school in Virginia. A decision not to proceed was respected, because the commitment to work for two school years was not to be taken lightly. Dan chose Maimana because he was determined to go as far from Kabul as possible and really be "out there with the people." In one hilarious story during training, Dan's mother wrote to him that in Rochester at a cocktail party at Christmas a journalist friend whom she hadn't seen for some time came up to her and asked, "So how are things in Afghanistan?" She matter-of-factly responded with how Dan was doing and what Afghanistan was like, and the friend almost collapsed with laughter. His question was a standard line for journos for, "how's it going?", and he'd no idea that her son was actually there!

I chose Kapisa Province because I had been there during training and liked the layout of the land, and it included the famous Panjshir Valley. It was also attractive to me because it was only three hours from Kabul and I looked forward to taking advantage of Kabul for R&R.

Alan Gold found himself in a Pashtu-speaking location and his job didn't work out. Tom remembers that he transferred back to Kabul and created a job for himself at the Kabul Zoo. This type of story in Peace Corps was not uncommon: if your first job didn't work out, alternatives were found.

One scary event that took place close to the end of training was the death from rabies of a Scandinavian woman world traveler who had been bitten or scratched by a cat and fell ill. She came to a veteran Peace Corps nurse for help in a waiting room opposite our training center. She ended up hysterical and screaming, dying after a terrible night. This was the first time any of us had heard of such a thing and, it sobered us up as to the dangers of life in Afghanistan.

During training we had also gotten to know some volunteer standouts. One was a nurse named Mary Simpson, working in a clinic in Baghlan. She had retired and joined the Peace Corps possibly in her late 60s. She was a good-looking woman with pure white hair, confidence and a ready smile. The Afghans loved her not only for her nursing expertise but also because she was a woman and could attend to women who were not allowed to be seen by a man according to their religious belief. The "normal" way for a woman to be diagnosed by a doctor was behind a curtain with a female nurse to answer the doctor's questions, generally inconvenient and ineffective. Mary was also a beacon for all of us young volunteers. When we met her during training, she was ready with advice and stories that lit the way for us.

Another was a man who had been working for Esso in Baton Rouge, Louisiana. He and I talked about the oil industry and his experience. He and his wife had joined the Peace Corps to do something of value in the world and help others, saying there would be plenty of time to work in industry. He took a positive view of China, comparing it to India, and saying that their communist system seemed effective at putting people to work and getting things done. We didn't know at the time of China's Great Leap Forward and famine of the 1950s or the Cultural Revolution then underway, both disasters for the country.

II

Science Supervisor
Year One in Kapisa

1972

Map 3: Kapisa Province

0   10   20   50 miles

Elevation in feet

59

11. Kapisa and Home in Baku Kham

The province of Kapisa is in the region called *Kohistan* ("mountain land"), making up part of the plain called *Kohi Daman* ("mountain skirt") north of Kabul. To the north and east are the Hindu Kush mountains and to the west is the *Kohibaba* ("father mountains") range. This broad, largely flat valley at 5000 feet elevation is about 50 miles south to north from Kabul to Gulbahar, 20 miles wide west to east between the two mountain ranges.

Kohistan is largely Tajik, a tribe centered in Tajikistan—at that time a Soviet Socialist Republic in Central Asia. Tajiks in Afghanistan were said to be prouder and more warlike than their brothers in the USSR. Provinces neighboring Kapisa are Parwan to the west, Baghlan to the north, Laghman to the east and Kabul to the south. The Panjshir River runs from the northeast from mountains that are over 19,000 feet elevation south to Gulbahar and then along the Kohi Daman plain, eventually joining the Kabul River and flowing to Sarobi where Afghanistan's first hydroelectric power plant was built.

The plain was broken by thousands of cultivated plots of land bounded by low earthworks that also served as paths for walking, bike riding and animals. Water supply came from the Panjshir River in open flowing channels called *jueys*. The preferred crop was wheat, while at higher altitudes in the Panjshir only barley could be grown. Few and far between amongst the plots were clusters of family homes, made of adobe and surrounded by high walls. Fruit trees grew along the intersections of the plots and in orchards. For weeks in springtime the countryside was stunningly beautiful, with green everywhere, brilliant white clouds, clear blue sky, and multitudes of bright red poppies amongst the wheat stalks.

Kapisa was reached via a turnoff to the east from the paved main north south road from Kabul to Jabul Saraj, a small village at the base of the *Hindu Kush*. From Jabul Saraj onwards, all roads were dirt. It was about 10 miles to Gulbahar, a village built clinging to the Panjshir River as it emerges from the mountains. Here were shops and houses covering each side of the road, gripping the rising mountains. From there it was only a few miles to the German Textile Factory (the Sherkat, or company), built by Germany in the 1950s as an aid project.

About 15 miles south of Gulbahar on the main road was the Kapisa Department of Education in the Provincial Government Offices in Mahmude Raqi. Along the road were small bazaars and villages every few miles. The towns where we would be working were Rukha in Panjshir, about 25 miles northeast from Gulbahar, then south to the Sherkat, Mirmasjadi, Mahmude Raqi, Nejrab and then east to Tagob. The total distance of our territory was about 70 linear miles. From Tagob to Sarobi on the Kabul Jalalabad Road was a further 25 miles. The Bagram Afghan Air Force Base was about five miles west of Mahmude Raqi on the other side of the Panjshir River, and was off limits, so I never saw this. It was the major military air base from the early 20th century until now.

I was met at the Sherkat Hotel by the provincial Director of Education, whom I had previously met during the training trip. He welcomed me and encouraged me to take a home in the sherkat compound, the only location in the province that had concrete houses and electricity from the Sarobi Dam power plant. He said living there would be safer and more convenient for me, and that there were German volunteers working in the factory that I could socialize with. This was the Deutscher Entwicklungsdienst or DED, a German version of the Peace Corps. I was diplomatic and thanked him for his suggestion but determined to do the Peace Corps experience and live like locals in the countryside. No doubt the Director as well as the Governor were also concerned because they were responsible for my safety.

I was directed to a house for rent in Baku Kham a couple of miles south of the sherkat, a hamlet with about a dozen shops on each side of the road. There I met the landlord, an elderly gentleman in local dress with a long beard, who had recently constructed the property. Soon we agreed on a deal and for the next couple of years he'd come and collect the rent. He had no children, and later I learned that he had taken a second wife and still no kids, so the fertility problem was his.

I was also introduced to a cook candidate named Mohamed Assif who previously had worked for German families at the sherkat. I was impressed, hired him and we agreed on salary and terms. He turned out to be a fine person, a skilled cook and servant, and he stayed with me for the next three years. He lived with his wife and children in a house a short distance away. As I look back on it, it was strange that I never met his family, but that was the culture. Nearly all servants for foreigners in Afghanistan were male. Muslims would never allow a woman to work at another person's house. Their belief was captured in the expression that a man and woman alone together are "cotton and fire", and they will catch fire.

It was essential to have a servant because of what, to me, was a primitive existence. Daily we agreed on food to be cooked, and Assif went to our local market to buy *naan*, meat and vegetables. He also drew water in buckets from the flowing *jueys* along the road outside our walls. He boiled the water for drinking and soaked vegetables in water with iodine tablets to make them safe to eat. He did the laundry by hand in large basins and hung the clothing on lines between my garden trees to dry. He cleaned the house with brooms and took the *tushaks* (cotton mattresses) to the roof to bake in the sun after dusting them with powder to kill the bed bugs which would crawl out to escape the heat. He kept the bathroom *bukhari* stocked with firewood bought locally so I could bathe. He bought kerosene for the lamps and kept them filled. And he would go to the Gulbahar bazaars for larger purchases. Finally, Assif was my guard, the locals knowing that the house was rarely left empty. We PCVs would have been hard-pressed to live without the help of a servant.

Assif knew how to cook a number of delicious German dishes such as schnitzel, dumplings, beef stew, roast potatoes and potato salad. His Afghan food repertoire included rice and *pilau* (pilaf), roast chicken, lamb kebab, roast vegetables in local yogurt, vegetable soup and much more. Afghan naan was a delicious and dark whole wheat unleavened bread that rises slightly and was full of flavor, body and fiber. It went well with soups and any kind of meat. The fruits were many and varied: grapes, watermelon, honeydew melon, pears, apples, pomegranates, figs. Fruit was often small and malformed, but usually very sweet and flavorful. Decades later working in Hong Kong and China, I discovered that the Chinese preferred small and misshaped fruits and vegetables to large and beautiful ones, saying that the natural ones taste better while the beautiful are simply engineered to look good and probably filled with chemicals.

The compound and house were completely organic, made of adobe mud, poplar beams and straw, with exterior walls that were several feet thick. The compound was about 60 by 75 feet with 18-foot-high walls. There was a short driveway along the south wall leading to the entrance and a small garage, big enough for a cart. There was a huge pair of solid wood doors eight feet high with a large hand-wrought iron knocker, a thick steel ring about eight inches in diameter. Inside the compound and across the internal garden and courtyard, the house had five rooms in a row: a storeroom and dressing room, bedroom, stairwell to the roof, guest and eating room, office, and kitchen. All the rooms but the storeroom had double doors opening to the courtyard, with small paned windows from floor to top.

My house in Baku Kham facing north looking over the 18 foot high walls at the Hindu Kush mountains in the distance

The flat roofs of the house were supported by poplar poles covered with woven straw mats, more straw and branches, and a thick layer of adobe. These roofs need regular renewing as the snow and rain wore them down, leading to leaks called chakak. I recall vividly the first rainstorm soon after moving in when the ceiling leaked in several rooms, and we had to put out buckets and stack furniture in the corners. The flat roof was for sitting, eating, and sleeping in summer. The house walls were whitewashed, all the floors were covered with *burria*—straw mats. The guest room was lined with *tushaks* and *boleshts* (pillows) to sit and lean on. In the center was an Afghan carpet, about five by eight. We sat *char zanu* (cross legged, literally four knees.) There was no electricity.

The bathroom was across the courtyard to the left, consisting of a narrow hall with a bathroom and a toilet on the left. The bathroom floor was the only concrete in the compound. There was a *bukhari,* a round wood stove with a water tank on top through which a stove pipe rose and turned, going out a tightly fitted hole in the glass window. The tank had a faucet to draw hot water. To bathe I used two buckets, one filled with cold water and one for mixing, and a dipper to pour water over myself while sitting on a small stool. There was also a table for toilet kit, soap, etc. and a mirror on the wall. The bathroom got hot quickly from the roaring hardwood fire in the *bukhari*, and taking a bath in freezing temperatures in the dead of winter with snow on the ground was very refreshing.

The toilet room at the end of the hall had a door and was raised several feet. It was so dark inside a lantern was needed, and I just squatted over a hole in the center. Night soil was collected from underneath by a man with large straw baskets on his donkey, who sells this "fertilizer." Hence the need to boil all water and use iodine pills to soak vegetables to kill germs.

The garden had a large quince tree in the middle with apricot and pomegranate trees to the sides. There were rows of vegetables on either side of the entrance walkway to the house. Assif hired a local farmer to plant and weed the garden, from which we enjoyed potatoes, carrots, and onions.

Assif purchased all necessary household items: straw mats, a kitchen table, a two-burner kerosene stove and metal oven, another table for preparing food and other necessities, trash cans, etc. He also bought plates, flatware, glasses, dishes, cotton tablecloths and napkins from the textile factory outlet. In the bedroom I had two single beds, with hand turned poplar legs and sides and a *tushak* on top of woven rope. There was also a simple chest of drawers, a couple of side tables, a rack to hang clothes, and a pair of large galvanized iron chests with locks for valuables. Kerosene lanterns were used for lighting, and wood stoves for heat. At 5,000 feet elevation and no electric lighting within miles, there were brilliant stars every night that was cloudless. It also could be 10°F in winter, or 90°F in summer, though fortunately it cooled overnight due to the elevation. The stoves heated the rooms quickly, the thick walls were excellent insulation.

Before I left America, I had bought a small, battery-operated Sony cassette tape recorder and spent a week going to various friends' homes taping music. I had a dozen long tapes with a tailored collection of rock and classical and jazz music that I enjoyed for three years.

Afghanistan at that time was one of only two countries in the 55 where Peace Corps served where we earned higher salaries than locals. Provincial volunteers made Afghanis (Afs) 9,000/month, or about $100. Kabul volunteers earned Afs 11,000, where costs were higher. The Prime Minister's salary was Afs 12,000! My budget was about $8 per month each for rent, servant and all the meat, fruit, and vegetables I could consume; the balance of over $70 was available for entertainment, buying books, radio, film, goods, carpets, etc. So, while I lived in a mud house along a dirt road with the only modern conveniences a camera, cassette tape recorder and a shortwave radio, I lived very comfortably, with a full-time servant and more money than I could spend.

Because I wanted to live like the locals, I asked Assif to call me "*aghai* Toby," a local form of respectful address, rather than using the English Mr. In retrospect this was neither necessary nor effective. I chuckle when I recall meeting a teacher in the Gulbahar bazaar once, and in my new and bookish Farsi said to him something like "do you diagnose me?" meaning recognize. He chuckled and made a comment about me being an *antique adam*. Adam, from the Old Testament, is Farsi for a male person. He meant that I was old-fashioned. He was right, and I easily assumed the role of a conservative country teacher.

I soon acquired a small female German shepherd mutt, a large black male German shepherd, and a gray cat, still a kitten. The cat was good for mouse hunting, the dogs for security, as well as yapping and creating nuisances of themselves. Visitors who heard their loud barking or saw the dogs were scared. But the animals were great companions. Unfortunately, as time went on the dogs would run around and make a mess of the garden, spoiling some of the vegetables.

12. Science Teacher Training

At the beginning of the Afghan school year, on April 1, 1972, the first order of business for me with my counterparts was to present my letter of introduction from the NSC to the Provincial Director of Education in Mahmude Raqi. My counterparts were Sayid Qamar, from Panjshir, and Mohamed Saied Khan, from Gulbahar. After this, we went with the Director to Lycée Mirmasjadi, the most advanced lycée in the province, to observe classes and get to know some of the teachers and students. Although this was my second visit to Mirmasjadi, I was excited to see the eager students and teachers observing their foreigner at work and enjoyed this startup day on the new job. We spent the rest of that week attending classes, making lists of the science equipment, and moving it from the school storehouse to the laboratory and library room in a separate building behind the school.

Afghanistan's secondary schools were patterned on the French system wherein students take up to 15 courses per year. The school year ran from the beginning of spring to the end of October with schools closed during the frigid winters because they lacked heating. We next prepared a schedule to visit the five boys' lycées and two girls' schools in the province with the plan based on geography.

The schools that we could travel to on day trips were Mirmasjadi, Mahmude Raqi and the girls' schools at Ushtegram *Neswan* (*neswan* means female) and Sherkat Neswan in the Textile Factory compound. I travelled to all by bicycle except Mahmude Raqi which was 15 miles south and was best reached by bus or jeep ride.

For the distant schools we needed travel days and to spend nights in the schools. Panjshir was 25 miles northeast, Nejrab over 30 miles south, and Tagob nearly 50. Of all the schools, only Tagob was in a Pashto speaking location. Finally, there were also middle schools at Hamzargah and Dehati Dasht, close to my home, and which we visited only a few times.

We planned a schedule of two-day visits to the local schools each month, and one day weekly in the office. For the longer trips we allocated one week per school. The Director of Education approved the plan. Travel and overtime money for trips to distant schools was important for my counterparts, so they wanted to travel as much as possible. My salary was about four times theirs, which I never told them, but they knew and no doubt rankled. Sayed Kamar argued determinedly on several occasions to receive payment of his earned allowances, which only the Director of Education could approve, and which he did somewhat begrudgingly. Money was short and always an issue. It didn't help that my counterparts were NSC employees and thus didn't report directly to the local Director of Education.

The office day was spent in the Department of Education at the Provincial Government Offices. We planned schedules, prepared guides, revised lessons, and agreed on roles. Soon, when not teaching, Sayid Qamar and Saeid Khan mostly skipped the office day and went to their more distant homes. Living centrally in the region, I could be home every night, which they couldn't. They also didn't need the Farsi study I needed to keep up with the program. It also became apparent that attendance for Afghan education employees was much less strict than in an American system.

I enjoyed the day in the office and took with me two large dictionaries: one from Afghanistan was Farsi to English and the reverse; the other Iranian and Farsi only. I studied the texts and experiment sheets and translated new words and continued with building my language skills. From time to time, I would go and chat with other department people, often with the Assistant Director of Education, who was local and more informal than others. I felt like a local teaching employee, ate lunch in the local kebab shop and took a waz (means open, used for a small truck), bus or jeep home at the end of the day.

Thus began the first school year, filled with activity. We trained teachers, taught and performed science experiments, regularly visited nine schools, and delivered equipment and books. We reported to the NSC and the Kapisa Director of Education, and interacted in Kabul with the NSC, Peace Corps, USIS, the Asia Foundation and on rare occasions the Royal Ministry of Education, working directly with hundreds of enthusiastic and respectful teachers and students.

The job was interesting and filled with variety, and I was beginning to understand the language much better and to experience what life was like in this new and different culture. I also could see how our work contributed to a large number of people.

13. Teaching at Local Schools

Sayed Kamar and I arrived by jeep at our first teaching day at Lycée Mirmasjadi, a one-story cement, light yellow-colored school building. The entrance was in the center, with a long row of classrooms on either side. Behind the school building were a volleyball court and soccer field, and behind this, the laboratory and library building.

Our first port of call was to the school principal, a serious person who received us with what seemed like a degree of solemnity. We had met this principal on the training trip to Kapisa during our introduction to the province. He asked about our program and told us that the lab and students were ready. We had expected to be instructing the teachers who would then teach the students. However, this was to be the standard going forward; we would train teachers and teach students all in one go. We dealt with this principal many times over the next two years, and he was always courteous, but formal, and I suspected that he would always take the side of the Department of Education in any dealings with the NSC.

The lab room was a large square room, with a blackboard in front, some educational posters on the walls, and a small library; a storeroom was at the back right side. The science kits were on a row of tables at the front, facing 50 students from different grades seated on chairs. Per the French lycée system, high school students take biology, chemistry, and physics concurrently for all four years. With up to 15 subjects yearly, each subject was taught only two or three days per week. Until now they had no practical or experimental work so students were tested on their ability to regurgitate the written text verbatim.

Our routine was to do experiments, take questions and give quizzes. Students who correctly answered eight or better out of ten were commended to the principal and visitors. In testing, cheating was common. Cheating was called *naqal*, which means transfer. The culture expects you to transfer answers to your friend if needed, to be helpful. After the experiments the kits and materials were locked up in the storeroom.

Lycée Mirmasjadi students at a biology demonstration, with Sayed Qamar on right behind student with chalk and teacher left

We had trained for many experiments. We started with a favorite, using direct current from a battery to hydrolyze water and collect the lighter-than-air hydrogen in an inverted test tube. Then we put a flame to the hydrogen, which would explode with a pop, once again forming water vapor. This demonstrated that water was a compound that could be split into hydrogen and oxygen.

Our second experiment was investigating air pressure using large bell-shaped glass bottles and balloons, which turned out to be condoms from the local market. We burned a candle inside the sealed bottle, which consumed the oxygen in the air, and the balloon deflected inwards. Black soot, or carbon, was also deposited inside the bottle as a combustion product, along with CO_2, which cannot be seen. We ended with a diagram and a demo of how soap works, cleaning by emulsifying oils which can then be washed away with water.

Interacting with the students was eye opening and fun. They asked good questions and were keen to see the experiments. They also asked me to speak English. Confused, I asked, "What do you want me to say?" They said just talk some sentences so we can hear the sound. So, I said something like, "I'm an American from Mamaroneck, New York, and am working in Afghanistan as a teacher trainer." They all convulsed with laughter and turned to each other with "ding, ching, bong, doe, cronk" noises in imitation of my speech, kind of like what we did as kids mimicking Chinese. I laughed, too!

They also asked me to write on the blackboard. I wrote some cursive, and they marveled. It was left to right, unlike their Arabic scripted Dari which is written right to left. Another student asked why we said the earth was round, as anyone can see from the horizon that it is flat? I did my best to explain the great distance needed to see the curvature, and how sunrise and sunset, and the moon hint at the shape.

Chemistry experiments included dissolving sugar in water and passing the mixture through a filter, contrasted with insoluble starch that won't pass through a filter. We showed that iodine solutions wouldn't dissolve in water, but would in alcohol, and that oil and water were insoluble. We demonstrated the boiling points of gasoline, kerosene and diesel and discussed how they burn in cars, lanterns, and trucks.

Other experiments included the chemistry of burning a candle, collecting carbon from the smoke and water; burning sugar with and without ash as a catalyst; the triangle of fire (oxygen, heat, combustible matter); using a microscope to examine my blondish hair and a student's black hair as well as bacteria, protozoa and paramecia in *juey* water. We also taught algebra, geometry, and trigonometry, and showed how this could be useful in daily life, such as in calculating the size of a building and the quantity of materials needed to build it. Our work was collaborative. My counterparts and I shared responsibility for demonstrating the experiments, and then helped the teachers to do it on their own.

With these mostly farm boys dressed in their western trousers and short sleeved shirts, in a place with no paved roads, running water, electricity, telephone, or television, and where it took three weeks to correspond with home, I felt that I was truly in another time and world. In truth, this was part of the motivation for the Peace Corps experience: to provide a service while learning about a new culture and to see an entirely different life, living close to nature. The boys were active and even mischievous, as well as respectful: a good combination for learning.

There was keen interest amongst us in who did what. Mohamed Saied often didn't show for work, and Syed Kamar, while mostly there, was competitive. In retrospect he no doubt thought I was too rigid. Both wanted me to teach them English but didn't put effort into it. We often started English lessons, but they would soon fizzle out. They didn't take notes or study, and the lessons lacked continuity. Today I wish I had been more disciplined and effective in teaching them English. I always carried notebooks and wrote down new Farsi vocabulary and studied it while riding on buses or waiting for transport, helping me to read the science and math textbooks. I guess I was looking for the same diligence in them.

Early on I was given a tour of the textile factory, known as the sherkat. To me, knowing little about this industry, it was quite modern, with huge areas filled with looms slamming shuttles back and forth to produce cloth from great spools of thread. Workers were busy everywhere and looked comparatively well dressed and fed. There were large shops, storerooms, and offices. On the main road was a factory outlet store selling cloth, bedspreads, napkins, aprons, shawls and many other fabric goods.

I met several of the senior executives who expressed an interest in English language lessons, and I agreed to meet with them. This began a fun and useful weekly meeting. They had been trained in Germany and spoke the German language, a big help in learning English. They also knew a lot about the West, though less about America. We were to have many enjoyable evenings and dinners together. We talked about life in Afghanistan and America, and they could answer all kinds of questions about the local culture and history. One evening, for entertainment, one of them invited one of his servants who was a country man to join us, and he delighted in showing his ability to bray exactly like a donkey, which was hilarious.

The streets in the Sherkat compound were paved, and the cinder blocks and concrete houses were surrounded with low walls and had electricity. I met a half dozen young German volunteers from DED. They were very friendly and welcoming. And they offered to buy liquor or other items for me from the German Commissary in Kabul. As Peace Corps volunteers, we didn't have US Commissary access, though it was provided for the Embassy, USAID, USIS and others. Their generosity was much appreciated, and I occasionally took advantage of it. They also partied a lot and gave me an open invitation. Beate and Ditmar Steuer were particularly welcoming. I taught English to a young German girl, Doris Kramer, who left the company environment and traveled two miles down the dirt road to my mud house for lessons. Assif told me I should marry her because I needed a wife and to him it only meant one thing when a man and woman were alone together.

The DED volunteers were trained textile and hospital workers, very good at their work and focused on their technical jobs. This was different from most of the American PCVs—university graduates without specialist training. In many ways this made the Germans more effective. Much later I learned that this model is widespread in

Germany. Many people take specialist technical training in fields from logistics to hotel management, manufacturing to transportation, and become titans of industry, without a university degree.

The girls' lycée at the factory was in a nice building, and the girls were well dressed in navy blue uniforms and wearing white head scarves. Many were attractive, with dark eyes and lashes, long dark hair. They were all very respectful and reserved, even shy, and many were clearly the children of educated people working in the Sherkat as engineers, accountants and executives. Having a foreign teacher was a big deal to them. Later they would be taught English by Denise Blake, whom they revered. The school's facilities were the best in the province, and the girls seemed the most prosperous.

Saied Khan and I performed the experiment on solutions using starch and sugar and filtration. Only sugar went into solution and passed through a filter. Then evaporation of the water leaves sugar. We discussed how solutions have a solvent and solute, with the solute

My counterparts Sayed Qamar and Saeid Khan first and third from left with headmaster of Ushtergram girls school in between with students doing a chemistry experiment

being dispersed on a molecular scale. We distilled alcohol and water, and solutions of the two, showing the effects on boiling point and drawing schematics of what happens in boiling.

We also brought a sheep's heart, lungs, and liver from the bazaar and talked about biology and the functions of organs. We treated marble with sulfuric acid to produce carbon dioxide, and ended up with experiments on osmosis and how chlorophyll works.

Saied Khan could be a bit of a devil. In a very serious and stern fashion he gave them a lesson in English on how to decline the verb "to go." The pronunciation of "go" in Farsi means shit, and "goes" means fart. Fully knowing what he was doing, he required a young girl to stand up and say "I go, you go, she goes" while keeping a straight face in a room full of giggling red-faced girls struggling to suppress their laughter.

About 10 minutes east by bike was the girls' school at Ushtergram, one of my favorites. The school was small and had a coed elementary level and girls' school from middle school through twelfth grade. We taught only the older students and teachers. Our initial visits were spent distributing Mendelev and other science charts, teaching heat and physics experiments, translating science vocabulary into local lingo and doing math problems. I learned that the Periodic Table of the Elements internationally was called the Mendelev Chart, first created by the Russian chemist Mendelev. The US didn't use this name, no doubt because of the Cold War.

The headmaster was a small and conscientious fellow, assisted by a serious and graceful teacher who was quite dark skinned. Skin colors in Afghanistan varied from quite light to very dark and meant nothing socially. Both these gentlemen were a generation older than I. The head of the elementary school was an attractive slightly plump young single woman who was mentally quick and lively. She wore a white sheer head scarf but not a veil, as did all girls and women we taught. I came to feel the tension between men and women in Afghanistan, as I was attracted to her without having any interest to be so. Normally we would teach and then have a lunch in midafternoon with only the men.

One day we went to an elementary class, where they were playing (teaching?) bazaar. Some children were shopkeepers, selling meat, vegetables, and household goods. Others were given play money to bargain with and buy. It was beautiful. These tiny little boys and girls, maybe seven or eight years old, would ask what meat was on sale and the price. The answer was mutton and 20 Afs per pound. The would-be buyer would then erupt with a full-blown confident tirade and hand waving with, "What? Twenty Afs? That is very expensive! I'll never buy it at that price," and on and on. These kids learned from a tiny age to bargain, haggling being a learned ability practiced in schools.

I mention the teacher was dark skinned because he taught me a lot about diplomacy and tact. He enjoyed talking about world affairs and would start discussions with, "Aghai Toby, we very much appreciate your coming here and teaching us, and we respect America, one of the great countries in the world. But please tell me how is it that America can support a nation like South Africa that by law discriminates against people based on their skin color? And why is America dropping bombs from its huge B-52 bombers on the rice paddies of Asians in Vietnam who are just trying to live? How is this making the world safe for freedom or democracy? And we respect the Yahud (Jewish) people and revere and believe in their prophets, Moses, Abraham, Masih (Messiah, which Muslims also use for Jesus.) But how is it right that they come from Europe to Palestine and take away the land of the Muslim people there? They should come in peace and live alongside the Palestinians."

We PCVs faced questions on these three topics throughout our time in country. I recognized truth in the criticisms but found myself defending my country. I said that we were trying to do good, to change apartheid, protect freedom and work for peace. I was surprised to find that even though I was against the Vietnam War, I defended our leaders saying they are not bad people, they just believe we must fight against communism. My sense of skin color disappeared over time and when I returned home in 1975, I was appalled to wake up again to the real situation in America and that we have not shed our prejudices. My teacher friend also said that he had no problems with

Americans, only with the American Government, a refrain repeated in many countries.

Ushtergram was famous locally for its hot chili peppers and chili powder. One day we sat down to a delicious lunch of soup, meat, vegetables and *naan*, and I sprinkled the powdered pepper on my food; it was indeed delicious as well as very spicy. Shortly afterwards, one of my eyes nearly exploded in pain, and I jumped up and ran to the *juey* flowing outside and rinsed my eye for minutes before it settled down. I had scratched my eye with fingers dusted with pepper without realizing it. The others roared with laughter at the American who shared an experience that everyone knew.

14. The First Anglo Afghan War

Working "on stage" as a science teacher trainer in a foreign language, while challenging and fun, left me mentally exhausted. So, I developed a habit of relaxing in the evenings reading (by kerosene lantern), particularly Afghan history and novels, the latter everything from Lord of the Rings to Dune and The Idiot. Fortunately, the Peace Corps library had an abundance of well-worn volumes from which to choose.

A book that lit my enthusiasm for Afghan history was *Signal Catastrophe: The Story of the Disastrous Retreat from Kabul, 1842*, written in 1966 by Patrick Macrory, about the First Anglo Afghan War of 1838–42. It was a failure for the British and reminded me in a variety of ways of the American Vietnam War.

In 1747, the Pashtun Ahmad Shah Durrani from Kandahar had united the Durrani Pashtun tribes and conquered eastern Iran, all of Afghanistan, and south to Karachi and east to Delhi in India, creating the largest Afghan empire that was to last until the end of the 19th century. British rule in India, dating from 1757, was then engaged with a struggle known as The Great Game, between the British Lion and the Russian Bear who both sought to control Afghanistan as a buffer state for their expanding empires.

In 1837, Emir Dost Mohamed Khan founded another branch of the Pashtun Durrani dynasty, known as the Barakzai (or Mohammadzai) dynasty centered in Kabul, which lasted to the modern era. The

British then made the mistake of believing that the exiled Afghan King Shah Shujah would be a better surrogate for them to prevent the encroachment on India by the Russians, who had been intriguing with Napoleon I of France on an invasion of Afghanistan (which never happened). So, in 1838, the First Anglo Afghan War began when the British invaded, placing Shah Shujah on the throne.

The Afghans however would not accept occupation or becoming vassals of the British. After increasing rebellion and failed negotiations, the British political agent (head of mission) was killed in 1841 and in January 1842, the British, who had unfortunately built their compound on indefensible ground below the Afghan fort on a nearby hill, were forced to retreat in the dead of the frigid and icy Kabul winter. History had it that the British army and legation numbering 16,500 souls, mostly Indian, were destroyed en route to India, with only one survivor to arrive in Jalalabad, as they were easily slaughtered in the high passes to the east. Some small children were taken by the Afghans, later recovered as happily converted good little Muslims.

The following year the British sent an Army of Retribution to avenge their loss and recover any survivors, of which they found several thousand. They attacked Jalalabad and Kandahar, and then decided to "retreat" via a long route north through Kabul and Kohistan and then east to India. There they destroyed the Kabul bazaar, one of the great sights of Central Asia, and attacked Istalif in Kohistan, killing all the males, raping many of the women, looting everything and destroying the buildings. Their military reputation reestablished, they then withdrew. (Ewans, p. 71)

For me, the history of this period was particularly fascinating, as the British were to fight three unsuccessful wars in Afghanistan, all while globally balancing their imperial interests in India, Africa, the Americas, and China. The narratives of British conquests and colonization included frequent references to their leaders and decisions around the world, and how these theaters influenced one another. And despite their prowess in creating perhaps the greatest empire in history, their failures in Afghanistan resulted from such factors as poor intelligence and judgment, political intrigues, and operational incompetence on top of the immense difficulties of what they were trying to achieve, which was to subjugate a large collection of fierce and independent peoples in a vast land of soaring mountains and large deserts.

15. Life at Home and Bringing Movies to Kapisa

We knew when we joined the Peace Corps that letters home, round trip, took three weeks, and that telephones were not available to us in Afghanistan. So, I wrote letters regularly, carefully and in detail, and cherished what came from home. We also were given subscriptions to *Time Magazine* and the *New York Times News of the Week in Review*, free for all PCVs worldwide. I read these nearly cover to cover and became a lifelong subscriber to both.

An exciting new discovery was shortwave radio. We were encouraged to buy a Japanese set, about the size of a lunchbox, with AM, FM and up to five shortwave bands. During all my years in Afghanistan, I explored the airwaves. On clear nights you could hear the BBC, Voice of America, and broadcasts from the USSR, Japan, Philippines, Hong Kong, Australia, Germany and others. It was fascinating to slowly turn the dial, listen to the crackling static and eventually make out a broadcast and figure out where it was coming from. It was also my first real introduction to propaganda, as each broadcast had its slant.

This also began my lifelong appreciation for the BBC. It always was the first with the news, the most reliable and to me, unbiased: simply reporting the facts. I also listened to BBC Persian, to learn more of the language and the Iranian pronunciation. I appreciated the excellent editing and succinct style, as well as "BBC English," a precisely scripted and educated way of speaking. It was obvious that the announcers were talking down to the listener, maybe even especially to Americans, but it seemed natural and didn't bother me. Some years later in Bahrain, British friends with strong regional accents told me that their speech would never be allowed on the BBC, but sometime in the 1990s, I woke up and realized that the BBC had all types of regional and international accents and had evolved fully to everyday speech. BBC's excellence and accuracy in reporting has remained, for me, without peer.

Living in this village quickly became thrilling to me. Several times a day I'd hear the *azaan*, the Muslim call to prayer, gently floating from the local mosque a short walk away. The road in front of my house often filled with people, animals and vehicles, but mostly was quiet. I watched people going about their business at the shops or buying on bazaar (market) days and children playing. Adjacent to my house women worked in the fields which the men plowed with oxen.

Transportation on the road was by walking, bike, Russian jeeps, small buses, freight trucks, flatbed vans, occasional camel caravans and, rarely, Russian-made Volga brand taxis. Astonishingly, the Russian covered jeeps would regularly carry up to 17 people: four in the driver's row, five in the second row, four in the back with two each side facing one another, and four standing on the rear bumper hanging on to the roof. The driver would hang halfway out the window and struggle to shift gears, reaching between the knees of a squashed passenger. The freight trucks were covered in colorful paintings and Muslim gospel with bells and garrulous chains hanging down the sides. The buses were crammed with people, including children and veiled women, bags of goods and foodstuffs, chickens in cages, lambs and more. The roofs were piled high with bags, metal trunks and more people, sometimes 60 in all.

Small boys moved along the road sitting on the rump of a cow or a donkey flicking long switches and calling out sharp cries to direct the animal where to go, with a trail of other beasts following. We PCVs were in awe of these little boys for their skill and confidence. There is an Afghan proverb, literally "donkey work is a world of knowledge." Donkey work means driving a working donkey, and world and knowledge employed a play on words based on the same root. The excellent meaning was that there is much to know and learn in this humble job and was a metaphor for much in life. There were also *gawdis,* horse- or donkey-drawn two-wheeled carriages with bells jingling to warn pedestrians.

Wheat was ground into flour locally using waterpower. There was a flour mill a short distance west of my house using an ancient design with *juey* water driving a wooden propeller whose shaft connected to a large granite millstone in the millhouse above. The millstone was fed from a kernel hopper and the flour collected in burlap bags from the rim of the millstone. The air inside the mill was thick with flour dust and smelled sweet and clean. Farmers paid with a portion of their grain for the milling service.

The Kohistan Road was a main thoroughfare for the *koochis* (gypsies, literally "movers") who travel in summertime by caravan from Jalalabad to the central high mountains in the Hazarajat. Sometimes we would get old *koochis* begging for naan at our door. One day during the spring flood as I was coming home, the road was blocked behind a caravan of six or eight camels that had run into trouble while crossing a canal from the Panjshir River that passed over a low flat bridge. A *koochi* boy had lost his footing in the fast-flowing flood water and had been swept away, nearly drowning. Wailing *koochi* women and men were clustered about the soaked, dazed boy on the muddy road. Small children were strapped over their thighs, sitting high up on the loaded camels. Though young, the women looked aged and wrinkled, had tiny braids in their black hair and wore tattered, dirty, brightly colored clothes. The men were not fierce looking Pashtuns but looked tough enough to survive on the moon without Apollo support. Two baby camels no bigger than large Great Danes suckled milk from their mothers. The mess was cleared up in a few minutes—the camels and people moved to a different crossing further downstream.

I soon welcomed a roommate named Mark Svendsen who was in the Food for Work program aiding the people during the severe drought and famine in Afghanistan in 1971 and 1972. He would be with me for most of my first school year. He had been a PCV in Afghanistan from 1968–70 and had responded when the Peace Corps reached out to him and others to return and work to distribute food. The program distributed American wheat in exchange for work on rural development projects and was funded by a global Food for Peace program of USAID.

Mark was an excellent roommate as I started my experience in the province. He was working with Kapisa provincial officials and was able to provide info and advice based on his previous experience. His dad was a professor at the University of Indiana, and he had a naturally thoughtful and positive outlook. One story he shared was that after a meal during one of their Food for Work trips, he used a small corner of uneaten bread as an ash tray. Afterwards he was told that those who saw this were mortified that any food could be used as an ash tray in the middle of a devastating famine. This type of experience was an example reminding us that we needed to think carefully about how we behaved in this new culture and difficult situation.

Mark's younger sister Carol also came to Afghanistan, and later his parents visited. Carol became friends with an English girl named Cathy Stephens whose father was with the UN, and they in turn connected us with a wide variety of aid and diplomatic workers, a great source for social connections. Carol and Cathy both found jobs locally with American and British agencies.

Soon PCVs John and Denise Blake moved to Kapisa and took a house in the Textile Factory. John and Denise had met in Brazil with Peace Corps where he was disqualified by the staff. They had appealed

Mark Svendsen, my Peace Corps volunteer housemate and later PC Staffer and a local bridge construction he managed in the Food for Work Program. Photo courtesy Mark Svendsen in Washington where they married and then were reassigned to Afghanistan. John was a graduate of Texas A&M and worked as an agricultural extension agent. He visited farms promoting the recommendations and programs of the Ministry of Agriculture. True to his Texas education he went with textbook in hand and referred to it for technical info. He soon learned that, to the locals, book reading meant inexperience. Calmly not agreeing, he joked about it. Denise was an excellent English teacher in the Sherkat school, and she was adored by her students. The Blakes would visit me in Baku Kham, and sometimes sunbathe on the roof in the hot sun, Denise in her two-piece swimsuit, no doubt shocking to Assif. But for them this was the only place in the province where they could relax behind high walls. We shared many happy times and meals together.

Toby with Denise Blake and new puppies from his dog Gurg (means wolf in Farsi) inside his Baku Kham compound

The Afghan people could be both worldly and naïve in their outlook. Many had met other foreigners over the years and were uniformly welcoming, hospitable, and friendly. It was said that this was because Afghanistan had never been colonized, and the people were proud and unbowed. Occasionally we volunteers would hear questions like, "A good teacher named Bill from America worked here, I think from New York. Do you know Bill?" Or, "What part of Germany is New York in?" We marveled at this but were happy that "Bill" was remembered and had been a good teacher. We never heard such comments about the USSR, but maybe that was because we were Americans.

US politics, even though distant geographically, still impacted me. In a letter to my parents in 1972, I reported learning about how Afghans did have opinions about American leaders:

> Just heard that Alabama Governor Wallace was shot. I suppose the NRA will continue to block gun control legislation, which is sad. Glad to hear McGovern is doing so well. The people here are down on America for "imperialism and destroying" Vietnam. And they all love John Kennedy. It freaks me out to walk into a mud house in the middle of nowhere, and have the host pull out an old magazine picture of JFK and say "now this was a true man…" The owner usually has only a couple of old magazines and perhaps a picture on the wall of *Khana Khoda* (House of God in Mecca) and a few photos of family elders. Many Afghans say Nixon was a bad man because it is reported that he called Afghanistan a nation of thieves after his vice-presidential visit in 1959. He undoubtedly made a bad impression, as the story has seeped into the very corners of this land.

While still in training in Kabul, I had learned about a service provided by the US Information Agency, USIA, to lend 16 mm projectors and films to American government workers and PCVs for showing to the locals. This was part of their communications and information (propaganda?) remit. I proposed bringing films to Kapisa and after approval of the idea with the Director of Education, I went to Kabul and brought back a half dozen films and a projector from the USIA.

Fortunately, the German textile factory had a large auditorium with a projector room available for use. The Director and the headmasters of the local schools spread the word, and we shortly were able to pack the auditorium with hundreds of students, boys and girls separated.

The films shown were *Washington Mosque*, *Last Decade in Space*, *Apollo 11*, *Boy Scout Jamboree*, *Handful of Soil* and *Art Heritage*. I showed them in two days over two weeks. The *Apollo 11* was most exciting, though a few skeptics questioned if the landing on the moon was staged and not real. I don't know how many of the students had ever seen a film, but there would have been quite a few for whom this was a first.

The *Art Heritage* film had footage from the Met in New York, the Louvre, Michaelangelo's *David*, and ancient Egyptian and Greek statues. The Director of Education afterwards admonished me politely but strongly that I should not have shown the art film because the nude statues of David and Greek women were unacceptable to Muslim culture. I apologized for my mistake and had indeed observed the gasps and giggles from the students at those shots. It was lucky that the *Art Heritage* film was the last film shown, because otherwise I might have been shut down for inappropriate content.

Of course, the whole exercise was a lot of fun, and my stock went up locally. The movies no doubt were long remembered and appreciated.

16. Teaching at Distant Schools

On the Kohistan plain and a half hour south by vehicle was the Lycée Mahmude Raqi, much like Mirmasjadi but more rural. The students were from the families of farmers, artisans and shopkeepers, as well as provincial government workers. My counterparts and I did a range of experiments, working with year 10, 11 and 12 teachers as we demonstrated for their large classes of boys.

Eid al Fitr celebrations in Mahmude Raqi with children riding a merry-go-round and revellers atop the hills. Notice the light brown hair of some of the children.

I really grew to like the principal there. He was an interesting and passionate man, knowledgeable and worldly, but also showing a great deal of humility and respect. He was a *Haji*, having been to Mecca, as well as other middle eastern countries, and had flown in airplanes. He kindly expressed his gratitude that we Americans came to his poor country to teach and give something to humanity.

He was a landowner with a sizable farm and large compound residence, like a fairytale castle surrounded by cultivated plots. The compound had great high walls, inside of which were clustered homes and feeding troughs and pens for milk cows, sheep, working oxen and donkeys.

He invited us supervisors and teachers from the lycée to a fascinating evening and dinner at his home, which we reached after a walk through farmland and orchards. We were served delicious chicken *pilau*, vegetables, tomato, radish and onion salad, *naan,* fruits, black tea, and steaming fresh milk, sweetened with sugar. We talked about Afghan affairs, regional politics, and America. At one point the

85

principal said he thought that Kabul was now quite modern with the biggest jets flying into the airport and asked me if this was true. I said that, actually, the Boeing 737s flown by Ariana Afghan Airlines had been upgraded to the larger 707 and more recently to a much larger 747. He was deflated, and I realized I could have been more diplomatic in my answer and by praising Ariana as a well-run airline.

During the religious *Eid* (holiday) days the village and nearby plains were filled with thousands of people strolling in their finest clothes, picnicking, playing games and gambling. Small children rode on handmade wooden Ferris wheels, squealing with joy. Rege Rawan ("moving sands") mountain, a vast steep slope of pure white soft sand on the side of a rocky mountain, was nearby. On one visit, we PCVs abandoned teacher mode and climbed up the rocks to the top of the sands. We took off our boots and socks and holding them while barefoot we ran straight down what felt like a cliff. With the sand giving way and sliding, we could take controlled long leaps, which was exciting and fun. We were just like a bunch of kids! The mountain is a geologic phenomenon, and the normally convective wind forever blows the sand back up the mountain.

At the end of June, the Asia Foundation supplied a large store of books that I had applied for, and I collected them in Kabul and distributed them to the schools and the education department. They were much appreciated.

All in all, work was going well, though not always smoothly. From a letter I wrote to home in mid-1972:

> The people joke a lot, my language is still miserable, and I'm often confused by culture as well as language. Currently we're working weekly one day at each of the two boys' and girls' schools, performing experiments and training teachers. Many of the kids are eager to learn, and very bright, however, the system here is rote oriented and it is difficult to teach science as we'd like to.
>
> The cultural experience here is proving to be interesting, at times trying. There is some animosity from those who view America as a rich nation of non-believers (infidels)

who help Israel, slaughter Vietnamese, and give little to Afghanistan. There is also the problem of not being arrogant while trying to assume the pride and toughness that is characteristic of Afghan people. And this is in a society where there is little chance for a non-Moslem foreigner to be accepted. Religion here has not yet budged from the letter of what the people call the "Books of the Sky"—the Old Testament and the Quran.

In Mahmude Raqi I sometimes witnessed hellfire and brimstone Islam. One mullah stood six feet tall, and in his fiery voice belted out the Quran, ending sentences in song-like uplifting tones, in the way that the scripture is memorized. He had glistening eyes and a confident, pious smile. His black beard added to the image of his peran and tunban, embroidered vest and turban. His parting words to me were in Arabic and always seemed threatening when in fact, he was asking Allah to keep me safe. It took some time for me to understand that he was offering words of kindness.

Trips to the Panjshir Valley were, for me, the most interesting. This feeling probably came from the combination of the sheer vastness and steep climb up the switch backed valley and the lycée principal and his staff, who were so interesting to talk to. The road from Gulbahar headed north on the left of the Panjshir River, then bending to the northeast. With the beginning of summer, the Panjshir river was a torrent raging through large boulders, fed by the melting snows high in the mountains, with green and lush cultivated land close to the river. Small plots and carved terraces rose up the mountainside growing wheat and barley alongside mulberry, apple, apricot, almond, cherry, pistachio and pomegranate orchards.

The road was often not wide enough for two vehicles to pass and on both sides were large boulders and steep dropoffs. It was easy to understand how years later the Soviets failed to subdue and hold the Panjshir, as the terrain is essentially impassable by heavy vehicle military convoys because of the narrow road easily attacked from above.

The lycée was in the village of Rukha, just before Bazarak, about 30 miles up the road, where the river flattens out for a mile or two. The lycée was a long unfinished brick building parallel to the road, mostly barren inside, filled with crude benches and desks, overcrowded with students, with some window frames not yet glassed in. The principal's office and the guest room were at the front. It would take a few more years to complete the construction.

Our work routine there was the same as on the plains. We taught and demonstrated to teachers as well as students, took questions, delivered equipment, and spent the night in the school. My Farsi was now a reasonable tool, being at an "accomplished beginner" stage. My Panjshiri counterpart Sayid Qamar uDin, being a Sayid —a descendant of the prophet—was a respected person by local tradition. For the people, the school was an institution of strength, tradition, and pride.

We took meals in the guest room, where we ate with the principal and several teachers. Food was served on a large tablecloth placed on the floor, around which we sat on *tushaks*. Lunch was soup with *naan* and side dishes. Each person had a single thick crusted *naan* about 18 inches long, 10 inches wide, square at the base and pointed at the head. The *naan* was dark whole wheat formed with ribs inside the crust and slits where the bread had been stuck on the inside top of a tandoor, a large earthen oven, something like a pizza oven. The bread was delicious and very nutritious.

A large bowl of steaming soup was placed in the center of the group. Each person would tear half of his bread into small pieces and drop them into the soup. We each had a small round dish of pieces of meat, potato, and purple onion. Meat could be beef and rarely donkey or camel, if that was all that was available, and was very tough. The bread in the large bowl absorbed the steaming soup, and we tore small wedges from the other half of our bread and scooped up the steaming wet glutinous bread from the bowl directly in front of us. Our host occasionally replenished our small dish with meat and vegetables. An unusual and rare treat was roasted sparrows. They looked like tiny chickens, about two inches long and were served whole in their juices. Head, beak, body, bones, wings, and feet were taken in one bite, which tasted like chicken with potato chips, from the crunchiness of the tiny, hollow bones and skull.

Condiments included spicy red chili pepper, ground purple grape powder and salt, which we took in finger pinches for our individual dish. At the end of the meal, depending on the season, we had fresh fruit: mulberries, honeydew melon, pomegranates, and individual small pots of black or green tea served in tempered glasses. After eating, some smoked, generally harsh Pakistani cigarettes or British brands.

Panjshir Principal
wearing a *karakul* cap

The evening meal was special, usually rice with chicken or lamb, all luxuries. Chicken was as special as in the day of George Washington. It was said that a *khan* (gentleman) prefers the wing, as the meat of the wing was the most tender and tasty. Chickens were all free-range and old, scrawny and leathery, and the dry, tough breast the least desirable. After dinner we talked culture, history and politics. The Afghans were interested to learn about America and the West, and the elders were worldly and knowledgeable. They talked of the days of the British Raj and the centuries-long tussle between Imperial

Britain and Tsarist Russia, the Russian Revolution, World Wars I and II, and current events. They knew a lot more history than I did, and I learned much from the conversations.

The principal was from the Panjshir and the same age as my father, 51. He had studied at the Teachers College in Kabul and then spent over 20 years teaching in various parts of Afghanistan before finally landing an assignment at home. His knowledge of Western history was remarkable. He described the Spanish Civil War and the "partisani" forces and the support Franco received from Hitler and Mussolini. One day I showed him a picture from a history book at the school of Chamberlain, Daladier, Hitler, Mussolini and Ciano. Not reading the caption, he named all except the last, saying that he was Mussolini's son-in-law, then replying, "Oh yes, that would be Conciano, the Minister of Foreign Affairs."

I stayed in a room for storage (or guests!), which had a small table, a cabinet closet, two small Afghan carpets and a *charpoi* bed. Per Afghan culture, the principal and teachers did not leave me alone except for sleeping, as this would "bring me sadness," meaning make me lonely. I slept on *tushaks* with ample blankets and a *chaprostie* (janitor or housekeeper) slept outside my room for protection, and in case I needed assistance.

The toilet facility was 20 yards away at right angles to the downhill edge of the school area. It was an adobe structure of maybe a dozen latrines about four feet high, each a small room with a wooden door with ventilation slits. Inside was a hole in the floor and a pile of pebbles used for toilet paper. The ceiling was so low that you had to stoop and squat, and I needed to bring my own toilet paper or use the pebbles. The smell was dreadful, made worse on hot summer days, and I learned to take care of business quickly. The waste was collected from behind and below for fertilizer.

17. Kabul Visits

Once when I left Lycée Rukha, I stood on the road outside the school, waiting for a vehicle—the way of travel throughout Asia, as any van, bus or truck will pick up travelers for a standard fare. Along came a well-polished, tan Russian Volga private car, which stopped and picked me up. The driver was a uniformed professional, and in the back was an affluent, well dressed, slightly portly gentleman who had the air of a strong type. We talked a bit, but he wasn't really interested in conversation and was simply being kind by offering a respectable looking foreigner a ride to Gulbahar. I much appreciated traveling in style and relative comfort down the windy, rocky, bumpy Panjshir Valley road. Later Sayid Qamar told me that he was most likely a "smuggler" of lapis lazuli from mines far up in the mountains. The who, what and how of this was beyond me for sure.

Soon after returning to Baku Kham, Marty Kumorek arrived with USAID Director Bart Harvey and his wife, on a trip up the Panjshir River Valley. They had wanted to see Mark Svendsen's Food for Work location, and then invited the two of us to join them. I was thrilled. They had a four-wheel drive vehicle and had planned to stay in the home of a head man far, far up the river valley.

Of course the drive was much easier and faster than the buses I was used to. The river was flowing more quietly because it was later in the season, and before the winter rains and snows. About five miles past Rukha we passed through the village of Bazarak, where the riverbed opens up and is wide and flat, with large, cultivated areas on both sides of the river bordered by steep mountains going straight up. It was an impressive expanse of farms, orchards, and houses. Then the Saricha road again narrows, heading uphill to the northeast, eventually reaching the Khawak Pass at 12,600 feet elevation. Alexander the Great reputedly passed there and at Nuristan, at elevations reaching 24,000 feet. Eventually we came to a big compound with mostly stone houses where we were welcomed by our important local host. It was clear that the head of USAID was a VIP in Afghanistan.

As per normal hospitality they first served us tea and allowed us some time to quietly rest. As evening fell, we were served a delicious meal with qabuli *pilau*, lamb, chicken, *naan*, eggplant with yogurt and salad of tomato and purple onion. I had become not simply used to purple onion, but a lover of this fragrant and tasty vegetable. For dessert we were served a melon like honeydew. Conversation at dinner focused mainly on the Panjshir Valley and future development work.

The main projects were schools, road improvements and repairs, and pedestrian bridges linking to the east side of the river. Later when we were alone, Bart and Marty somewhat unconvincingly but very affably commented that they had not at all missed having their evening cocktails.

Along the road both going and coming we had seen men walking who were wearing sandals made from leather uppers stitched onto soles made from tire tread, extremely durable footwear. Later I'd see that flip flops and buckets were also made throughout the country from old tire treads.

We were probably at around 10,000 feet of elevation, surrounded by mountains reaching up to 19,000 feet. The air was thin, but we were told and could observe that the men here could tirelessly walk up and down steep roads and mountains all day long. Bart told us that he'd read there were three places in the world well known for the greatest longevity of the people. These were in Chile, Tajikistan and Pakistan, near Afghanistan's Wakhan Corridor. The people in these three locations had three things in common: all were at very high elevation with very clean air, the people constantly exercised by walking up and down the high mountains, and all had diets rich in lamb meat and fat.

The Lycée Rukha principal had also told us that these Panjshir folks, who were farmers, hunters and sometimes fighters, carried with them a food called *talkhon*, a mix of equal parts of walnuts and dried mulberries, ground into a solid paste and formed into the shape of a brick. This all-natural food is mostly sugar and protein, and with ample river water for drinking, men can survive on this alone for days, even weeks. Operating in the high and steep mountains with their stamina, knowledge of the mountains and trails, adequate ammunition and *talkhon*, Panjshiri guerrilla fighters were a formidable almost unconquerable foe, which the Soviets were to learn much later.

This trip up the Panjshir was a welcome new experience, learning about the work of others, and being able to share time with important people in the development game.

With Kabul less than three hours away, I often went monthly for R&R, to pick up mail, and for work—checking in and getting equipment from the NSC, books from the Asia Foundation and Peace Corps library, and movies from USIS. This was something of a battle for me, the Kabul vs. Baku Kham life, and I did feel a bit guilty for being able to get to the city regularly. But it was what it was.

Most often I'd stay with Heidar or Marty, who both generously invited me to come stay with them anytime. Heidar's home was stately and his family diverse and interesting. Marty was interesting and knowledgeable, and his home modern and filled with antiques and artwork, books, and a well-stocked American kitchen and bar. Both frequently invited guests, including Europeans, American government people and prominent Afghans.

Kabul had a cinema in Share Naw that showed mainly Indian films in Hindi or Urdu language, which many Afghans could follow, and some had English subtitles. Urdu is a language of Pakistan and is written in the Arabic script and includes many Farsi words. The Indian (now called Bollywood) films were three hours long with an intermission in the middle. They were filled with Asian beauties and song and dance, love affairs, and villains and heroes.

There were also movies from the USSR, typically war movies showing the great Soviet war machine grinding down the Nazis in World War II, or the Red Army fighting to victory during the Communist Revolution. Occasionally there were British or American films, sometimes with Indian themes. One particular movie was about a famous Indian classical dancer, with a well-known British star playing the lead part. She was beautiful and played in "dark face" makeup, but her dancing was not a patch on the real thing. Heidar was highly critical of this laughable approach of not using Indian dancers and actors in lead roles.

I also really liked having dinner at the Kabul Hotel. It was a very reasonable and civilized affair, served in a large dining room with a high ceiling, by waiters of skill and dignity trained in the British colonial style. They served a four or five course fixed price meal of European food. It tasted slightly different from the real thing but was good. They also served drinks, typically whiskey, gin or sherry, as

93

well as wine from the Afghan winery, established by Italians decades before. It was cheap drinkable everyday wine.

Another favorite food experience was kerai, a kebab dish. Heidar and I often went to a famous local spot in the heart of the Kabul Bazaar, just off the Kabul River. It was near workshops of carpenters, metal workers, toy makers in small open shops with men sitting before tables or hearths, banging red hot chunks of steel into shovels or metal parts for machines. We'd walk down the narrow, dark, covered paths in the bazaar to the kebab shop, which had the cooking on the first floor and seating on the second. We would order and then climb the stout wooden ladder stairs and await the meal. Kerai consisted of chunks of tasty lamb kebab and tail fat fried in oil with an egg, onion, tomato, and spices, served in a small skillet with a large piece of *naan*. Delicious!

USAID in Kabul had a Staff House which PCVs were allowed to use. They served hamburgers, French fries, and beer, and lots of other American food that we missed and couldn't get in the provinces. Volunteers often met there to party and let our hair down. I remember one time whooping it up, and when the Afghan waiter asked if there was anything else I wanted, I replied are there any girls? His face turned to stone and eyes narrowed, for such a thought insulted his honor and I realized I'd made a huge faux pas. I immediately apologized deeply and turned back to the others.

AID also had a Club with a swimming pool and tennis courts. I was fortunate to be able to make some tennis friends and play some of the tournaments, great exercise and a chance to get outside of the day-to-day.

In July we had a PCV Math Science Supervisor conference where we spent a full day on site reports, learning about how each of us was working in Kabul, Ghazni, Kapisa, Baghlan and Maimana. We were asked to compare our experiences and make recommendations for training the incoming cycle of teachers. This included NSC supervisors and science teachers and trainers then being brought for the Kabul school system. One of our concerns was the improvement of relations with the NSC, as we volunteers felt left out of the mainstream.

Dan Kugler from our group suggested that we work with the lower classes of grades 7, 8 and 9 in a progressive sequence, with the goal to turn out better teachers in four to five years. This was a good idea, but depended on what the NSC and department of education wanted us to do. We did reach a consensus that our objectives were to:

1. Teach teachers
2. Introduce a scientific approach with student experimentation and enquiry techniques
3. Increase lab and library supplies
4. Institute lesson planning for the teachers
5. Recommend that classes be separated by age and ability

Other work assigned to us was preparing experiment guides, periodic tables of the elements and science charts for classrooms, answer guides for the textbook homework and tests, and translating these into Farsi. We also made lists of science equipment and English books that the schools had and what more was needed. We then wrote requests for funds to meet these needs to the provincial Departments of Education and the NSC. Unfortunately, it would turn out that we never received any funds.

We all agreed that a challenge to our work was trying to change a system of education that was based on rote memorization and not teaching science as an experimental, dynamic process. The best educated Afghan student was one who could flawlessly recite the Quran, Farsi poetry and school lessons by heart. Recitation was done with students rocking forward and backwards on a chair or cross legged on the floor in a sing song sort of chant. We were not used to this, although our American education had also involved a lot of memorizing.

We finished our conference by meeting with Mr. Matin from Peace Corps and then visiting the NSC together to present our list of recommendations. Matin was very diplomatic and patient and did a good job of helping us to understand the challenges facing the NSC and education departments, as well as bringing our points of view to the both of them.

18. More Teaching at Distant Schools

From late July to September, we continued with a busy schedule of training teachers and delivering the NSC kits and books. The NSC now also provided some international equipment for secondary education known as Singer (yes, from the sewing machine maker) Kits and Oddo-Carini Physics kits. While teaching, we enjoyed seeing the light come on in students' eyes even though much of what they were learning had little application in their lives.

Our team, for the most part, worked well together, and we were received warmly and positively in all the schools. Sayid Qamar and I worked together on chemistry and biology most of the time, and Mohamed Saeid focused on physics. Both were good teachers. From locally available materials, Saeid put together simple experiments complementing the textbooks and covering inertia, centripetal

School construction in Kapisa Province with precise brick and stonework, and poplar wood beams awaiting installation

96

motion, moment arms, action and reaction, falling objects, liquid pressure and density, surface tension and more.

The weather in late September was beautiful with occasional rain while the Hindu Kush (east) and Kohibaba (west) mountains were now covered with snow; the summer dust that had obscured the mountains was gone. The cultivated areas were covered with greenery and trees, and in places rocky barren mountains rose into the clouds, shrouded with mist. Probably the only thing I missed was seeing the ocean.

On a moonless night, the stars could be seen in all their splendor from my humble mud roof, which I had just had re-mudded for the winter. The stars were brilliant, and I could see some two dozen constellations.

To complete the year, we needed to travel to the distant south and easterly towns of Nejrab and Tagab. Nejrab was famous for its hospitality and lush green valley with five fingers that reach up to the towering mountains. Arriving in Nejrab by bus, Sayid Qamar, Saeid Khan and I were met with enthusiasm. We delivered the books and equipment, did experiments and attended eleventh grade chemistry and twelfth grade biology classes. We were impressed with how the teachers presented their lessons. Our experiments included analysis of organic matter, production of hydrogen, generation of static electricity, pressure and elastic forces, and mechanical advantage. After school we were provided a delicious dinner with a variety of fruits for dessert, and delicious hot, sweet milk.

In Nejrab, I was taken to the home of a German DED volunteer named Werner Strohhecker who was working in agriculture. He was tall and strong looking with a full head of blonde hair. Like the Germans at the Sherkat, he was generously welcoming. In time we visited one another, and later in my last year, he and other DED volunteers came to my house in Kabul for dinner. He and his father also visited me in New York City in 1975 after I returned from Peace Corps. They were on their way to buy a farm in Ontario Province in Canada, having given up on West and East Germany being reunited. They sold their small German farm for a huge sum and bought a massive farm in Canada with the money.

We spent two weeks in Nejrab, with a weekend at home in between. I went to Kabul and met other volunteers for a picnic and mountain climbing, including leaping off short cliffs onto gravel, where I fell and broadly scraped my left leg below the knee. Returning for week two, I waited for transport in the Mahmude Raqi tea house on the main road in my wool suit in stifling heat. Drinking hot, sweet tea taught me that hot tea in a hot climate is refreshing and cooling, something Asians have known forever. We had to sit on top of the small bus as all inside seats were occupied. I got the feeling that Sayid Qamar was bearing with me on this undignified way to travel, as I was solely focused on getting there, whereas he, as an educated local, would have preferred to wait another day and travel properly.

We arrived tired and dusty so delayed work for a day. We carried on with experiments on fermentation of grapes, distillation of alcohol and properties of hydrocarbons. We also plated zinc with copper, demonstrated the heat of solidification of paraffin and delivered the Singer Discovery Kit. I learned that everyone knows that when fresh washed mulberries are left wet in baskets for a few days, they ferment and when eaten make you drunk. Apparently, this is okay because it's natural, or maybe because nobody talks about it.

Midway through the lessons I realized that my left trouser leg was all wet and saw that my leg was quite swollen and oozing from the fall on the weekend. I was guided to the local clinic. The "doctor" was a local man of some learning with a clinic in his mud home with glass cabinets and a few bottles and medicines. He put alcohol on my calf and wrapped it in gauze. For me it was a wakeup call to see how little medical support was available for the local people in distant villages. Worried, after work I left for Kabul and the PC doctor's office. It all turned out well, and I got a lesson about not jumping off hills on picnics and behaving like a teenager.

Back in Mahmude Raqi for the next week, we did another dozen experiments, delivered books, made year-end plans, and arranged our final trip to Tagab, which was the only Pashtun village in the province.

From my journal:

I am sitting here in Mahmude Raqi, just below the hill that, though desolate and barren, houses all the government offices and is the political center of the province. It is warm, yet crisp, much like Afghanistan was a year ago when I first arrived. In the sun you warm comfortably, and in the shade, you're almost cold. Sayid Qamar and I are waiting for the country bus to Tagab, to complete our year's schedule for all seven provincial lycées. Tagab is the southernmost village of the province and is Pashtun.

It was the second day of the holy month of Ramadan, so no one was eating, drinking, smoking or taking snuff. Breaking the fast at sundown is called eftar, when people have a small amount to eat and drink, then go to pray. After prayer they enjoy a leisurely meal and music, and the company of family and friends. During the fast a man is not permitted to see his wives at night. As the month wears on, people eat less as this is more comfortable. Everyone wakes at 3:00 a.m. to eat the sahr (early morning meal) and to get ready for the day.

As it was Ramadan, our travel and arrangements were complicated. Fortunately, in Islam travelers are exempt from fasting, so we could get on with the work as well as eat. However, the locals go to work early and finish early, and are sleepy from about noon onwards. We were provided for, but it was strange to eat alone inside without the teachers. We taught in Farsi which was translated to Pashto by the teachers, so everything took a lot longer.

We allocated two weeks for Tagab, and in that time we taught classes in three sections: seventh to 9th graders, 10th grade and 11th grade. Experiments included neutralization of acids, heat of melting paraffin, analysis of organic compounds, and properties of soaps.

We slept in the school, and in the morning some local boys watched me shave, wash and brush my teeth with water from the juey outside. They looked at me with wide eyes like I was some kind of exotic creature, compounded by my English and our team's Farsi, neither of which they understood. By now such things didn't bother me as we volunteers were on display all the time. That's no doubt part of the reason why, at home in Baku Kham, I often spent the evenings when I had no roommates writing letters, reading history, studying Farsi, listening to music and having a drink. Down time outside of the fishbowl was essential.

On our final day, we found that the chemistry and biology teachers had "escaped": they had left early to wait out the fast at home. So, we worked with the other teachers. We found that they had a microscope and demonstrated its use, looking at onion cell structure and blood cells, and comparing my fine, blondish hair with a student's thicker coarse, black hair. We also set up an experiment to see the effects of growing two dishes of beans, with and without chemical fertilizer.

19. Language, Religion and Women

One of my goals in joining the Peace Corps and accepting the offer of Afghanistan was to see the world and live in a different culture. From the beginning it was clear how remarkable this experience would be. As my first year of service progressed, I was learning much about the language and religion of the Afghans, and their way of family life.

Afghanistan's two main languages were Pashtu and Farsi (or Persian), which the government officially called Dari, the original name meaning court language. Persian was created from Pahlavi (middle old Persian) and Arabic in the 8th to 10th centuries in what is now Iran, Afghanistan and the Central Asian kingdoms of the Samarqand, Bukhara, Balkh, and Seistan. Farsi developed far and wide, and each of the countries speaking it today—mainly Iran, Afghanistan, Uzbekistan and Tajikistan—had a role in the heritage. Interestingly there are parallels between Farsi and English, in that the backbones of the languages are Pahlavi and German for the vernacular and Arabic and Latin for the literary.

We science supervisors were sent to Farsi speaking locations, and hence never learned Pashtu. Given that the Pashtuns were the dominant ethnic group in the country, this meant that we ultimately identified with the minority Farsi speaking groups, even as Farsi was the language of Kabul and the educated elite.

Peace Corps language training was very effective for speaking fluency. We memorized short conversations by rote, followed by learning the meaning. To this day, we can recall many of those lessons, such as, in translation: "from here to Castle Fatullah Khan is how much road? ... This bicycle behind tire appears low in air..." The language also revealed how outgoing and friendly the Afghans were. When meeting, they always exchange a cheerful barrage of greetings: "are you good, are you well, are your children well, is your family happy, where have you been, your whereabouts don't exist, why have we not seen you, we miss you, come visit us...", etc. We naturally aped this as well as being creative. For example, the past tense of to go is "raft", so we'd say, "Let's raft." "Far out" was a hip statement of the era, so we'd say "dur kharij", literally "far outside" in Farsi. And so on.

I loved the challenge of learning Farsi and spent a lot of time reading textbooks from British scholars and UN magazines in Farsi. On the job in Kapisa, my language learning accelerated rapidly. It was a thrilling experience to be conversing with local teachers and suddenly understand even sophisticated new words simply from the context. Gaining meaning-by-association was like being a child again. Mostly, however, I learned from the effort of reading, listening, writing down and memorizing vocabulary lists, and working with dictionaries.

Farsi is an Indo-European language, the grammar is simple, similar to Spanish without gender. The alphabet and much vocabulary come from Arabic, a versatile and mathematical language, with words built from roots. For example, "salaam aleikum" is the Muslim greeting meaning "peace upon you." *Salaam* is from the Arabic root S L M meaning peace and from which are derived *Islam*, submission to God; *Muslim*, one who has submitted to God; *salaam*, peace; *salamat*, health; *tasleem*, surrender, and more. Knowing roots, I could understand new meanings quickly.

Farsi also uses auxiliary verbs formed by a noun plus to do, or to become, etc. So, one can say "write do," "play do," "live do," "work do," "steal do," "sleep do," or "hungry become," "cold become," "angry become," "sad become," etc. This provides automatic rhyming in poetry. There are also many Persian words in English: checkmate from *shah mat* or king died; *maadar* and *padar* are mother and father; cummerbund from *kamar band* or waist band; pajama from *pa jame* or foot shirt; khaki from *khak* or earth; *adam* for person, from the Bible.

During training we built language skills both from lessons and lectures about Afghan culture and how what we say is bound to customs. This led to constantly arising questions and insights into our American and English language ways. An example was the word "tonight." To Afghans this means the night just passed, because Allah created the world from darkness, and a new day starts from night. They also do not make statements about the future, preferring "inshallah," meaning "if God wills." So, when asked if it will rain tonight the answer is no, it didn't. If pressed about the coming evening, the answer would be "inshallah."

With more than 90% illiteracy, the spoken language was very simple. Typically, they use only one or a few words for things so, for example, there wasn't a feeling of profanity for basics, like bodily functions. They don't have feces, bowel movement, crap, poo, number 2 and shit, the word for it, phonetically, is simply "go." Illustrating this is the expression for freckles: "go-i-magas," literally fly shit. People may chuckle at this, but it's not rude. Incidentally, Afghan people in general don't have freckles, so when they see a red headed westerner covered with freckles, it's strange to them. Simplicity of language actually makes life easier, and friendlier. At the same time, they also had many subtle ways of saying things. For example, if you need to go to the toilet, you say you need to "joab-i-chai," literally "answer to tea."

I also became interested in Persian poetry during training and friends Heidar and Marty and teacher Zarghuna were keen to teach and share. Heidar was a real scholar, often quoting Omar Khayyam, Saadi, Hafiz, Mowlana—famous Persian poets from the 10th to 13th centuries, an era when Persians and Muslims were world leaders and highly refined. I hadn't much interest in English poetry, and it was a surprise that the Farsi poetry became interesting to me.

Omar Khayyam wrote meaningful yet simple quatrains. He was an astronomer, mathematician, poet and advisor to kings, a fascinating and brilliant person. One quatrain that I cherish is (my clumsy translation):

> Since there's nothing from everything that is, but
> wind on the hand
> Since there are for everything that is, flaws and fault
> Suppose what is, everything in the world isn't
> Imagine what is not, everything in the world is

The meaning is that since the end result of everything is nothing and nothing is perfect, imagine that everything that is isn't, and what isn't is. The worst may be the best, or wrong may be right. The most honest person may be the biggest crook, and vice versa. It also recalls the famous Mark Twain statement that it's not what you don't know that hurts you, but the thing that you know for sure which turns out not to be right.

Another famous quatrain is:

> They say that heaven in Aden is happy with angels
> I say that grape water (wine) is happy
> Grasp this cash, and leave your hand from that credit
> Because the sound of the drum, brother, from a
> distance is happy

The common saying is "the sound of a distant drum (of a wedding party) is very enticing." This is the same as the grass is greener on the other side of the street, or the promise of what you don't have is more alluring than what you have in hand.

There were also sharp insights about people: "even if Jesus' donkey goes to Mecca, when he returns, he's still a donkey." And another: "if you come to a low doorway, go bent over." It means avoid low minded or troublesome people.

In Farsi, *khan* is a suffix for the traditional English lord or sir or mister, used for a village leader or person commanding respect. *Jan* is a suffix showing endearment. One or the other is normally used with names in polite conversation. So, an important person might be Heidar Khan, and a close friend or child, Assif Jan. The other honorific is the use of Sayid as a prefix for a person descended from the family of the Prophet Muhammed. Normally people are addressed by a shortening to two words, for example Sayid Qamar uDin becomes Sayid Qamar, and Muhammed Saeid Khan becomes Muhammed Saeid or Saeid Khan. But you don't use a single name only, like Qamar, Toby, or Muhammed, as this is not polite.

In Britain today there are many last names of *Khan*, like recent Pakistan Prime Minister Imran Khan. To me, this has always seemed absurd, the same as calling someone Mister Mister. I've wondered if this was because the British in the past used their own naming conventions for colonial people without understanding their effect.

Islam is central to life in Afghanistan, and our training focused on the religion of Islam. The Arabian Peninsula neighbored and was intimately connected to the Persian, Babylonian, and Egyptian empires. The religion of the Arabs prior to Islam was mostly idol worship with various gods, and Mecca has a holy site centered about the Kaaba, a large, sacred black stone thought to be from a meteorite. The Prophet Mohamed lived in Mecca and had a vision in 610 CE whereby he was called to serve as God's messenger. Over more than 20 years he had additional revelations that ultimately were consolidated after his death in 632 CE into the Quran, the holy book of Islam.

Following his death, Islam spread rapidly, with a struggle for control of the movement between the caliphates in what is today Syria who were not of the family of the Prophet Mohamed, and in Mecca, who were led by descendants of the Prophet. This struggle came to a head in 680 CE with the Battle of Karbala in Iraq, in which Hussein ibn Ali, the grandson of the Prophet, and many of his followers were killed by a large army of the Umayyad Caliph Yazid. The result of this battle was the permanent and bitter split in Islam over the leadership between what became known as the Sunni and the Shia, the latter followers of Hussain ibn Ali. The Shia revere him as a martyr and grieve his death annually on the tenth of Muharram, often flagellating themselves in processions and chanting religious gospel. The split between Sunni and Shia is tragic and can be deadly to this day.

The practice of the religion requires obedience to the five pillars of Islam, which are the Creed, praying five times a day, giving alms (10 percent), fasting for the holy month of Ramadan, and making the pilgrimage to Mecca, called the Haj, for those who can afford this. On the Haj, the faithful pray and circle the Kaaba over a number of days. There are two major holidays, Eid al Fitr and Eid al Adha or Eid al Qurban. The first celebrates the breaking of the fast following the holy month of Ramadan. The second is the Feast of the Sacrifice, commemorating the willingness of Ibrahim (Abraham) to sacrifice his son to the will of God. The Islamic calendar starts from the Hejira when the prophet Mohamed fled from Mecca to Medina to escape persecution. There he started the first Muslim community which grew to become the center of the religion. Our year 1972 corresponds to 1351 in the Hejira calendar.

Allah means "The God," who is indescribable and to whom one must submit. All names relate to this. There are 99 names or descriptors for God, and people's names come from these names. e.g. Kareem meaning Kind or Compassionate is a name for God and Abdul Kareem means servant (abdul) of The Kind. Jabbar means all powerful and Ghulam Jabbar means slave (ghulam) of the All Powerful. With the Sunni Shia split this becomes complicated because the Shia use a name such as Ghulam Hussein (who was a man and relative of the Prophet Mohamed) and the Sunni say you cannot be a Ghulam of a man, so this is heresy.

We volunteers were constantly asked about our own religion. As a Unitarian, I said that I believed in one God that is, using their words, indescribable and undefinable. They assumed that I was Christian, although while Unitarianism did come from and is often described as Christian, Unitarianism is not a dogmatic religion, and mostly we do not believe in the divinity of Jesus of Nazareth. Afghans would respectfully say that Islam is the one true religion and that all you need do to become a Muslim is to repeat and believe in the Creed, "La ilaha il Allah, Mohamed Rasool Allah," meaning "there is no god but The God, and Mohamed is the Messenger (seal or last of the prophets) of The God."

To explain why they did not believe in the divinity of Christ, they offered the analogy of an ash tray, man, and God, saying that because man makes the ash tray, it cannot be the same as man, nor could an ash tray ever make a man. Likewise, since God created man, so man can never be the same as God or make a God. Hence Jesus was a man and cannot be God. Afghans were respectful and tolerant of Christians and Jews, seeing them as people of the "Books from the Sky": The Old Testament and the Quran. Their name for Jesus is Isa or Masih (Messiah), and he is revered, as are the Old Testament prophets.

We PCVs were stunned at how strongly the Sunni, about 80% of the population, were prejudiced against the Shia. My servant Assif, a very fair and sensible person, told us the "true" story taught by the mullahs: the Shia practiced *charagh kush*, meaning "kill the lantern." They said that Shia gather together at night, snuff the lantern, and in darkness have sex with whomever: their mother, sister, or daughter. The Shia were mostly Hazara people, physically resembling Chinese and said to be descendants of the Mongols who invaded Afghanistan in the 13th century. Most Hazara were humble and hardworking laborers and servants, and we were sorry that they suffered from discrimination.

For all Afghans, being Muslim is at the center of their existence. They believe that people are either Muslim or *kafirs*, non-believers, and that only Muslims will go to heaven. Their Islamic civilization teaches them how to behave, whom to respect and what is right and wrong. Their beliefs are fundamental to their conservatism. This makes reform and change for many difficult, whether in 1929 or 2002.

Muslims call the Crusades, from the 11th to 13th centuries, "janggi saleeb," the War of the Cross. At that time, Muslims were refined and highly educated, unlike the European Christians whom the Muslims viewed as barbaric terrorists invading their lands. This deep divide extends to the age of imperialism beginning in the 15th century. Even today many view the British, Portuguese, French and Dutch colonizers as pirates who, by force, gained control of their lands and for centuries robbed them of their wealth. In the 20th century, even as they emerged greatly weakened from World War I, the British and French aggressively expanded their Mideast empires from the lands of the defeated Ottoman Empire, but soon proved unable to manage or maintain them. The humble Afghans that I lived and worked with, even as they recognized our superior standards of living and education and thanked us for our help, privately believed that throughout history the West has been the invader and terrorist, while they are true believers living independently in their own land.

As I became more aware of Islamic history, I also read a great deal about the foundation of Israel, and the Israeli Palestinian conflict. I was coming from the point of view that we Americans were strong supporters of Israel with no tolerance for terrorism by the Palestinians. A book that was particularly meaningful for me was *The Emergence of the Middle East: 1914–1923*, by Howard Sachar, an eminent professor at George Washington University. I learned about the rise of Zionism at the end of the 19th century, and how the movement used religion, idealism, pioneering spirit, money, and ultimately terrorism (or para-military activity, depending on who is writing the history) and war to create Israel, supported by Europe and America who were unwilling to open their borders to the Jews. In time I came to the opinion that a lasting peace in the Mideast will depend on concessions by both sides, and that this is of the utmost importance.

Finally, Afghans had plenty of jokes about religion. One was: why is it that Christians always tell the truth, work hard and are dependable, whereas Muslims tell lies, steal and cheat? The answer is that Muslims are virtually guaranteed to get into heaven, whereas for Christians it is as difficult as walking a tightrope of a single silk thread over an abyss of flames in hell. So, they must do everything they can to be good to have even that small chance of going to heaven.

Another was the story of the Muslim judge and Hindu merchant who lived side by side and were good friends. One day the son of the merchant appeared in the judge's court and converted to Islam. That evening the judge said to the merchant that his son had been in court that day and converted to Islam. The merchant didn't know this, but acted unsurprised and said he knew. Asked how he knew, he said that three months ago his son started drinking alcohol, two months ago he started gambling heavily and last month he started hanging out with prostitutes. So, he said it was just a matter of time before he became Muslim.

Then there was the joke about hell in which there were great cauldrons of people from each nation heating over the fires of hell. In the cauldrons, the people in the French, German, American and other nations' cauldrons were building human pyramids and helping individuals to climb out the top and escape from hell. In the Afghan cauldron, people were climbing up the walls, but when one got close to the top, the others below would grab him and pull him back down.

There is much written about the veil or the burka. The veil in Afghanistan is the *chadri*, a garment that completely covers the body from head to toe full length in the back and half-length in the front with a mesh over the eyes. It is made of light-weight fabric, is embroidered on the head and the face section, and is fully pleated from top to bottom allowing it to become as full as needed. Most *chadris* are colorful, with a bright purple being most common, in addition to light and dark blues, gray, almond, white and black.

Women in Afghanistan seemed like ghosts, floating down the street in their head-to-feet veils. In 1973 in Kabul roughly a quarter of the women had shed the wearing of the veil when outdoors, but many more wore it in rural areas like Kapisa. The custom is that the public is a man's world where women should be covered up. According to Islam as practiced by many in Afghanistan, the faces of women past puberty should never be seen by males not part of the immediate family. In truth there are many interpretations of this custom, which even today is a source of controversy.

One of the worst insults that can be levelled at a man is to call him "beysharaf," meaning without honor. This normally refers to a man who does not protect and honor the women of his family, or to women in his family who are not honorable, meaning that they have affairs with others or are available. Another severe insult is to be a "razeel," which is a scoundrel, a vile person, also possibly beysharaf.

The home and the family were the stronghold of women. When families got together, the women, from toddlers to grandmas, would go into the interior of the home with free rein of house and garden. They would talk about families, children, clothing, cooking, education, as women the world over do. They see the newborns and the growing children. They dance and sing, play music and listen to the radio together. Male visitors, on the other hand, are kept in a guest room with a door to the outside and do not have access to the interior of the house. Related to this is the saying that you never ask a man about "zar, zan or zamin," which are gold (money), women and land (wealth.)

Later, when I was married and would visit traditional homes like this, I felt like a second-class citizen, with my wife free to enjoy our host's home. Somewhat sadly, when I returned to the Middle East from living in Japan in the 1980s, the magic was gone, and a lot of this was because of the inability to connect with families.

When it comes to marriage, women play a crucial role. Marriages are arranged, and elders choose the partners to wed in order to keep families together and to meet landholding and business needs. Often it is grandmothers and mothers who decide which son will be good for which daughter and call the tune for these family alliances, which are amongst the most important family decisions. Weddings are large happy events that take days. The bride's family deliver her on horseback or in a carriage to the groom's home, with drums and music playing and big celebrations, men outside and women inside. A significant bride price is paid by the family of the groom to the family of the bride. It can be made up of various forms of wealth: animals (sheep, donkeys, horses, camels), jewelry, land, cash, etc.

Islam requires that the men of a family look after the women. If a man dies leaving a widow, the brother or nearest relative of the deceased is obligated to offer to marry the widow. She is not obligated to accept this offer; it is her choice. If she accepts, then they marry and the new husband must give her equal treatment as his first (or second, or third) wife: same size house, same amount of money, and same attention and love. The Quran says a man may have four wives.

Map 4: Afghanistan, Crossroads of Ancient Kingdoms

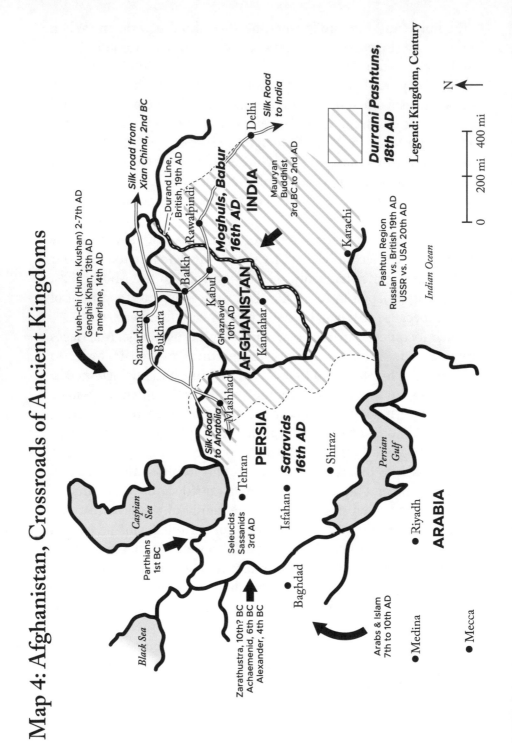

Silk road from Xian China, 2nd BC

Yueh-chi (Huns, Kushan) 2-7th AD
Genghis Khan, 13th AD
Tamerlane, 14th AD

Durand Line, British, 19th AD

Delhi

Silk Road to India

Rawalpindi

Balkh

Moghuls, Babur 16th AD

INDIA

Mauryan Buddhist 3rd BC to 2nd AD

Samarkand

Bukhara

Kabul

Ghaznavid 10th AD

AFGHANISTAN

Kandahar

Karachi

Silk Road to Anatolia

Mashhad

Safavids 16th AD

PERSIA

Pashtun Region
Russian vs. British 19th AD
USSR vs. USA 20th AD

Indian Ocean

Parthians 1st BC

Caspian Sea

Seleucids Sassanids 3rd AD

Tehran

Shiraz

Isfahan

Persian Gulf

Riyadh

ARABIA

Black Sea

Zarathustra, 10th? BC
Achaemenid, 6th BC
Alexander, 4th BC

Baghdad

Arabs & Islam 7th to 10th AD

Medina

Mecca

N

Durrani Pashtuns, 18th AD

Legend: Kingdom, Century

0   200 mi   400 mi

Generally, only the wealthy marry more than one, and modern thinking is that having multiple wives is difficult.

Some female volunteers in the north had good experience with the veil. Walking to school daily they went through the bazaar and boys would often taunt them, pinch them, and occasionally throw pebbles at them. This was, of course, infuriating. Their local counterparts said, "Why don't you put on veils and walk with us?" So they did. It was a revelation. The bazaars, filled with men, parted before them like the proverbial Red Sea, and they walked unbothered straight to school. They also felt empowered seeing all while being invisible.

Years later at a Halloween party I wore a Japanese Noh mask, a serene, carved wooden visage with but two small eye holes. Everyone freaked out after talking to me for only a few minutes, asking me please to take off the mask because they felt so uncomfortable not being able to read my expressions. I, on the other hand, felt advantaged over those I talked to. I learned that this is what wearing a veil feels like, and it is surprisingly empowering.

The Farsi-speaking *Kohistanis* in Kapisa placed a high value on education for their girls and women. The girls were keenly interested, diligent and proper, full of life and a lot of fun to be around, and proud not to wear chadri. However, honoring tradition, our after-school lunches were hosted by the men teachers and the principal, and the women went home.

20. Afghan History from Antiquity to Zahir Shah

One of the reasons I'd joined the Peace Corps was being intrigued by the history of Central Asia, at the center of the ancient world, connecting India, the Fertile Crescent—"cradle of civilization" in the Middle East—and Central Asia, including the famous capitals Bukhara and Samarkand along the Silk Road from China. Afghanistan for millennia was not only a crossroads of civilizations and kingdoms, but also a scene of violent confrontations, called by some historians the cockpit of Asia. For here there were continual battles and regime changes from the beginning of recorded history.

The first named leader in the region may have been Zarathustra (Zoroaster) who seems to have been born in Persia and later settled in Balkh sometime between the 15th and 10th century BCE. By the 6th century BCE, Afghanistan had become a satrap of the Persian Achaemenid empire led by Darius I. Today at the Persepolis ruins in Iran, one can see stone carvings of vassals bringing and presenting gifts of camels, cows, jewelry, fruit, vessels of oil, slaves and more to the Shahen Shah, the King of Kings of Persia. The kings of the satraps were called Padishahs, hence the Afghan Shah in our time was known as either the Padishah or King Zahir.

Following the defeat of the Persians by the Greeks in the 4th century BCE, Alexander the Great conquered Central Asia from Bukhara to the Indus Valley. Following this the Mauryan Empire brought Buddhism from India. The Ghandara ruins of Buddhist temples near Jalalabad show a glimpse of their splendor. After this, came the Yueh-chih (later called Huns), known as the Kushans, whose greatest king Kanishka ruled in the 2nd century CE. The Kushans ruled for five centuries, while yielding territory to the Persian Sassanid dynasty beginning in the 3rd century CE.

The modern era of history began with the Arab conquest bringing Islam to Persia, Afghanistan, and Central Asia over the 7th to 10th centuries. Local peoples fought many wars and repeatedly returned to their old beliefs before eventually adopting Islam. By this time Afghanistan had already been on the Silk Road from Xian (at the time the largest city in the world) in China for more than a thousand years.

The Farsi, or Dari, language emerged over this period. In 998 CE Mahmude of Ghazna (modern Ghazni) established the Farsi speaking Ghaznawid Empire extending from Kabul to India, said to be one of the richest empires in history that lasted for a century and a half.

The Ghaznavid empire was then conquered by Mongol emperor Genghis Khan in 1210–1220 CE, who destroyed most of the cities after his favorite grandson was killed in battle. Some historians say that Afghanistan has never fully recovered from this destruction. Genghis Khan built the largest empire in the world extending from Mongolia to the Middle East and Eastern Europe.

After Genghis's death, this vast empire fell apart until his descendant Timur (Tamerlane) conquered much of Afghanistan in the 14th century. The Timurids ruled until Timur's great-great-great grandson Babur the Great captured Kandahar and Delhi in 1526, establishing the Mughal Empire with its capital in his beloved Kabul. Meanwhile to the west, the Safavid Empire in Iran from 1501, stretched from the Persian Gulf north to Herat and Bukhara.

Afghanistan was thus split for two-and-a-half centuries, by the Shia Safavid and Sunni Mughal empires, both Farsi speaking regimes. This explains how the territory came to be an orderly and traditional monarchy, with a state religion, a regulated economy, mandatory army service for men, and government services and permits, prepared by scribes for the illiterate.

In 1722, Hotaki Ghilzai and Abdali Pashtun (Afghan) tribes led revolts against the Persians, conquering Kandahar and Esfahan, and holding off Russians from the north and Ottoman Turks from the west. But then an officer of the Safavids drove the Afghans from Persia and had himself elected Nadir Shah of Persia in 1736. However, in 1747 he was assassinated by his officers and Pashtun Ahmad Shah Durrani in Kandahar then united the Pashtun tribes and conquered eastern Iran, all of Afghanistan and India to Delhi, creating the Durrani empire, the largest Afghan empire.

Britain began to trade, organize, and rule in India from 1757, and thus began The Great Game, the struggle between the British Lion and the Russian Bear to control Afghanistan as a buffer state between them. As British India expanded, they began paying large subsidies to the Afghan kings and to the Sikhs in the Indus to keep them from cooperating with Russia.

Ahmad Shah died in 1772, followed by intrigue and violence amongst his descendants, with successive leaders murdered, blinded, and cut to pieces. First came Timur, then Zaman Shah, followed by Mahmud and Fath Ali Shah. In 1803 Zaman's brother Shah Shujah ascended the throne when Napoleon I of France was rumored to propose an invasion of Afghanistan to Alexander I of Russia. In 1837, the younger brother of Fath Khan became Emir Dost Mohamed Khan, founding a branch of the Durrani dynasty known as the Barakzai (or Mohammadzai) Pashtuns centered in Kabul, which lasted until the 1970s. The Russians had subjugated the Shah of Iran and set him to attack Afghanistan, which, with the threat of a British force in the Persian Gulf, failed at Kandahar in 1838. Having lost faith in Dost Mohamed and having close relations in the Indus with Ranjhit Singh, who opposed the Afghans, the British invaded Afghanistan and put Shah Shujah on the throne.

As written in chapter 14, this gambit soon failed with the stout resistance of the Afghans, and the British mission under Mountstuart Elphinstone failed to conclude a treaty of friendship. They were forced to retreat in early 1842 and were largely slaughtered. They then returned in 1843 for a war of retribution during which they inflicted much damage on Kandahar, Kabul and Istalif in Kohistan. The feared invasion by the Russians never took place.

Water carriers in Kabul, showing the humble station of the father of the *Kohistani* Tajik who led a civil war and briefly became King Habibullah after overthrowing Amanullah Khan in 1929

The British then launched the First Anglo Afghan War, which ended in failure as covered in chapter 14.

The second Anglo Afghan War, 1878–1880, was much like the first. Afghan king Sher Ali, a son of Dost Mohamed, received the Russians in Kabul, but not the British. Again fearing for their Indian empire, the British decided to attack. The Russians advised the Afghans to make peace, which they did in 1879, as well as agreeing to conduct foreign relations in accordance with the wishes and advice of the British. But the British envoy in Kabul was soon thereafter murdered, so the British, in retaliation, then sent forces and occupied Kabul, but withdrew in 1881 after they and the Russians agreed on the international boundaries of Afghanistan, set by the Durand Line. The British in India however did manage to retain some control over Afghan foreign policy.

In 1880, Emir Abdur Rahman, known as the iron emir, came to power. A strong ruler, he centralized the government, army, and legal system, established a conservative regime and put down over 20 wars of rebellion. In 1896 the international boundaries were fixed when the Durand Line Agreement was signed with the British creating the Wakhan Corridor, a finger of land reaching northeast to the China border, confirming no border between Russia and India. The Durand Line also severed Pashtunistan between Afghanistan and India, and cut off Beluchistan, thereby creating intractable problems for Afghanistan that exist today. Long opposed, Abdur Rahman finally only signed the agreement to the Durand Line when his subsidy was substantially increased.

His son Habibulah Khan became king in 1901 and kept Afghanistan neutral in World War I. But he was assassinated in 1919, when another son, Amanullah Khan, the reformer king, came to power. In May 1919, the Afghans invaded India to expand their territory and eliminate the influence of the British Indian Empire. This was not successful, and after three months, an agreement was reached that guaranteed Afghanistan independence and confirmed its eastern border along the Durand Line, in exchange for Afghanistan promising not to interfere in India's northwest frontier.

This agreement also freed Afghanistan from British control over foreign affairs. Amanullah Khan then introduced constitutional reforms, compulsory elementary education, abolished compulsory wearing of the veil, began the import of western technology, and opened coeducational schools. He also made Afghanistan one of the first nations to recognize the USSR following the Russian revolution, continuing the tradition of closeness with Russia, balancing relations with the British.

Conservative religious groups however opposed these reforms and, led by the illiterate Bache Saqao ("son of water carrier"), a Tajik from Panjshir, overthrew the regime in late 1928. He proclaimed himself Habibulah Khan ("beloved of Allah") which led to civil war. He was soon defeated and then executed by Mohamed Nadir Khan, cousin of Amanullah, who became Nadir Shah in November 1929. Pashtuns were back on the throne, after less than a year.

Nadir Shah produced a more conservative constitution and began industrial development. But he was assassinated in 1933, and his son Mohamed Zahir Shah became Padishah, and ruled until 1973.

Pashtuns have ruled continuously in Afghanistan since 1747 and have never submitted to outside control, except for short period in 1928–29, the USSR-supported communist governments from 1978 –92, and the US and NATO sponsored coalition governments from 2001–21. Their rule however has been bloody, with repeated assassinations of rulers, rebellions and violent regime changes, accompanied by a long-term struggle between conservative religious elements and those favoring reform and modernization.

21. Year End 1972

In the last month before the schools closed for the winter break, we finished our list of lessons and experiments for each school in Kohistan. We met the Director of Education, who praised our work, and asked us to submit a request for equipment requirements. Talking about funding, he told us that corruption is rife in Afghanistan, but that for the decades that he has been on the "chowkee" (chair), not once did he ever take even a single pen as a gift. Later Sayid Qamar explained that this is a common expression and sarcastically it really means that officials accept cash, sheep, chickens, etc. but never a pen. In later years I learned that this refrain plays in many other Asian countries as well.

In Kabul we met Dr. Ghaznowi who requested a report of our activities during the school year with the endorsement of the provincial Director of Education. He also asked us to identify 10 science education problems with recommended solutions and a proposal for the coming school year 1973. He also asked us to make a plan for science seminars to be held over the winter for teachers and helpers either in the province or in Kabul. This was to include schedule, list of attendees, laboratory exercises, teacher incentives and logistical details: sleeping and eating arrangements, heating, availability of laboratories and travel allowances. Lastly, he said, "Don't promise anything." We told him that we wanted to invite 32 teachers from the seven lycées. In the end, there was no funding, and no seminars.

We reported that in Kapisa Lycée Sherkat was the only school in the province with running water and electricity and only Mirmasjadi had any equipment and reagents at the start of the year. In addition there was only one science teacher in the province who was a college graduate and that most science teachers were simply assigned to fill an empty slot even if they had no qualifications for this. Finally, it was a problem that the location of our offices at the Directory of Education in Mahmude Raqi was close enough to be accessible to only one of our seven lycées.

Despite the above, we had brought science teaching and teacher training to all of the schools, distributed supplies and showed that experimentation does not depend just on money, equipment and stocked laboratories. For the coming school year, we proposed to divide our time equally between teaching and developing the science center for distribution of equipment, materials and funds in conjunction with the Department of Education and the NSC.

For Dr. Ghaznowi, we identified these 10 problems in science education:

1. Little or no lesson planning
2. No scheduled lab periods

3. Little student participation in experiments
4. Problem solving by rote
5. Little note taking by students
6. Lack of creative questioning by teachers
7. Little use of scientific principles to solve practical problems
8. Testing in schools that is not uniform or creative
9. Grading based only on the mid-term and final exams—not including quizzes and homework assignments
10. No separation of students by interests and abilities

Back in Kapisa, we had a rude awakening in early December. The Director of Education told us that he had been out of contact with us and our work, and we had not gotten his approval for what we had done. We had reported to him and discussed our work from time to time, but he evidently was not satisfied with our communication. Most likely this reflected the turf battles between Kapisa, the NSC and the Royal Ministry of Education in Kabul. My counterparts did not take orders from the province and were proud of reporting directly to the NSC. No doubt, the Director's criticism was partly because he did not want to use his budget for our program or for travel pay to my counterparts. However they persisted and eventually were paid, presumably with pressure from the NSC .

Dr. Ghaznowi also gave us a schedule of time off over Christmas and early January, an NSC Seminar for supervisors from mid-January to mid-February and more time off before the start of the new school year on Nowroz at the spring equinox. So, I planned trips to Iran and India for my holidays.

I was fortunate to have college and grad school classmate John Boepple visit from Bahrain, where he was working in the oil industry, for a nine-day vacation trip. We had a great time, seeing Kabul, Kapisa, and Jalalabad, as well as enjoying Afghan kebab, pilau and Czechoslovakian beer and Russian vodka purchased from literally under the counter of a pharmacy in Share Naw. In just a few years after our participation in anti-war demonstrations at college, John noted ironically that he was now working in a refinery that produced vast quantities of jet fuel for the US Air Force in Vietnam, and I was teaching in a USSR-leaning medieval state. We were encouraged about news that the Vietnam War might be about to end, though negotiations soon failed. When he left for New York, I sent with him a beautiful small Mauri carpet for my parents for Christmas.

I also met volunteer Ed Madinger, whose father worked together with my father in the research and patent department. Ed was a dynamic guy and a very good guitar player. He was plugged into other PCV musicians and a fun social scene, and we enjoyed getting together. Unfortunately, he later came down with hepatitis and had a tough time recuperating.

For Christmas I was invited to join Mark and Robin Luce and Juris in Ghazni, about 70 miles south of Kabul, along the main ring road from Kabul. Ghazni was different from Baku Kham and *Kohistan*. It was a large, vibrant town, with some paved roads, a famous castle and many shops and schools. Juris had a very active science center, where they were making new equipment and preparing lessons in novel ways. Mark and Robin were English teachers, each very good at what they did. We were friends from training and really enjoyed partying together.

Robin made a delicious ham (sourced from Kabul) dinner for us, in a small kerosene oven, with many of the trimmings we would expect at home. It was a cold and snowy winter, so we spent a fair amount of time under the *sandali*, a low coffee table used for warmth in winter. A pan of hot coals (or electric heater) is placed under the table, which is covered with a large quilt, extending on all sides. People sit cross-legged under the quilt and sling a coat over their shoulders.

At the end of my first year, I wrote to an elderly aunt:

> … by this time I have concluded that the best course of action for me is to write saying "can't possibly tell you what is happening here, see you in 2 years." A Chinese fellow at Union Carbide told me that Afghanistan is like the Middle Ages. For every old car, bus, and truck, there is a donkey, a cow, a chicken, and a shop several times over, even in modern Kabul. Mud houses, turbans, *karakul* hats,

119

and baggy pants and shirts far outnumber modern looking apartments and western dress. Recycle is not an ecologist's phrase, but a way of life. No bottle or can is wasted.

The terrain here is best described as a crater on the moon. The dust is unimaginable and Kabul is surrounded by jagged, treeless mountains. Afghanistan is in a second year of a severe drought and famine, yet the bazaars are filled with fruits and vegetables. Buying anything is an interesting game of language and bargaining skills. Lamb carcasses hang on hooks in open-air butcher shops, where the butcher cuts off meat and hands it to you dripping blood or if asked, wrapped in newspaper.

The people here are poor yet have a strong spirit. Beggars are very rare. Men are carpenters, metalworkers, woodchoppers, food merchants, house builders and more, using the ancient methods of their fathers. They work hard for six or seven days a week and live on a diet of whole wheat unleavened naan, vegetables, meat, fruit when in season, and on special occasions enjoy rice and chicken.

Afghan hounds are scraggly beasts and quite rare, not the handsome and well-groomed hounds we know. Locals are mostly cruel to dogs and children throw rocks at them. This is surprising to me because the Prophet Muhammed was a shepherd, and in Britain and other western countries, shepherd dogs are highly trained and much loved, and pet dogs are prized. Here they say that dogs are unclean, and that the reason that dogs get stuck together after copulation is because they broke Noah's prohibition against sex on the Ark during the great flood. And this is God's punishment.

Thus ended my first year. I was well on the way to understanding the culture and history and believed that the work that we were doing was valuable. The roles of America and other leading nations in Afghanistan were slowly becoming more clear, and I realized that I still had much to learn.

III

Year Two in Kapisa

1973

22. January trip to Iran

Juris and I left Kabul on December 29, traveling by bus to Herat. This largely Shia city was famous for impressive old mosques and shrines, large open spaces, and tall pine trees. We met an American architect along the way who taught us a good deal about the structures of Islamic domes and buildings. There Juris and I went our own ways, and soon I arrived in Tehran, a huge city of 3 million people, expanding all the time and, in many ways, indistinguishable from an American city. Its covered bazaar was said to be the world's largest, where almost anything could be found. I spent three days with Don Croll, our former language director, his wife Marcia, daughter Nora, and recently adopted Iranian son Ehsan. It was wonderful to benefit from a well-rounded view of Tehran and Iran from a knowledgeable American. I also met his good buddy Ehsan Lavipour, a Jewish

The Herat Grand Mosque in Western Afghanistan

Iranian whose father was a successful businessman and money changer in the bazaar. Iran's minorities were an accepted part of Iran's diverse society, and included Jews, Christians (Armenians and Assyrians), Parsis (Zoroastrians), Bahais, and Sunni Muslims.

Don told me the latest joke going around Tehran which spoke of the Iranian's confidence and closeness to America. The US had named former Head of the CIA, Richard Helms, as the new ambassador to Iran. The USSR ambassador immediately requested a meeting with the Shah and said to him that America had named its number one spy as ambassador to Iran, that this was an outrage, and what are you going to do about it? The Shah replied, "Well, I guess that makes you number two."

I left Tehran, traveling to Isfahan on TBS, a bus company with luxurious modern buses booked like an airline. It was snowing as we drove through the mountains and shortly, around a bend, the speeding bus began sliding sideways on the icy road, directly in the path of an oncoming Mack truck towing a long, heavily loaded flatbed. All our hearts jumped and the Iranians in unison repeated a deep chant of "blessed be the Lord and keep all his people especially the family of Ali," a Shia prayer. The driver vigorously worked the steering wheel left and right and brought the bus under control and back into our lane. The danger immediately evaporated and there was an audible sigh of relief throughout the bus.

In Isfahan, the small two-story guest house I stayed in was modern and swank, completely different from any hotels in Afghanistan. It was filled with conveniences: telephones, electric heaters, TVs, comfortable chairs, electric kettles. The staff spoke Farsi, and I could communicate. Wow, it felt so good.

Isfahan was a mix of the medieval and modern, with many stunningly beautiful mosques, madrassas (religious colleges), shrines and other historical sites covered with intricate blue mosaics and Arabic religious inscriptions. It also has a very large, covered bazaar made of brick arches and domes, filled with Isfahan's exquisite carpets, Persian miniatures painted on ivory, inlay work, and brass and silver works, jewelry, carvings and more.

Many young people proudly said to me "Isfahan, *nesfijahan,*" a rhyme meaning, "Isfahan, half the world." Persians repeated this rhyme, often arrogantly, saying that Iran is the greatest country in the world. Of course, they have much to be proud of, with 5,000 years of civilization, peer to Egypt and older than their ancient adversary Greece.

After Isfahan I went to Shiraz, the resting place of Hafiz and Sa'adi, giants of Persian poetry. Hafiz's tomb is under a stone dome in a peaceful garden, a glimpse of the past. Next was Persepolis, one of the capitals of the Achaemenids in ancient Persia, aptly described in *The Heritage of Persia* by R. N. Frye and *Persia, An Archaeological Guide* by Sylvia Matheson, which I read on the long road trips. The ruins of Persepolis are still striking after 2,500 years. It is huge in scale with many halls and structures. The entrance hall was about 200 feet wide with two ramps sloping upwards to left and right and then turning back to the center, joining and entering the hall. Ten-foot-high stone walls along these ramps were adorned with bas relief sculptures of processions of the satraps and tribes bearing gifts ranging from camels and horses to jewelry, furniture and slaves to the Shahen Shah, King of Kings, from the known nations of the world at that time in North Africa, the Mideast and Central Asia.

This trip dazzled me—much like the continuously edifying and startling first five months in Afghanistan—and charged my imagination, recalling Lord Byron's fascination and eloquence for Persia. Although I resented it, it also became clear why Iranians looked down on the Afghans as poor neighbors. Iran was far more developed, and they judge Afghan Farsi speech to be mostly illiterate with an unsophisticated country accent. Iranian Farsi was mellifluous, sounding to me like French, while Afghan Dari was harder edged. Persians also, no doubt, harbored historical grievances against the Afghans for the defeat of the Safavids by Pashtun Ahmad Shah Durrani in the eighteenth century, ending their rule in the east. And importantly, Iran was majority Shia while Afghanistan is Sunni.

124

23. NSC Winter Seminar

Back in Kabul, the NSC Winter Seminar was well run and attended and reinforced for us that we were part of an important effort in raising the educational standard in Afghanistan. For five weeks we were together with all our NSC counterparts and PCVs, plus NSC and UNESCO Kabul staff. It enabled us volunteers to review each of our results, successes, and failures. We also were able to spend time drinking beer and eating hamburgers at the USAID Field House. This was really fun as we had many stories to tell and discussions about adapting to life in Afghanistan.

The seminar covered all aspects of our program and work, starting with reports from each location and discussion of successes and problems. Following this were modules on laboratory design and safety, then on to the physics curriculum, with experiments, laws, formulae, and problem sets. It was like being back in college: blackboards covered with proofs and lab demonstrations. We also were shown educational movies with insights into teaching methods.

Then it was on to mathematics: how to solve equations, statistics and their use. Following this we learned about ecology, poverty and underdevelopment, the Afghanistan physical environment, and the biosphere. Much of this was new to me and very interesting. We had lectures on bacteria and fungi, geology and life zones of Afghanistan.

Next was chemistry, including methodology, experiments, mixtures and compounds, and magnetism and the structure of the atom. We wrote chemical reaction equations and talked about how all of this could best be taught.

At the end of the seminar, we were given another three weeks off, and as planned, I headed to India.

24. February Trip to India

Hindustan was described in books as a land without beginning or end.

Charlie Ferrell and I flew to New Delhi on February 26, and our first experience was being driven way out of the way by a shifty taxi driver. We managed our way out of that and after several days parted company, as we'd made separate travel plans.

I took advantage of the Afghan and Asian hawala money changing system for the India trip. The money market in Kabul was an enclosed courtyard with money changing shops on the first and second floors all around. I went to the merchant recommended by friends, and he quoted me a black market rate for Indian rupees which was far better than the official government rate. I paid for the amount of cash needed and gave a delivery time and place. A short time after checking into the hotel, there was a knock on the door with a man delivering the money. At that time this could be used for as far away as London, and no doubt the system was old if not ancient.

My first visit was to Dr. Dixit and family. His daughters were part of my social scene with Heidar in Kabul. He was a retired Indian agricultural official, recently home after a two-year tour of foreign aid service to Afghanistan. I stayed and enjoyed the company of his daughter Jaya and the Lodhi Hotel and nightly discotheque scene and enjoyed the food. We ate at Moti Mahal, a famous north Indian restaurant, with delicious *naan,* kebab, rice dishes, vegetable curries, and many different spices and chutneys.

I was soon on the way to Agra and the Taj Mahal. Sterile pictures from high school geography classes did not do justice to the Taj— one of the Seven Wonders of the World. The Taj Mahal is the most beautiful, incredible architectural structure and work of art. Passing through the outer Great Gate of red sandstone arches, into the inner courtyard, about a thousand feet from the Taj, I stood speechless. The Taj Mahal (meaning crown or pearl palace) was built by Moghul emperor Shah Jehan (meaning king of the world) as a mausoleum to honor his beloved deceased wife. It is built on a 300-foot square marble platform with a massive dome mounted on an octagonal building and four open sided ivans inscribed with black Kufic, Qur'anic script. On the roof are four more small domes, ivans and cloisters mounted by slender minarets. The geometric proportions and symmetry combined with the beauty of the marble and inlaid stone materials are stunning.

I next visited the Red Fort of Agra, like the Red Fort of Delhi—with its massive red sandstone walls, parapets, immense gateway doors, moats, palaces, audience halls, mosques, baths, and harem palaces, made of white marble with flower inlays of semi-precious stones. How enduring to build in stone and how beautiful is the splendor of the East! In America we spend our money going to the moon, and less on magnificent buildings. Yet here, it must be recognized that in antiquity magnificent structures were built with legions of workers working by hand from dawn 'til dusk for only bread and tea.

Next was the "pink city" of Jaipur, made from red sandstone. The city palace museum was a magnificent testimonial to the days of the maharajahs (local hereditary rulers) with sumptuous gardens, marble audience halls, silk clothing from China and Persia, tiger hunting and elephant riding, the arts—music, miniature painting, traditional dancing. The garden at the old Maharajah's palace was inhabited by servants, gardeners, monkeys, birds, bats, and dogs. At the rear of the garden was a Hindu temple with men washing, practicing yoga, and playing classical music.

From Jaipur I took a short trip to the huge Amber Fort and palaces. The private quarters of the maharajah's 20 wives and harem of 250 concubines were off a common court, joined by a secret passage leading to the king's chambers.

Next was Udaipur, a "white city" made of white limestone. It is also called "city of lakes" with the famous Lake Palace Hotel on an island in the largest lake, a former palace visited by Queen Elizabeth, Jackie Kennedy, and the King and Queen of Iran, among others. I stayed in a hotel owned by the brother of the present maharana (higher than maharajah), stripped of power but not wealth, and educated like an English gentleman. His personal photo album was filled with celebrities, and his bar included potent liqueurs made from saffron and rose petal. The food in Udaipur was also different, with spicy fried vegetables, mangoes and other fruits, and breads like roti and papadum.

After Udaipur, it was off to Mt. Abu and a long-distance train ride in one-meter gauge Indian trains reminiscent of old westerns. Seating in third class is on a wooden plank, staring out the window at rolling dry Rajasthan hills and stone fences, sheep and cow herds, tents of the poor. On curves I could see the small cars ahead, the chugging coal burning steam engines and from every window, door and rooftop passengers' feet, heads, and arms sticking out and soaking up the breeze. Layers of dust turned our hair gray.

At station stops the train was assaulted by vendors of all ages selling water, tea, liquor, food, reading material, cold drinks, cigarettes, games, children's toys. The beggars played music, sang songs, distributed small sheets spelling out their plight and asking for alms, Hindi on one side, English on the other. In third class I met a variety of people, many of whom spoke English: a merchant marine officer, a PhD from Indiana University, self-made businessmen, a marine biologist for the Royal Science Society of India. Those trained in the UK or the US would take me under their wing, buying me tea and snacks and seeing that I was taken care of. And there were the families—massive, sprawling, with children of all ages. The train rides, though often uncomfortable, never seemed to last too long.

From the train station, I boarded a country bus for the long, winding, treacherous road trip to Mt. Abu, at about 4,000 feet elevation. It was a beautiful town with a lake, palm trees, central soccer and cricket fields, houses, hotels, eating spots, tourist shops and the famous Dilwara Temples. These are Jain temples carved of white marble with floral, statue, and epic designs of great artistry. Jain is, perhaps, a branch of Hinduism founded by Mahavira, a contemporary of Gautama Siddartha, the Buddha. The 24 saints or gods (Tirthankars) of Jainism are carved into three major temples at Mt. Abu with depictions of their lives and legends. Jains believe in non-violence and non-killing. Mt. Abu was a favorite honeymoon spot for Indians, with several couples asking me to photograph them.

From Abu it was off to Ahmedabad and Baroda, a harrowing drive with a speeding bus driver. Baroda is the hometown of my MIT classmate and roommate Sanjay Amin and where his family owned a pharmaceutical factory. It has a great deal of industry and many classic buildings, a former maharajah's palace, an excellent museum and lovely gardens. The faculty of engineering at the University of Baroda was an Indian palace, complete with colonnades, arches, balconies, and spires. The museum included the Maharajah's collections of art and household effects from Japan, China, India, Persia, the Middle East, and Europe. Sanjay was still in grad school in

Cambridge and his parents were in the Himalayas, so his uncle was my very hospitable host. We toured the town and had an evening at the theater.

There was rail construction work on the trip to Bombay, with exceedingly long lines of single-file refugees carrying railroad ties, sections of rail, and earth in baskets on their shoulders and heads … another glimpse into America's past when railroads were built by hand. The views on the train line south to Bombay were my first views of an ocean in 16 months.

Bombay's downtown was marked by huge 19th century Victorian buildings, traffic circles with statues and monuments, expansive parks, modern skyrise and conventional apartment buildings. I was surprised that I was not struck by poverty as I saw the shanties built along and within feet of the train tracks, a bustle of clothes washing, men working on machines, children playing, tiny gardens under cultivation. There were smiling, happy people everywhere. Perhaps living in Afghanistan amongst very poor people had changed my outlook. Material poverty is not spiritual poverty, unhappiness, or purposelessness. There is a vast disparity between rich and poor, with short life expectancies and rampant disease for the poor compared to the wealthy, yet the poor seemed to have mastered the struggle for existence, even as unjust as it was.

During this trip I read several books about Indian history, philosophy, and religions, all eye-opening. Islamic culture is new, and in the Judeo-Christian mold, with influences of Middle Eastern culture. India, however, has at least a five-millennium long continuum of cultural evolution, and where this evolution has arrived is bewildering. Islam tells the illiterate peasant that fate is God's predetermined will, and that we are all equal and will meet as brothers in the next world. India's pantheism says that everyman's position in society is sacred and fixed, be it high or low, and that all evolutions—cultural or biological—are also sacred, and that man's life is fundamentally the same as all living things. The mere process of living is a determination of the future, that all actions automatically contribute to fate—sans judgment or the concept of sin. Poverty is accepted by the poor not only as fate but as sacred. But the beggars, the paraplegics, the diseased still appall us who do not understand the Eastern acceptance and philosophy.

The Hindu religion has three major gods: Brahma, the Creator; Vishnu, the Preserver; and Shiva, the Destroyer of evil spirits and forces. Hindu scripture is prolific, the most famous of which are the Vedas and the Upanishads. The most influential of these may be the Ramayana and the Mahabharata – often called the Iliad and the Odyssey of Hinduism. The Ramayana is the epic of Rama, and the Mahabharata is that of Krishna. Rama and Krishna are two incarnations of the god Shiva who were sent to mankind as messiahs or saviors in times of need. So, the savior concept is fused with the reincarnation theory to create epics, whose fiber provides the stories which teach honor, duty, justice for all strata of Indian Hindu society.

The Bombay Prince of Wales Museum had a collection of Rajasthani and Moghul miniatures, sections on natural history, archaeology, armaments, Chinaware, European art. I also visited the massive cave temples carved out of rock on the Island of Elephanta, close to the Gateway to India, built by the British in 1911 to commemorate the visit of King George V, the first British monarch to visit India. The Elephanta Caves were largely destroyed by Portuguese artillery practice, but still have impressive carved remains from nine scenes from the life of Shiva.

I also visited the Ajanta and Ellora Caves, some hours from Bombay, close to Aurangabad, a strategic city in the central Deccan plain of India. This region was the historical key to the North India-South India balance of power and finally took its name from Aurangzeb, one of the last powerful Moghul Emperors. The caves are Buddhist, Jain and Hindu, carved from second century BCE to the tenth century CE. These massive hand-carved underground dormitories stagger the imagination: assembly halls, huge Buddhas, frescoes of the life of the Buddha, Hindu temples, bas-reliefs of the Ramayana, and representations of the Tirthankars of Jainism.

In Bombay I met Raghava Pai, the brother of my boss at Cyanamid who had advised me about Afghanistan and Peace Corps. They are a Hindu Brahmin (the highest caste) family who worship Krishna. It is not uncommon among Hindus for the father to primarily worship

Vishnu, say, while the mother reveres Shiva, and the children perhaps Brahma. Hence family members can have different holy days and special days, all tolerated and appreciated because they believe that all roads in religion are true roads. I also learned from Raghava Pai that many Indians believe that you must not kill even a mosquito, because all creatures have a right to live, and that reincarnation will mean that you might come back as a higher or lower form of life.

I also met a Parsi, or Zoroastrian, girl. Originally Persian, Parsis emigrated from Pars province of Persia to Gujarat during the eighth to tenth centuries CE when Iran was converted to Islam. The Parsis have long been influential and wealthy—the Tata family being the most famous industrial family of India. This young woman had a Persian name, Feroza Dastur, and neither she nor her parents looked Indian, though her mother wore pretty saris. Feroza spoke English as a mother tongue, and was fluent in French, German, Gujarati, Hindi and Marathi. She hoped to join the Indian Foreign Service soon and was then a Bombay India Tourist Organization Guide—which is how I met her. She was an excellent swimmer. We enjoyed Juhu Beach, as well as the internationally flavored, one-time imperialist stronghold, Wellington Club. The family was very kind to show me hospitality for a few days.

Last was the Daulatabad Fort, a vast structure about 200 miles east of Bombay and which was probably unconquerable without some sort of treachery or intrigue. It had seven sets of walls, an outer moat, and an inner moat, all on a large hill of rock smoothed off on the sides to make sheer, precipitous drop offs of a hundred feet and more. On crossing the second moat, you had to ascend a completely unlighted tortuous secret passage defended from 50 feet overhead before coming out 200 yards below the inner fort.

My trip to India was quite an eye opener. Iran was a rapidly modernizing Muslim country, steeped in ancient culture yet also closely related to the Judeo-Christian world. It has a western feel to it, with bustling activity, modern styles of shops and bazaars, and police forces and other civil services that were easily recognizable. Iranians were also very entrepreneurial with many businesses having sprung up doing and making most everything that modern economies require.

India on the other hand was completely new in many respects: religion, architecture, history, food, many ethnic groups with different beliefs and racial or physical characteristics. I was happy to be returning to Kabul, but at the same time was still absorbing so much that was new and came away somewhat in awe of India.

25. Back in Kapisa Teaching with New Confidence

After three months of exciting travel, I was depressed—typical for PCVs—although still keen to stay in country. Back in Kapisa, this quickly dissipated as we set about preparing for the new school year.

It was once again a gloriously beautiful spring. During my first week back, there was a terrific hailstorm with hail the size of golf balls literally assaulting the earth. The apricot blossoms were badly damaged—my apricot liqueur production would be low this year. The mountains were snowcapped and rugged, the weather, whimsical: alternately bright and crisp or misty and wet. The hailstorm was followed by a beautiful rainbow, calm, and bright sunshine. The remaining blossoms were fresh and fragrant. The tops of the compound's walls sprouted red wildflowers and the house roof grew grass. The quince tree had green buds pushing out and the recently tilled garden had flowers, potatoes, onions, carrots, lettuce, cabbage, tomatoes, eggplant. Soon there would be hot green peppers.

Our first task was to send NSC letters and photographs from last year to the schools, set up our provincial office and deliver books from Kabul to the Director. We were honored to meet with the Governor, who was kind and attentive and thanked us for our work. My counterparts and I wrote lectures on science education methodology, laboratory safety, and lesson plans by grade and subject. We also set the schedule for our school visits and sent letters of advice to the schools.

I felt my confidence growing that work would be good this year, and my language adequate. Our plan was to spend two weeks per lycée, one week per middle school and three months in the distant schools. We planned to focus on teacher training, meaning long days preparing materials, observing classes in the morning and teaching in the afternoon.

It was a pleasure to be back at Mirmasjadi to teach and spend time with the teachers. We faced the new school year determined to cover a great deal of ground. Being with teachers and in front of classes never lost its appeal. Seeing bright eyes and minds of those who had so little was a real stimulus to us in our jobs. While we never received any budget for science teacher training, or for seminars, equipment, and materials, we made do with what we had—essential for the large job of upgrading national education, and we were proud and happy about that. The lack of training of local teachers was a nationwide fact that we had been assigned to help address. And of course, we were not perfect; when our experiments failed, local teachers would

Headmaster of Lycée Mirmasjadi third from right in front with teachers on the back steps of the school. The teacher at the top right in the white jacket was a good volleyball player.

see this and question us. This too was a learning experience all in its own, as experimentation and practical arts always have failures.

One afternoon after school we played volleyball, and the teachers were good players. It was a great sport for Afghanistan, needing only a ball, two poles and a net to set up a court on a hard dirt surface. We played barefoot. One of the teachers whom I knew well was about my age, charismatic and athletic; he enjoyed spiking balls down at me. I had last played volleyball in middle school and struggled to be competitive. He knew a lot about America from his older brother who had lived there. He was married and told me the local expression that being married was having a "scabbard for your sword", and that unmarried males are "boys" until they marry. This was humbling for me, as I was single with marriage still an unknown. His comment was not so subtly letting me know one aspect of my social position. I no doubt imagined myself as the educated foreigner doing service work in their country, and above rather than a peer to the teachers. I realized that I needed to relax and be more down to earth.

Though we worked effectively, our counterparts' problems remained. Unfortunately, the three of us even quarreled from time to time. Mohamed Saeid Khan disdained the job, calling it "very small work," and saying he was only staying to learn English from me. But neither he nor Sayid Qamar made much of an effort at this. My view was that if you wanted to learn English you had to work at it, and that good high school science teachers in America would not consider their jobs to be "small work," and they generally loved teaching young people.

Saeid was often absent and saw himself as something of an aristocrat. His father, who had died six or eight years prior, had been a successful merchant with close ties to governors and some money, now gone. The previous year he was engaged to the daughter of the Commandant of Kapisa but I don't recall if he married. This was part of the cultural mystery of Afghanistan where men and outsiders never got to know local families or about their women or marriage. It was a cultural barrier for Americans to get close to the people.

Sayid Qamar uDin could be difficult, even saying that Saeid and I were not needed, could teach him nothing and that I was a spy. I once arrogantly (and foolishly) replied to this by saying spy on what? Mud houses? But he also could be cooperative and friendly, though occasionally moody. One day he asked me why I thought Muslims were not allowed to eat pork. I said that pork could carry a dangerous disease, so likely in ancient times a rule was made not to eat pork. He flew into a rage saying that it was written in the Quran that you must not eat pork, and this was the word of God, not man. I answered that there are different interpretations of the holy books, but he argued vehemently that the Quran is the word of God and that there are no disagreements as to what is written. I thought this exchange was just looking for an argument.

The Panjshir Principal had told me that Sayid Qamar was with the communist students when in college in Kabul. On returning to Kapisa he was the serious Muslim, and proud of being a Sayid, a descendant of the Prophet Mohamed. I recognized this as not unlike my generation, with people moving from anti-Vietnam war positions to the establishment. Sayid Qamar also had a tendency (like all young people, including me?) to say more than he knew. One day in Panjshir a teacher asked what an ocean looked like. Although he had never seen the ocean, he said it looked like a mountain, piled up on the horizon. I said, no, it's not high, simply flat as far as you can see. I spoke too quickly and caused him loss of face, not to mention that describing an ocean truly was not simple.

Mohamed Saeid often was absent from work, and while Sayid Qamar was more regular, he too would sometimes not show up for a week or weeks at a time without explanation until he reappeared. This was possible in part because they did not report to the local Department of Education, but time and absenteeism in Afghanistan were different from my experience. People were often late or absent, and that was life. I, on the other hand, always showed for work, both in schools and the office, and this added to friction, along with my position and wealth from being an American.

As I think about counterpart relations today, I recognize that my inflexibility and hard driving personality was obviously part of the problem. I wanted to do everything "by the book," and could be stubborn. My friends Juris in Ghazni and Charlie and Tom in

Baghlan praised their counterparts and worked happily with them. Others in our NSC program also had mixed experiences like mine.

In truth in Kapisa, we did have many good times together over the years. However, I didn't socialize, drink or carouse with them, wanting to maintain my seriousness and commitment to the job, and feeling uncomfortable with behavior not consistent with the strict Muslim way of life. Some teachers and helpers at schools had even said to me that they understood that it was okay for me to drink alcohol because it wasn't forbidden in my religion. But I didn't want to be the target of criticism and gossip and knew that boozing with the locals surely would get around and produce that. I still wonder, was this behavior stiff and uncooperative? And was it a paradox that at the same time I was so taken with the country and the culture, and drank regularly with the elite in Kabul?

Once when I was in Kabul, Marty told me of a famous Afghan poet named Burhan who had been to university in America. When he returned to Afghanistan, he said that the magic in Afghanistan was gone. He was referring to the mixture of the mystical, historical, and religious culture of society that was heightened by an environment that was so simple and close to nature. The spirits, legends and ideas of antiquity had vanished for him.

I also learned that some Afghans hid their insecurity about Afghanistan's underdevelopment. For example, when asked by foreigners what bathrooms were like in Afghanistan, they would reply that they are big and beautiful, with gardens and trees, not saying that actually they squat in the fields. I had thought romantically that the locals were strong and coping with their meager quality of life, including 60% infant mortality rate, mud houses and no electricity, phones or TV. In truth life was hard for them, and I was beginning to understand the reality.

Later I received a note from a Westchester, New York, acquaintance of my parents, Mary Niles. She was visiting Kabul with her husband, a senior American lawyer working on behalf of the State Department to resolve the land and water rights dispute between Afghanistan and Iran along the Helmand River. They kindly invited me to dinner at the Kabul Hotel, and luckily, I was in the right place at the right time to quickly respond. Mary later wrote to my parents:

> within a couple of hours Toby was here at the hotel in response to my note … we had a pleasant cocktail hour in our room and dinner together downstairs … We all think your Toby is an exceptional boy. R (her husband) wishes he could see him again to ask questions … Toby has already learned much, and it's current. His information comes from sources quite different from R's and Asa's (another lawyer on the assignment). He'll not be bored here, interested as he is in the past, as well as the present, of the country.

Mr. Niles was in Afghanistan on a legal and diplomatic mission, with Iranian relations also involved. Mrs. Niles's comments point to the difference between knowledge gained by PCVs on the ground and official sources. We PCVs would joke about the CIA in trench coats and Stetsons, not speaking the language or really understanding what was going on. With age I see this as naïveté and cockiness, but it's also true that history has shown the USA has not excelled in understanding foreign countries or in intelligence work.

I also received a letter from Bob Carrubba, my Union Carbide supervisor in my last job in New Jersey, advising that the research department had disintegrated. The two top chemical engineers were transferred to South Charleston, 13 divisions were consolidated to eight, and many familiar faces had departed. Bob himself had moved to Engelhard Industries to work on a new combustion process. He said my decision to join the Peace Corps was good: this was welcome reassurance and a lesson for the future.

In a letter to my parents:

> Happy to report that last year's roommate Mark Svendsen is returning as a Peace Corps staff member in Kabul. And I will gain a new roommate, Jim Wheatley, in the Food

for Peace program. He is from Colorado and a gun-toting conservative, bringing with him a pistol bought locally.

I wasn't happy about the gun and suspected it was against PC rules but accepted it. Soon after that, Assif acquired a shotgun for us which we shot several times in our compound so that people in the bazaar could hear it and word would spread, hopefully scaring off potential burglars. Jim was with me for a few months and then moved on.

26. Possible Job Transfer

From Juris, I learned of a possible opportunity to teach at Kabul University in the Faculty of Engineering—either immediately or the next year. This college had been built and staffed by Stevens Institute of Technology in New Jersey, with funding from USAID. Their contract would end in 1973. In May I returned to Kabul to meet with Dean Zewari about a possible transfer to this faculty, and to meet staff from UNESCO, Peace Corps and the NSC. Dean Zewari was an upbeat and professional person, and the prospect of working for and with him was attractive.

I was interested in the Kabul University job because it would be a more advanced level of work. My commitment to Peace Corps service and to Afghanistan never wavered. I also was not lonely living alone in Kapisa, largely because I worked long hours and kept busy in the evenings listening to music and the shortwave radio and reading. But I had also opted for Kapisa, a location close to Kabul, where, in two-and-a-half hours I could be with friends and other volunteers, and no doubt I did this much more often than supervisors in more distant locations, and sometimes felt guilty about this.

However, the word from Dr. Ghaznowi was that if I wasn't happy in Kapisa, he could offer a transfer to Charikar, west across the Panjshir River from Kapisa, where a supervisor position had opened up. Charikar is a big town on the road to the Salang Pass and a stopping point for buses with tourists, including the World Traveler (hippy) traffic. As WTs are not respected by the Afghans, the town could be rough on westerners. Larry and Sue Bennett had been assigned there. Larry was a standout in our original Science Teacher Training cycle and was an excellent organizer and presenter. Sue was a very capable RN assigned to the local medical clinic. They both were serious Christians and conservative. Unfortunately, locals harassed Sue, often taunting, grabbing and pinching her as she walked to work. Not willing to tolerate this, they requested a transfer to Kabul.

The advantages of working at the Faculty of Engineering were obvious: Kabul University was the pinnacle of education in Afghanistan; teaching was in English; it would be good professional experience, had better students and facilities, and I would work alongside American and Afghan professors. But I had committed to two years in Kapisa developing the NSC program, teaching many teachers in many schools, and helping to establish the new NSC program. Disadvantages of staying included the carefree attitudes of some teachers and students and a lack of funding and support. Kapisa's Assistant Director of Education, Mr. Einy, also told me that my wanting a transfer could reflect badly on the province.

In the end, I applied for the transfer, got PC staff approval, and this request was then rejected by Dr. Ghaznowi, so I stayed in Kapisa. I had also been influenced by learning of Dr. Ghaznowi's decision to discontinue the PC program after our groups finished our assignments, which may also have been partly political, reducing American involvement while retaining UNESCO support. The NSC had requested 20 supervisors per year from the Peace Corps, but we had managed only eight and four in the first and only two cycles of volunteers.

We PCVs believed that we were more capable and responsible than our counterparts. Not involved in NSC planning, we had spent our first year figuring out how to do our work within the educational system. We also doubted that the Kabul staff had much experience working in the provinces. PCVs in the boonies worked hard and gained local respect, but we didn't know if this reached Kabul. We did know that we brought headaches with requests for equipment and materials. Finally, we were not bound by local administrative rules, and some may have viewed us as being on a two-year "junket," the celebrated and reviled comment once made about Peace Corps by President Nixon.

Later in the spring, Washington Peace Corps sent a woman named Susan Biddle to visit me in Kapisa to take pictures and collect stories. This was fun, and two pictures of me with Sayid Qamar teaching at Lycée Mirmasjadi and eating a meal on my roof with other PCVs were later published in *National Geographic*.

27. Tragedy at Lycée Mirmasjadi

One night in mid-May, eight or nine boys broke into Lycée Mirmasjadi and tried to steal the large carpet in the principal's office. They failed because the janitor fought barehanded against their knives to protect the 10,000 Afghani ($111) carpet. The janitor slept in the school and was responsible for security and protecting the property. His salary was 500 Afs per month or $7. He was stabbed in the stomach and the next morning was taken to the hospital in Kabul. He died four days later.

In the Muslim religion a person who passes away must be buried within a day or as soon as possible. I attended the large open-air funeral and wake held behind the school. We all sat on carpets and kilims beneath trees amid the farmland and nearby farmhouses. The day was sunny and bright with blue skies, the Hindu Kush mountains imposing. The body was brought in a plain wooden coffin from the Kabul hospital where he died, perched atop a wood and rope bed carried by four men at the posts, covered by a blanket and bunches of flowers. Mullahs, teachers, laborers and religious students attended. The Qran was read by the mullahs. Prayers and blessings were followed by eulogies and remembrances, tears were shed. A plaintive cry from the Mahmude Raqi principal was particularly moving. We pressed forward to see the victim's face, and then the deceased, wrapped in a white sheet, was removed from the coffin and buried in the ground.

The janitor was considered a martyr entitled to all the glories of martyrdom because he died as a man of honor protecting the people's belongings which were entrusted to him. Though I did not recognize his face when the coffin lid was opened, I later recognized him from his small son and his sister's son. He one day had gone out of his way in the bazaar in a village south of here to give me his salaam and pay respects: I was new at the time and known to school people far and wide. It was common that ordinary people like janitors and shop keepers would say hello and be welcoming to foreign workers like me. He was a dedicated servant.

Perhaps his bravery, which to us would be senseless, was what kept the lid on society there. Maybe Puritan honor and willingness to sacrifice life for property eroding to a state of rational pragmatism in America contributes to our murder and mugging statistics. It was a sad and difficult time for the Kapisa provincial officials, and it looked as if the culprits would not be caught. The day before the crime a student said to be of "bad character" had asked the janitor how many janitors slept in that room. This boy was apprehended and beaten for several days but swore no knowledge and was released. There were no witnesses, and the school was pitch-black, having no electricity. Mr. Einy had gone to Kabul to comfort the man and be at his side, and to question him hoping to learn who might be responsible, but the man was unable to respond.

I believed I was safe in my home in Baku Kham, less than a mile from the Mirmasjadi Lycée. Unlike the school, my house was next to a bazaar with a dozen shops either side of the main road just north of me. The shopkeepers slept in their shops to safeguard their goods. I also had two dogs and a shotgun. And I had no intention of being a martyr, given a choice. Asif told me that if someone had wanted to rob me, it would have happened already. I realized that he had given this a lot of thought from the very beginning. He also said that the dogs barking would awaken him in his nearby house, and he would come. If I hadn't felt safe, I would have moved by then.

The janitor's murder was a sad story and made me appreciate that there was little crime in Afghanistan. Certainly, in the province where I lived, murder and robbery were very rare. Local people generally knew one another in their villages and nearby surroundings, and they were vigilant and traditional, growing up with strong beliefs that crime was unacceptable and must be opposed.

28. Culture—Sex and Humor

My age group was the last in America to grow up before the pill and sexual freedom came to society. Girls were trained by their mothers not to trust men and always say no, as boys were only looking for one thing. Homosexuality was not acceptable and a shame for families. It was also grounds for dismissal from the Peace Corps, in part because it was supposedly taboo in Afghan society. One trainee was sent home for this.

Most Afghans were rural and lived in villages where the children grew up together. Boys and girls played games like hide and seek, marbles using pebbles, rolling a bicycle rim along the road with a stick, climbing trees, hopscotch, and playing bazaar shopkeeper. Also, as Muslims considered marriage to a first cousin the perfect match, it was common for parents to betroth first cousins from infancy. These children grew up knowing their spouse and happily accepted this.

When they reached puberty, however, boys and girls were separated. Women began to wear the veil and no longer played with boys who were forbidden to see their faces. But the boys knew their favorite girls at a distance from their walk, their talk, their height, even their shoes or ankles. And they could talk with them when they were wearing chadri. Boys and girls lived in sexual suspended animation, awaiting marriage, generally by arrangement, in mid or late teens.

Boys naturally had hormones and appetites that couldn't be bottled up. So, their first sexual experiences were with other boys. I'd heard talk about this but still learning and being uncertain about the language and being a bit naïve, I didn't believe it, saying there's talk but Afghans don't really do that. I said this to John Blake one day and he contradicted me and said it was both true and common. He and Denise had arrived home unexpectedly one day and found an older servant boy fully aroused and about to penetrate a younger boy bent over the kitchen table with his trousers on the floor. They were aghast, and this story woke me up to reality and to comments I'd heard that I hadn't taken for real. I was shocked.

The bigger boys would "do" the smaller boys in the ass, "koon" in Farsi, and a "kooni" was one who gives ass. That was a common insult for boys. Worse was "kushad", meaning broad, for those often "done." A few years later in New York, I said to my dad that I was going out with some buddies to meet some broads. He sharply told me not to use that word. Surprised, I instantly realized what this meant about women to his generation.

This is called "bacha bazi," literally boy play. Bacha bazi was no doubt discouraged by "good" families, but nonetheless inevitable female substitution. Anthropologists in America know this is common in societies where the sexes are segregated. Grown Afghan men often became fast friends as well as lovers, but nearly always would get married and have children, even as these earlier relationships persisted, especially since socializing outside the home was men only.

I never talked about this subject with Heidar, who was my best friend in Afghanistan, or any other of my Afghan friends or colleagues. It was too large a cultural gap and another barrier to getting to know the people, like some of the differences in religion, such as polygamy, women being covered up and out of the public eye, praying five times a day, and alcohol and pork being forbidden, or *haram.*

Country boys also talked about sexually mounting sheep, or, mostly unsuccessfully, donkeys. They also joked about the prodigious length of a male donkey's organ and watched horses and donkeys mating. A donkey "in flagrante" was quite a sight. The Iranians had a joke: what's the difference between a Turk and an Arab? They're both donkeys, the Turk from the waist up and the Arab from the waist down.

There were rumors of "houses of ill repute", one in Nejrab, in the south where we taught. Sayid Qamar mentioned it to me one day when we were there. I wondered why. But I saw no hint of it. Some *koochis*, the nomads who travel from lowlands to highlands in summer riding camels and camping along the main country dirt roads, did give sex for money.

Afghans love jokes. A lot come from stories about the mythical Mullah Nasruddin, also known as Juha in Arab countries. He is the local mullah who teaches truth through jokes, many political, and where he is often the butt of the jokes.

A few examples:

Mullah Nasruddin borrows a medium-sized pot from a neighbor. Some days later he returns the pot and inside is a small pot. Surprised the neighbor asks, "What is this?"

The Mullah replies, "Your pot had a baby."

The neighbor is delighted. Some weeks later the Mullah again asks to borrow a pot, and the neighbor happily gives him his largest rice cooking pot. After some weeks the neighbor asks the Mullah what happened to his large pot. The Mullah replies that unfortunately it died. The neighbor says asks how can a pot die? The Mullah says, "If a pot can have a baby, it can also die."

*****

Rich Ahmed and poor Mohamed live next door to each other. One day Mohamed wants to speak to Ahmed so he goes out his door and walks along the outside of Ahmed's large garden, where over the wall he sees Ahmed sitting at a table under a tree reading the newspaper and drinking tea. Mohamed knocks on the door and the servant answers. Mohamed says, "I'd like to speak to Ahmed."

The servant says, "I'll see if master is at home," closes the door, and returns a few minutes later. He says, "I'm sorry, master is not at home."

Angry, Mohamed returns to his house. Some weeks later, Mohamed is sitting at home when there is a knock on his door. He answers the door and there is Ahmed, saying, "I'd like to have a word with you."

Mohamed says, "I shall see if I'm at home," and closes the door. Returning a few minutes later he says, "I am not at home."

Ahmed says, "But you're standing in front of me!"

Mohamed replies angrily, "How dare you doubt my word when I have to accept the word of your servant!"

*****

Another story shows the independent streak and guts of Afghans. The king wants to find out what the people really think of him and

144

his kingdom. He disguises himself and goes into the bazaar to talk with people. At one point he asks a merchant, "What would you do if the king were to raise taxes and take away your shop?"

The man avoids answering several times, but finally when seriously pressed he says, "My donkey's dick in his woman's pussy."

Some weeks later there is a public event where the no-longer-disguised king comes face to face with the same merchant, and he asks the same question several times. At first the merchant does not recognize the king but soon realizes who he is and that he must answer. Thinking, he carefully replies "That little donkey in that little doorway." My interpretation of this is that the proud Afghan changes his language but not his tune.

*****

Churchill, Hitler and Stalin are in heaven before God and are asked to justify their terrible wars and killing of so many people. Hitler replies that his people were poor and suffering, and he was only trying to get some elbowroom for them. Stalin replies that he was viciously attacked by Hitler and only defended his homeland. Churchill replies, "We English did nothing, we just brought the Indians, Australians, New Zealanders and South Africans to fight Hitler."

Older Afghans said that America was really a puppet of the British, who were the masters of empire and politics, as well as founders of the American colony. One proof offered was the huge British Embassy compound with beautiful gardens, tennis courts, swimming pool and fine buildings. America, on the other hand, had a large, less imposing, modern, almost industrial building for its embassy on smaller grounds.

*****

Abdur Rahman was a powerful Emir of Afghanistan in the late 1800s fighting the Hindus to regain northwest India. One day the Sikh ruler from the Punjab met with Abdur Rahman telling him that India had too great a population for the Afghans to resist. Taking out a large handful of wheat kernels he tossed them on the carpet and said, "We will cover your land like this and what can you do to resist?"

Abdur Rahman whispered to an aid who left the room, returning minutes later with a large cockerel. Abdur Rahman set the cock down and it immediately began gobbling up the grain. He said, "This is what we will do to you."

*****

One day a Hindu was walking along the road with his wife when a fierce Pathan came upon them. The Pathan decided he would rape the wife. As he dropped his tombon (baggy pants), he said to the Hindu, "When I am fucking your wife, I want you to get down behind me and hold my testicles and not allow them to touch the ground."

Sometime later the Hindu bragged to his friend that he had recently taken advantage of a Pathan. Recalling the story, he said proudly, "I let his balls touch the dust!"

*****

On a trip to Mazar-i-Sharif at *Nowroz* I was on a long bus ride north with a loud *kilinar*, who collects money from passengers, cleans the bus, changes flat tires and serves the driver. The *kilinar* found that I spoke the lingo and started loudly calling me "mistar" and asking me questions such as where I lived. When I said Kohistan, he went into a long diatribe about how he'd come and take me to the Panjshir where we'd go hunting cows, and a lot of other nonsense. He was entertaining the passengers who were all laughing at me, the brunt of his humor.

*****

Pathans told the joke about the Hazara wise man. A Hazara farmer found his cow with its head stuck in the large pottery feed pot and he couldn't get it off. He went to the Hazara wise man and asked what can I do? The wise man told him to cut off the cow's head, which he did. Then the wise man said, now break the pot. Afterwards the wise man shook his head and asked, "What would these people do without me?" This was an example of prejudice against the Hazara.

*****

One day the mullah is invited to a grand dinner at the home of the Wazir (minister to the king). He arrives at the palace in ordinary clothing straight from his farm. The guards at the door refuse him

146

entry, saying he cannot come in wearing the clothes he has on. Disgruntled, he leaves and goes home.

There he changes into his finest clothes and returns to the palace where he is shown in and takes a seat amongst many others, cross legged on the floor covered with carpets. Food is brought to him, and he starts to shove handfuls of rice and meat into the cuffs of his shirt. Surprised, one of the hosts asks him, "What are you doing?"

The mullah replies, "The invitation was not for me, but for my clothes, so I am feeding them."

*****

The mullah has a toothache and goes to the dentist, who tells him the tooth needs to be extracted. The mullah asks how much it will cost, and the dentist replies "one dinar," which at that time was a large amount of money. The mullah asks how much it would be if he had two teeth extracted. The dentist replies also one dinar. So the mullah directs him to extract two teeth, the rotten one and a good one.

When he returns home, his wife asks, "How did it go?"

The mullah replies, "Ha, I took advantage of the dentist, and had two teeth out for the price of one!"

29. Baku Kham Bazaar

Perhaps Dr. Ghaznowi's refusal to let me move was a blessing in disguise. After a year's low profile and speaking the language well now, I started spending a lot more time in the Baku Kham bazaar on the road outside my home, mulling over life with the shopkeepers and farmers. It was exhilarating. Though I had thought them to be unworldly, they were wise and sensitive, and relished the simple country life. We exchanged stories, told jokes, and answered each other's questions. Some of the children in the bazaar were now salaaming me, as an adult worthy of respect, usually reserved for Muslims.

They often asked after my parents and brother Peter, saying that my mother indeed must be sad not to have her sons at home, and that my father must be a *paisadar* (having money, i.e. wealthy.) They were disappointed when I told them our land was small, that we did not cultivate it, and had no cows, horses, or asses. But they concluded that shops at home must be big, able to meet all our needs. They often asked about hunting and agriculture, and I confessed ignorance, as a "city sitter," though I loved to tell them about the avocado, orange, peach, and fig trees we had in California when I was a boy.

They asked what we say when we kill an animal. Muslims say "*Allahu Akbar*" ("God is Great") and hold the animal so that it cannot move while they hold the mouth open so it can't make noise. Headless chickens running around were viewed as barbarism.

The men also highly approved that my father didn't permit my mother to work outside the home. In fact, at this time my mother in New York was opening up to the currents of women's liberation, and when I returned home, I was to learn how America was changing and modernizing. In talking with the locals, my biblical knowledge was constantly taxed for the stories of Noah, Abraham, Isaac, Moses, and for church rituals and ceremonies: marriage, death etc.

With an abundance of big juicy white wine grapes in season, I started making wine. Asif and I crushed the grapes and poured the juice into a 5-gallon glass carboy, a very strong bottle used to ship sulfuric acid

Baku Kham shopkeeper on the main road near my house

148

from Germany for car battery acid. We sealed the top of the bottle with a balloon (rubber condom), tubing and a test tube filled with water. The carbon dioxide produced from fermentation bubbled into the test tube and when the bubbling stopped, it was finished. It took about ten days. After letting it settle, we decanted the wine into a couple dozen bottles, sealing them with wax. My first vintage was pretty good, and I thought maybe I was a born vintner! However, batch two was mediocre and the third tasted like mud, so I concluded my first success was just beginner's luck and that there's a reason winemaking is an art. I also hadn't realized that winemaking grapes, vitis vinifera, are very different from table grapes grown for eating.

Meanwhile, the Watergate affair was unfolding like a Dickens novel as I listened to the BBC news and waited anxiously for weekly updates in Time and the Week in Review. Local folks found our politics shameful. They said, "Politics is all lies and treachery, but the revelations of Democrat and Republican lies in recent years is very bad." Shopkeepers, though uneducated and illiterate, understood some of the nuances better than I. For example, from BBC Persian they heard that Congress was seeking to question or put Nixon on trial. They said this wasn't right. "Nixon is your king, and you first must depose a king before you can try him. You can't try a king." Shortly thereafter I read in Time of the constitutional problem of attempting to interrogate a sitting president, along the same lines. They also knew, and had a long history of, intrigue and treachery, saying that when Kennedy traveled to Johnson's territory of Texas, Johnson had him killed so he could become President. Afghan history is replete with murders and assassinations.

Getting to know the locals made me appreciate that wisdom is not all about education and literacy. These illiterate people knew about history and right and wrong, and they were quite capable of making judgements about political and international affairs. In my mind, this showed the fallacies in thinking around some of America's efforts at nation building in the post-Soviet era in Afghanistan. Afghans of all stripes were not ignorant or unintelligent. They simply operated according to different rules and understandings.

30. Visiting Kabul and Logar

Staying with Heidar's family in Guzargah was always special. Family dinner was served on a large table in the family dining room off the back of the kitchen. Sometimes six or eight brothers and cousins ate together. The men always ate first, with many dishes on the table, and the women would stand behind, making sure we had plenty of everything and adding delicacies to our plates. Heidar's sister Nadera and niece Nahid would lead the way and were always making sure we were happy with everything. When we finished and left, the women would sit down and enjoy their meal together.

Heidar's mother treated me so kindly, like a son. She was my mother away from home. When I had my wisdom teeth pulled and was in pain, I visited Guzargah and Shirin Jan asked me with a smile if now was I "beyaqel," meaning witless or foolish. She called me "bachem," my son. Heidar, on the other hand, more often responded to my errors with "khar asti bachem," meaning "you are a donkey, my son." This gets the message across but admits we're of the same stock.

I slept in Heidar's bedroom upstairs, which had a bed and a tushak on the floor, usually for me. The room was ample size and his niece

Nahid (elder sister's daughter) who was about 10 would serve us tea in the morning. She was bright and attentive, and always ready to help. One night there was a strong and frightening earthquake. The house was made of very thick adobe walls, with roof beams of large poplar poles. The house shook violently for some minutes, and luckily the house held. Earthquakes are infrequent but common in Afghanistan, and

Heidar's mother, Shirin Jan, at his wedding

150

very dangerous because the heavy walls and roofs are lethal when they collapse.

Anne Masterson was an English teacher who arrived just after our cycle and became part of our social group. She was from Cazenovia, very beautiful country in upstate New York, not far from Ithaca where I'd gone to college. She had three siblings that were Peace Corps volunteers, and she landed on her feet from the beginning. She also began dating Heidar, and we spent a lot of time together at parties, dinners, trips, and hikes. She had a great sense of humor and could give as well as she got. She was often a guest at Guzargah also.

There was an International Club in Kabul, set up by foreigners as an eating, swimming, recreation and tennis club. Once in a tennis tournament there, a Prince of Zahir Shah beat me in the semifinals in front of PCVs enjoying R&R, an exciting day for me. I also played a tournament at the British Embassy on fine clay courts in a beautiful garden and managed to beat a very good young French diplomat in a close three-set match but did not win the tournament. I also

played mixed doubles at the AID Club with Ann Macy, an AID staff member a few years older than I. She was a good player, and we also socialized together.

One weekend Heidar took me and a few others to an international football

Heidar Nowrouz and Anne Masterson at their wedding in 1976. Heidar is in fine Afghan dress of the elite.

151

(soccer) tournament in Ghazi Stadium opposite the Kabul carpet bazaar. The match we saw was Afghanistan against the USSR. The Soviets won, even though the Afghans gave a good fight. It was exhilarating to see international level soccer. We supposed that the Soviet team was perhaps not one of its strongest, and that the tournament was mainly for goodwill.

Heidar invited Juris, me and friend Bill Frank from Pittsburgh to a wedding in Qala-i-Logar, his family's ancestral home ("qala," meaning homestead). It was about 50 miles south of Kabul. The entrance to the estate was a long dirt road lined by huge plane trees, opening to a big tree-lined party area. To the left, another driveway lined with plane trees led to the compound entrance. The compound was huge, with walls 40 or 50 feet high, and three stories of rooms all around an internal courtyard. The courtyard had kitchens, storerooms, servant quarters, animals, and chickens. It was like a medieval castle.

The wedding guests were seated at dozens of tables, and Afghan musicians were seated cross-legged on a carpet at the front playing music. We were at a side table sipping whiskey from our teapots. Whiskey is the same color as black tea, and this is how men managed drinking in a culture where alcohol is haram, forbidden. I doubt the elders were fooled, but appearances mattered. We had quite a day.

The Qalai Logar family compound of Nowrouz Khan in Logar Province. He was Heidar's father and Secretary to King Zahir Shah.

152

31. History from King Zahir Shah to Prince Daoud's 1973 Coup d'Etat and the Republic of Afghanistan

In the 1950s, Afghanistan's King Zahir Shah approached the Eisenhower administration seeking a defense treaty with America, which was turned down. The US was an associate member of CENTO, the Central Treaty Organization, whose members were Iran, Iraq, Pakistan, Turkey, and the UK. Afghanistan then made a defense treaty with the USSR, aligning with India, who was also the leader of the newly formed non-aligned movement, following independence from Britain in 1947. With the Afghan-USSR treaty, most Afghan military officers were sent to the Soviet Union for training, with a small number to France, the UK and the US. Over time, the Afghan military became pro-Soviet, a key factor in later developments.

In 1953, King Zahir Shah appointed his cousin Prince Daoud Khan to be Prime Minister. Daoud took Afghanistan closer to the USSR, turning to them for military and economic aid while keeping Afghanistan neutral in the Cold War. He supported political liberalization, used American aid to develop the Helmand River project in the southwest along the Iranian border, introduced educational reforms including women's education, and made the veil voluntary. But he also maintained a repressive control of the country and pushed a harder line with Pakistan hoping to unify the Pashtuns. This led to an economic crisis when Pakistan closed the border, and he was forced to resign in 1963.

In 1964, Zahir Shah approved a new constitution with a legislature of an upper and lower house, and political parties from across the spectrum. At that time the People's Democratic Party of Afghanistan, PDPA, was established along communist principles. In 1967, the PDPA unofficially split into the "Parcham" (flag or banner) and "Khalq" (masses) factions aligned with the USSR and the "Sholei Jaweid" (eternal flame) faction affiliated with the People's Republic of China. Parcham was led by Babrak Karmal and consisted mainly of Farsi speakers from urban areas. Khalq, of more rural Pashtu speakers, was led by Nur Muhammad Taraki. "Taraki wanted to model the party after Leninist norms while Karmal wanted to establish a democratic front." (Wikipedia.) The PDPA factions grew and enlisted key people in the military and government sectors. They were strongly influenced if not controlled by the Soviet Union who opposed the CENTO nations surrounding their southern border.

The leaders of the PDPA had all come under the influence of communist ideology: Taraki with the Communist Party of India in the 1930s, Babrak at Kabul University in the mid-1950s and Hafizzulah Amin in the late 1950s at Columbia University where he joined the Socialist Progressive Club. Amin was to become the second to Taraki and eventually to displace him.

The international world was very unsettled at this time. China was in middle of its Cultural Revolution, while France was wracked with demonstrations and riots against capitalism and American imperialism. The US was struggling with anti-Vietnam War demonstrations, as well as civil rights riots in cities throughout the country. Meanwhile there was an ideological split over Marxism-Leninism as the USSR began de-Stalinization and advocated peaceful coexistence with the Western nations, which China, under Mao, viewed as revisionism.

The border problem with Pakistan continued to fester, dating from Afghanistan's loss of much of Pashtunistan and all of Beluchistan during the time of the British Raj.

Cold War regional alignment had Iran, Pakistan, the United States and China on one side with the USSR, Afghanistan and India on the other. The 1967 border war between China and India was an added problem. It appears clear that the US Pakistan-Iran military alignment trumped any concerns over Afghanistan's borders. It also didn't help that Afghanistan had a strong cultural affinity to India in music, art and films.

Conditions were ripe for Afghanistan to be essentially delivered to the USSR. On July 17, 1973, while King Zahir Shah was in Italy for medical treatment, Prince Daoud Khan took over the government in Kabul in an almost bloodless coup with a small, well-organized cadre of army lieutenants and the support of PDPA Parcham leader Babrak Karmal. All the action was over in a few hours of the early morning. For about a week there were tanks, armored personnel carriers, and machine gun toting soldiers in the streets close to the Presidential Palace and the Ministry of Defense. Air Force MIG fighters buzzed the streets and helicopters flew about for a few days, sometimes directly over houses near where I was staying. This coup was called the Saur (the local month) Revolution and established the Republic of Afghanistan.

To us Peace Corps volunteers the coup was startling, and I went with others to the downtown areas to see crowds amongst the tanks and troops, being careful to stay at a distance. There were no hostilities, and it seemed that most people looked favorably on the coup hoping for modernization from a government that had done little since Amanullah Khan in the 1920s. I do not recall any discussion of the need to pull Americans or the Peace Corps out of the country at that time, and we were not afraid, but I'm sure there was a lot going on behind the scenes. We were witnessing history and were of the naïve opinion that nothing could happen to us.

There was concern for safety and the stability of this regime, however. For weeks there was no news, just signs on the streets proclaiming the new regime and a government order forbidding people above a certain civil service rank to be officially invited to foreigners' parties. We expected this to impact who we could see and socialize with, which didn't happen, no doubt because we were the lowest rank of foreign guest workers, and we posed no threat.

The new regime was thus strongly influenced by Parcham, and we anticipated that the Soviet Union would gain greater influence in the future. Iran and Pakistan opposed the coup, and both had disputes with Afghanistan: Iran over the western border and the Helmand Valley, and Pakistan over Pashtunistan. Both, of course, were much stronger than Afghanistan.

The new Afghan government under the royal blooded President Daoud seemed cautious, and the feeling was that all would be well. Preparations were begun for a massive *jeshun* (independence celebration) but were scuttled for security reasons. A new cabinet was chosen, and a constitution framing committee was at work. The old cabinet, prime minister, and military officials were locked up in

Kabul Zoo for the first night and later transferred to the city prison, where they remained.

A celebration of the Saur Revolution in July 1973 parading a picture of Prince Daoud Khan, who overthrew his cousin King Zahir Shah by coup d'etat

32. Visits of Senator Chuck Percy and My Parents

Our PC Director, John Guyer, was the brother-in-law of second-term Senator Charles Percy of Illinois who visited Afghanistan during August. He, along with his and the Guyer families, had planned to visit me in Kapisa and then take a trip up the Panjshir Valley. My location was only a two-hour drive from Kabul, making it a convenient place to see how Peace Corps operated. However closely following the coup d'etat in July, the Ministry of the Interior wouldn't give permission for him to travel outside of Kabul.

So, happily, I was invited to come to Kabul and play tennis with him at the Ambassador's residence, as the Senator was a keen player. We played singles and then doubles with his son and nephew, all good players. I was honored to be asked, which was probably because the Guyers knew that I had played in college.

Afterwards we had drinks and a social evening with Ambassador Eliot. When he learned my hometown was Mamaroneck, NY, Senator Percy asked if I knew Thomas Watson, the founder of IBM. I replied that I didn't (and hadn't even known or remembered who he was). The conversation turned to the upcoming presidential election cycle and who might be likely Republican candidates. Senator Percy himself was in the mix, and others included George Romney and Nelson Rockefeller. Chuck Percy was an energetic Republican Senator who had become the president of Bell & Howell corporation before age 30. He had a long and influential political career, several times a potential presidential candidate during an era of liberal Republicans in the North and a conservative Democrat South. This exposure was a new social league for me. Nonetheless I was thrilled to be invited for the day, and it was a highlight of my time in country.

A few weeks later, a long-discussed trip of my parents to Afghanistan came together. I sent my parents a list of necessities to bring, including college textbooks, a sleeping bag, liquor, a camera and impossible-to-get delicacies like smoked oysters and fine cheese! I also really looked forward to being a rich "mistar" for awhile, accompanying and guiding my folks.

They arrived on September 26, at the beginning of Ramadan. I picked them up by taxi at the airport and it was, of course, wonderful to see them. They stayed at the Kabul Hotel, and on the first days we went to the PC offices and met Peace Corps medical head Dr. Johnson. He took a shine to my parents and later invited us to a fun dinner. He was a middle-aged, vibrant and charismatic person with a welcoming wife. I thought it must have been difficult for him and his wife to leave their family in America, but in time realized that his zest for life was like that of the volunteers.

We also met welcoming volunteers who said how lucky I was to have my parents visiting. How true! My mother told them of their visit to my brother Pete who was a volunteer in Guatemala and that they sure enjoyed the "Vacation Corps." I was annoyed and later asked her not to say this because there were anti-imperialists who viewed us as just that, as well as being spies. In retrospect this was ludicrous, as people would think for themselves. We also had my dad fitted for a suit at my favorite tailor and ordered lapis lazuli and silver earrings to be made by a jeweler for my mother.

We then spent several days in Baku Kham. My parents were impressed by my primitive home. We invited the Afghan textile executives who were my English students for dinner. They were fasting for Ramadan and coming to me for dinner was not convenient. But they did so out of respect for us and had to cut the evening short. I was disappointed with the shortened dinner, but it was my mistake. I should have realized how important the month of Ramadan is, and that it is not a time for entertainment. It is a time for prayer and thinking spiritually and renewal by staying home, slowing down, relaxing and eating less.

During the day, we visited the Director of Education and Lycée Mirmasjadi, meeting the principal there. We took a day trip to Lycée Rukha in the Panjshir where a new school building was under

My parents Charles and Jane Marion, on a trip to the Panjshir Valley, accompanying the Director of Education inspecting school construction in 1973

construction and were joined by Peace Corps Director of Programs Mr. Matin and now staff member Mark Svendsen from Kabul, and the Kapisa Director and Assistant Director of Education. While it was not possible to serve us meals, all were very gracious and hospitable.

Work commitments required me to stay in Kapisa for a few days, so my parents took a bus over the Salang Pass, where they stayed in Baghlan with some volunteers, and met Charlie and Tom, among others. I had hired for several weeks one of the drivers of two Russian Volga taxis in Golbahar, and headed up to meet my parents. When I arrived, I was stunned to see my parents' faces swollen, making them almost unrecognizable, like prize fighters after a big fight. They had been bitten by bed bugs and suffered allergic reactions.

This was an eye opener for me because I was often kept up at night scratching from the bed bugs in the *tushaks* at home and in the schools on trips. These cotton mattresses were filled with raw cotton stored and sold from small mud shops. The mattresses were filled by nadoffs, who used a large bow about six feet tall and fluffed the cotton by skillfully twanging it on the twine string of the bow, exploding the collapsed balls into fluffy cotton. In the bazaar you can hear this loud twanging during the day. We regularly had to spread the mattresses powdered with an insecticide out in the sun to try to kill the bugs, with limited success.

I wondered how my folks, who had traveled extensively, were so sensitive, and I was not. Was it possible that the "Greatest Generation" mostly had only American food and lodging, even in the Navy during WWII in America and the Pacific? This would have been more sheltered than modern-day Peace Corps volunteers? Of course, the experience cannot be compared to the danger of fighting in the Second World War.

When my brother and I were small in the 1950s, we had been on vacation in Mexico, and on a tour we ate delicious sugar cane straight from the fields. It made us violently ill with bloody diarrhea for days. We were staying in our camping trailer, and our dear mother had to carry buckets back and forth to the bathrooms. Whether because of this or not, my brother and I both ended up being asymptomatic to amoebic dysentery during our Peace Corps service. I tested positive

159

several times but didn't get the violent stomach cramps that most volunteers did. Treatment with tetracycline killed the bugs, and we always could carry on with our work.

From Baghlan we headed north by taxi, passing through Tangi-Khulm (Khulm Narrows) to Mazar-i-Sharif, a beautiful city with a Friday Mosque and shrine to the Sunni Moslem Caliph Ali ibn Abi Talib. This huge complex with many domes was entirely covered with brilliant, deep blue mosaics, and is the center for huge celebrations at *Nowroz* (New Year) on the first day of spring.

From there we drove on remote dirt roads to Bamiyan, sometimes able to eat from shops that were open because travelers and the ill are permitted to eat during Ramadan. Along the way, claiming that he needed to rest, the taxi driver stopped at the side of the road and went off to some *koochi* tents nearby. My mother said that she had read in a travel book that some *koochis* are prostitutes. When he returned, he said to me in Farsi that he'd smoked some hashish and had sex. I felt bad about this and thought it was disrespectful, while also realizing how sharp my mother was. Later in an even more remote location we

The 175-foot tall Buddha sculpture in Bamiyan, carved in the 7th century during Indian Mauryan rule. The sculpture was destroyed by the Taliban in 2001

passed a compound, and several large vicious fighting and security dogs ran out and chased the car. The driver didn't slow, callously ran over one, and kept going, while it howled. I felt terrible.

In Bamiyan we stayed in a large yurt, one of many that the hotel had for tourists. We enjoyed the splendor of Bandi Amir, which means "dam of the king," a series of lakes formed by naturally depositing limestone that builds up high walls fed by upstream rivers from the high Hazarajat mountains. The lakes are a deep, brilliant blue color, and a wonder to behold. We visited the two large sandstone Buddhas carved into the cliff face in the sixth and seventh centuries during the Buddhist era. One Buddha was ten stories tall, with the face shaved off by Muslims who disapproved of the statues as idols, forbidden by Islam. These statues were both destroyed by the Taliban in recent years.

Late that evening we tuned into BBC and learned that Egypt had attacked Israel across the Suez Canal. The Egyptians had planned routine exercises near the Suez Canal during Muslim Ramadan and Jewish Yom Kippur. They launched a surprise attack using pontoon bridges to cross the canal with mechanized forces and used water cannons to wash away the high banks of sand, breaching the Israeli lines. The war raged for days and then became a stalemate, with Egypt regaining control of the canal and its eastern shore, which they had lost to Israel in the Six-Day War of 1967. Their honor was restored, and they announced proudly that it was not a surprise that the war ended in a stalemate because they could not match the might of America, which had quickly come to the aid and resupply of the Israelis.

After returning to Kabul, I had to go to Kapisa for our final commitments in Tagab to the south, which turned out to be a bust. The Lycée's principal and assistant principal, as well as many teachers and students, stayed home during Ramadan. After a day each at Mirmasjadi and Mahmude Raqi I was back in Kabul with my parents.

We went to a *buzkashi* game at the national playing grounds. The players were Turkoman and Uzbeks from the north, large men with leathery skin wearing chaps and riding big strong horses. We saw two players fighting for control of the goat, galloping off at a spreading angle between them. Eventually one overpowered the other, who was pulled over sideways, his horse rolling over him, both on their backs. I thought we had just seen a fatality, but the rider got up, shook it off, and got back on his horse and continued to play.

We next took a bus trip to Peshawar in Pakistan through the famous Khyber Pass. Alexander the Great and many conquerors since his time have marched over this pass, which cuts through high rugged mountains with checkpoints on both sides of the Pakistan border. Along the way a man broke a chunk of hashish into small bits and emptied a cigarette of tobacco. He mixed the tobacco with the hashish, restuffed the cigarette and proceeded to smoke it and get high. My mother was paying close attention to this and raising her eyebrows.

Peshawar was a busy city with many paved roads and vehicles, a large population, and was filled with the noisy sounds of crowds and honking vehicles. We stayed at Dean's Hotel, famous among tourists. It was British style with a western bar where we enjoyed scotch and water, the scotch obviously diluted.

We returned to Kabul, collected my dad's suit and my mother's earrings, and the next day I sadly put them on the airplane. They headed

Buzkashi (goat pulling), the national sport of polo, played at the Kabul Stadium. The tomb of Nadir Shah is in the distance.

162

off for a short stay in Scotland. I was proud of my parents' indomitable spirit which is what imbued me and my brother with wanderlust and fearlessness, notwithstanding their reaction to bed bugs!

33. Friends Moving On

At about this time, Heidar was accepted to the Iranian Center for Management Studies (ICMS) in Tehran, a joint venture with the Harvard Business School. He left Kabul for an exciting one-year program. His experiences in Tehran were both positive and frustrating because Iranians saw Afghans as their backward and poor eastern neighbors and looked down on them. The program was first rate and Heidar an ideal business student. However, when he received his degree, his job prospects were poor, as Iranians were not hiring Afghans. Iran was modernizing rapidly and looked to America and the West for inspiration. The Iranians were starting businesses in all fields. Success stories were common, such as the electrician who started out repairing refrigerators and ten years later was the biggest distributor, repair service and retailer of refrigerators in the country.

I visited Tehran that year and by then was fluent in Farsi. When I met Iranians with Heidar, they would praise my language while largely ignoring him, which was ridiculous as he was a Farsi scholar. Heidar liked to tell the story of his eldest brother, Hussain, who got into a friendly argument with an Iranian one time while flying back from Europe. The Iranian claimed that the famous poets were all from Iran, none from Afghanistan, which wasn't fully true as the language and literature developed over a large area of Central Asia. He said that even the fictional Mullah Nassruddin was Iranian. Hussein laughed hilariously and said, "Of course he is Iranian" (as he always plays the fool).

My former teacher and friend Zarghuna had been tutoring US Ambassador Eliot for some time and with his help received a scholarship to go to Vermont to study Teaching English as a Foreign Language (TEFL). So, she was soon off to the States, taking with her a fine small carpet from her father, as insurance should she need to raise money.

I began to spend more time visiting with Bill Frank, who was close with Heidar, and Ted Emerson, from Concord, MA, and a descendant of the great writer. They were very hospitable to me in my trips to Kabul. For me, life in Afghanistan had become a moveable feast, with young academics, government agency workers and tourists coming and going. I enjoyed many young people stopping off in Kabul and sharing stories about travel between Paris to Delhi. From them I learned about ashrams in India, hiking in Nepal, best places to visit in Istanbul and Turkey, and much more.

Fellow science supervisors Charlie Ferrell and Tom Schillinger, based in Baghlan City, told me that as their service was finishing, they planned to hike over the Hindu Kush Mountains to the Panjshir and hoped to see me in Kapisa. Unfortunately, I wasn't in Kapisa at the time, so we didn't meet then. They hiked over the Khawak Pass crossed by Alexander the Great at an elevation of 12,600 feet. Charlie recently explained that by that time they could "deal" in the country, speaking the lingo, understanding the people and being comfortable anywhere. They had already taken two horseback trips east to locations unreachable by road to teach in distant Khost Wa Firing, for which they needed the governor's approval. This was deep in the mountains in a region that had been badly hit by the drought and famine and where they'd seen skeletons of horses along the road.

After working in a school in Doshi, they set off east to the trail. The head of the school said they could make it in a day. They had no map and there was no road, only trails, but they had a compass and asked people directions along the way. Charlie said that at the highest elevation they were above the level of agriculture and saw almost nobody. The road at the top had large stones on either side. They believed it had been constructed by Alexander the Great. On the way a man came up to meet them and asked if the king was still on the throne, as he'd had no news of the coup.

Tom said that farmers there would dry farm by broadcasting leftover seed in spring, returning in summer to harvest. He and Charlie bumped into another man who looked at them with bewilderment wondering who they were. At first, they weren't even sure if he recognized them as khorijis (foreigners.) He told them, "You can't make it over the pass in a day, you had better stay here with us." So they spent the night in a stone hut with a thatched roof, ten men sleeping shoulder to shoulder. One pulled out a pistol he'd bought from a Pakistani, and asked Tom if it was real because if it was a fake, he wanted to take it and get his money back. Tom saw a backward S on the Smith & Wesson brand but told the guy it was real and not to take it back, knowing this would be a mistake. Then the other men all pulled out guns. Tom and Charlie were the only unarmed ones.

Another fellow pulled out a treasured plastic ViewMaster that used daylight to show a circular slide disc of Hawaiian hula dancers, which was thrilling to them. At very high altitude in the middle of nowhere, Charlie and Tom were amazed. The next day, they hiked down to the Panjshir River and spent the night in a local teahouse before heading to Kabul and then returning to Baghlan for their last few weeks of service.

Recently, Charlie, Tom and I had a Zoom call, reminiscing about our time with the NSC and amazing two years of experiences. Charlie recalled having great counterparts, and how they worked cooperatively and were able to run the show on local admin and budgets. They, too, wrote an answer book for teachers and distributed it directly to the schools outside normal channels. Tom recalled their counterparts as good guys, one with strong English, though they didn't want to work too hard or travel to distant schools. This was opposite to my counterparts who wanted to travel and earn more money.

Charlie's feeling at that time was that Afghanistan was moving away from fundamentalism, which is supported by only part of the population. But he said that Afghans are incredibly capable of fighting against authority but cannot organize or govern. Indeed, they outlasted the British, Russians and Americans from 1839 to the present day. Many today want reform like that experienced under Amanullah Khan in the 1920s. Ironically, the shift to fundamentalism owes much to American arms support to the mujaheddin fighting the USSR in 1979, and Saudi money to financing arms and madrasas in Pakistan. The USA sadly lost interest in Afghanistan after 1989, and thus lost the ability to influence change there.

Tom told me he thought when he left Afghanistan at the end of 1973 the Afghans were eager to modernize and move ahead, like an airplane revving up to take off. Today they have regressed, and it will again take time for change to come. He said that Afghanistan has always been a crossroads in Asia, buffeted by the movement of people and wars. How tragic history can be.

34. Finishing as Science Supervisor

School visits picked up as we approached the end of the school year. We added middle schools not seen the previous year at Dahati Dasht and Bazarak close by, and Panbatuniar in Panjshir, performing a full range of experiments. Working with the Asia Foundation also paid off when they awarded us a large number of books, and a grant of 20,000 Afghani (about $300) for laboratory equipment. We developed a list of locally sourced materials for each school: a basin, bucket, black cloth for curtains, safety blanket, safety glasses and lab coat that we had tailored, a large washing brush, a carton for storage, a stove with alcohol burner, cheesecloth, gallon cans for kerosine and alcohol.

Amazingly, all together this cost only about $45 per school. I was amazed at how far money could go, and ever since have thought about how cost-effective local aid can be, including stimulating the economy. Next, we asked for permission to use a Peace Corps truck for delivery because volunteers were not allowed to drive or use PC vehicles. Fortunately, Director Guyer was happy to give permission.

After getting a local driver's license, I picked up the PC truck and with Sayid Qamar and Mohamed Saeid began delivery to the schools. It was exciting to be behind the wheel and made me feel important. Beyond the irrigated valley of the Kohi Daman was a relatively flat and treeless stretch of land along the dirt road to Nejrab and Tagab. This was a very safe place to drive. I let Sayid Qamar and Saeid Khan, who had never driven, drive for a short distance. It was fun, and they loved it. Showing up in a big American truck also enhanced our profile throughout the province.

Getting to drive a big truck in Afghanistan reminded me that we PCVs were both fortunate and privileged. Afghan people, to show humility, sometimes introduced themselves using *khak* (earth or dirt, from which comes khaki) before their name. This recognizes our common religious heritage of ashes to ashes, dust to dust. I once jokingly said to Heidar's older brother Rahman that I was "*khak* Toby." He slyly laughed and said, "We know the truth." He reminded me of the American School teacher in Kabul who was seriously injured in a car accident, and a US military hospital airplane was flown in from Germany to evacuate him.

An interesting aside about *khak*, or dirt: it is not considered unclean, unlike in English where dirty means just that. In Farsi, dirty means dirt-like, and clean, as the earth is what sustains us. Khaki means the color of earth and was adopted by the British Raj for the color of its uniforms.

Another story was of a volunteer who accidentally drank a strong local insecticide stored in an old, recycled food bottle. He became gravely ill, and Dr. Johnson medevacked him by plane to Tehran. Clearly, we volunteers had immense support. At the same time, many PCVs worked far out in the boonies with exposure to a variety of health risks, which was all part of the challenge.

Around this time Standard Oil Company of California (SoCal) ran a full-page letter in the New York Times about improving Arab relations and searching for peace through evenhandedness in the Israeli and Palestinian conflict. By this time I believed that we Americans hear mostly only one side of the story. Don Croll once described the great gulf between the west and Islam. It went all the way back to the Crusades, and he mentioned Crusader Rabbit cartoons on TV were biased against Muslims, and how this affected us growing up. Sadly, SoCal was heavily criticized in the press, and thereafter withdrew from making such political comments.

Winding up was a busy time and nostalgia got lost in the excitement of work and moving to Kabul. I spent the last week of October writing final reports and guides for the teachers and saying goodbye to the provincial and school staff.

My final report started with a summary of the monthly reports submitted. Discussion focused on practical work with the schools' teachers and office work establishing the science center. I hand-wrote in Farsi a 22-page chemistry guide for teachers. The write up described the Center's formal work plan, ordering furniture and listing the teachers who were expected to run the science center. We documented the correspondence with the NSC on laboratory design, materials, seminars and accepting funding. I also listed the additional help from the Asia Foundation and their contacts.

This part of my memoir was mostly taken from notebooks I wrote in Farsi, which were not as thorough as English would have been. This plus my forgetting a lot of content and language has made the writing difficult.

Our conclusions and recommendations were for a closer bond with the Director of Education and planning together with the NSC. This would require a strong admin office to plan and record work with the schools. We suggested a uniform program for all schools with study outlines. At the end of each school year the teachers should be tested, and results given to the Director of Education. Finally, we recommended that the science supervisors write 20 percent of the exam questions for mid-terms and finals.

I was under no illusions that differences between the NSC, the Education Department in Kabul and the provincial Department would be resolved. Sayid Qamar and Saeid Khan were focused on keeping some distance from the local department of education, being representatives of the NSC in Kabul, which was resented and criticized indirectly. In the end it was the job of the Ministry of Education in Kabul to resolve any contradictions.

Saying goodbye to many people was heartwarming, as we had enjoyed our work together, and people were kind with their thanks and good wishes. Saeid Khan and Sayid Qamar and I were truly sorry to say farewell to each other, recognizing that despite squabbles, we had been through a lot together and appreciated our time together.

I also realize that I had often been too inflexible—they had been more relaxed. After all, they were in long term jobs, earned smaller salaries, and had to navigate local politics. I wish I had done more schmoozing with them, but so it was.

I left Kapisa with mixed emotions. My large adobe castle had been home for two years, and seen many visitors, friends, meals, and fun. It had also been the archetypical Peace Corps experience, living remotely and like a local. The Baku Kham bazaar had become my neighborhood, and the people friendly and outgoing. I also had fulfilled my two years of service to the educational system, while learning about a foreign culture and serving American interests. By this time, I was also fluent in Farsi and had learned a fair amount of the poetry and philosophy of a few of the greats in Farsi literature. But I was excited to be headed to Kabul, to more challenging work, a more cosmopolitan life, and more creature comforts. So I moved on with great anticipation.

IV

Reupping for a Third Year of Service, Teaching at Kabul University in Faculty of Engineering

1973-1975

35. Move to Kabul and the Faculty of Engineering, Fall of 1973

My first Peace Corps contract was ending on October 31, and with approval from the Peace Corps I was accepted to re-up for a third year, to teach at the Faculty of Engineering at Kabul University.

I was very happy to be staying in Afghanistan. I spoke the language fluently, had some good friends, enjoyed the social life, food and opportunity to travel that was part of the experience, and believed I was continuing with my original goals of being a PCV and useful to the host country. The only downside was having a salary of about $100 per month, when I could be earning about twenty times that in the States as well as building a long-term career. I was just turning twenty-four years old, so not overly worried about career.

Moving from Kapisa to Kabul was a whirlwind. Kabul is a city split in half by mountain ranges. To the northeast is the Kohe Asamai mountain, dropping off in the middle of the city to the Kabul River that cuts through the mountains. To the southwest is the Kohe Sherdarwaza mountain. I was directed by the faculty to a good house in Karte Char, Precinct Four, on a side street south of Asamai Road which runs west to east. Across this road to the north was Kabul University. My street was lined with houses and, like all Afghan houses, my house and small entryway garden were surrounded by walls. The house had electricity and was made of concrete, with a living room and dining room area to the right, a kitchen, bedroom and bathroom to the left. The bathroom had a western toilet and a shower. It was the lap of luxury. I could ride my bike to work in about 10 minutes. Juris found a house in a more local neighborhood up the hills of Kohe Asamai, with good views looking down to the university.

Mohamed Assif came with me and did a fine job of moving all the furniture and goods to Kabul using a local waz (open truck) for transport. He asked if he could keep the dogs in Baku Kham, for security and because they would not do so well in the city. I said I couldn't part with them, a big mistake. One day the next year someone came to the door and they both managed to run out, never to be seen again. It was sad, because no doubt they would have been captured subjected to the often cruel treatment of dogs.

The sights and sounds of Kabul of course were totally different from Kapisa. There were city buses, old and basic, but they ran all the time and could be taken all across the city. There was also an abundance of taxis, bikes, trucks and private cars and jeeps with a steady noise level.

I enjoyed going with Assif to buy firewood. The merchant would have a great pile of wood chopped to the right size for a *bukhari*, and you'd order a quantity of 20 or 30 *charak* (about 4 pounds). Using a big balancing scale with large iron pieces of machinery of known weight in a pan on one end and a platform for piling the wood on the other, he'd weigh *charaks* continuously calling out 1, 1, 1, 1, 1, 1... and pile them on his waiting karachi (cart on a truck axle), then 2, then 3, etc. Ever since I use this method at home, for example, when making rice and counting the cups of water, or ice cream counting

South Kabul. Faculty of Engineering is the serrated rooftop in the lower right. My home was across the main road a few blocks to the left.

the cups of milk. It can't go wrong. No arguments. The counting is continuously audited!

The Faculty of Engineering ran quite efficiently. Dean Zewari was in command, and ably assisted by Assistant Dean Nazeer Ahmad Pashtoon. The Dean was an impressive and affable man, and always very smart in a dark suit and tie, with a short haircut, very businesslike. More importantly he put people at ease and had a genuine personal interest in people. Once we were discussing the use of an English word that had been modernized to become a verb by adding "ize" at the end, and I said I didn't think that was good English. He said that he was surprised as he would expect engineers to be in favor of change and updating language, like technology, which is always progressing. It made me think twice and be more open-minded. He was very welcoming and supportive of Juris and me joining the faculty.

We were still volunteers, paid by the Peace Corps, and with all the support of the American mission in Afghanistan. We still had to abide by the PC rules, as well as the requirements of the university. The faculty

On the steps of the Faculty of Engineering, from left Dean Zewari, Hamid Ghazanfar, Ted Tumelaire. From right Toby and Asst Dean Pashtoon

had four departments: Mechanical Engineering & Chemistry—MECh; Mathematics, Electrical Engineering & Physics—MEEP; Civil Engineering—CE; and Agricultural Engineering—AgE. The department had committees ranging from scheduling and academic standards to curriculum review and research coordination. We had regular staff meetings dealing with faculty issues, teaching assignments, student problems and upcoming activities.

The atmosphere at the faculty was energized and professional. The professors were mostly young, from late 20s to mid-40s, with interesting backgrounds and experience. Quite a few had attended Stevens Institute. One was a distant member of the royal family, which I figured out from his accent, which was unlike common speech. Another studied in the USSR and had an attractive blonde Russian wife. We asked him about his education in the USSR, and he showed me his course transcript which included Communism and Marxist theory. I later told my office mate Hamid Ghazanfar that the Soviets were teaching them propaganda. He said, "Not really. When we studied engineering in the USA, we were required to take electives, and our advisors usually suggested that we take a course in American History, so it's the same thing."

Early on I got to know faculty members Abdullah Kakar and Ghulam Rasool Kohistani, who were outgoing and interested to hear about my and Juris's experience in Afghanistan and to talk about their time in America. Abdullah told Juris and me that he was planning a hike across central Afghanistan during the summer break and asked if we'd be like to join. Naturally we did. Ghulam Rasool's family was from Panjshir, so we shared experiences there. He and Hamid Ghazanfar had a lot of good jokes and insights into how Afghan people behave.

My work schedule was to teach for the fall semester and then go on home leave in the winter. For me, teaching at the Faculty of Engineering was like being a duck back in water. The professors were nearly all American-trained using an American curriculum and the students, by and large, were well prepared and very intelligent with good-to-excellent English. In addition to Afghans, there were a few Indians and a Palestinian.

From my journal:

> Nov 16, 1973. My job at the University has worked out extremely well thus far, now teaching 75 students Thermodynamics I and 12 lectures in Manufacturing Processes, Polymers (Rubbers, Plastics, Fibers), Ceramics and Glass. In spring, I will teach Thermo II. Instruction is in English, which makes life easy. I also took on as tutor for my Farsi a former professor from the Faculty of Literature.

36. Home Leave

Peace Corps required volunteers who extend their service to take a home leave trip, enforced by making the travel settlement payable only for a flight to home. My home leave began on January 10, with a week in Tehran. The Crolls had kindly invited me to stay with them, and Heidar was also there studying at the ICMS.

We enjoyed the Armenian restaurants, and their excellent chicken and lamb kebab, robust local beer, and Russian Stolichnaya vodka, stored in the freezer and which poured like a thick syrup. The custom was to take turns offering toasts of shots of "Stoli", which lubricated dinners brilliantly. At that time, Don Croll was working with Ehsan Lavipour, whom I'd met on my Iran trip the previous winter, setting up a copper pot manufacturing business. The pots and pans of all sizes were beautiful, made of thick shiny copper, with stainless steel handles.

The nightclubs in Iran were magnificent. It was said that if you visited Tehran from Paris or Beirut, it was not much, but from Kabul, it was like Paris. I could confirm the latter. They had singers, dancers, magicians, and comedians. The custom at that time was to park Don's car on the street outside the nightclub, paying local men to wash and protect the car for the evening. Failing that, hubcaps would go missing.

This was the heyday of Googoosh, Iran's most famous female singer, who was like a cross between Umm Kulthoum of Cairo, Janis Joplin and Ella Fitzgerald. After years in the wilderness following the Iranian revolution, Googoosh left Iran in 2000 and now lives in California and performs to great acclaim once again.

I flew to New York on an empty Pan Am 101 flight, overwhelmed by the attentiveness and attractiveness of my stewardess. I immediately wrote a gushing customer appraisal of her. I was the proverbial world traveler who was returning from the boonies. My parents greeted my arrival in New York. They had prepared wonderfully for my visit, starting with dinner with best friends from the neighborhood, the Rosenbergs. Fred was a great raconteur and as witty as ever. He said, "welcome to civilization," which jarred me. I showed only how delighted I was to see them, but silently thought that despite its poverty, Afghanistan was civilized and cultured, reflecting its institutions, religion and history. My dad later took us to a New York Knicks basketball game, and Mom on another evening prepared a lobster dinner. It was great being home.

My parents suggested I visit my older brother Peter, a Peace Corps volunteer in Guatemala. Unable to contact him, we decided I should simply go and find him there. They had previously been to Guatemala and seen his village while getting a sense of the country. No doubt my own Peace Corps experience had given me the confidence to travel to faraway places, so I took my chances, flew to Guatemala City and went to the Peace Corps Office to ask about his whereabouts. They said that he was in Totonicapán, 110 miles to the west at 8,200 feet elevation.

I spent the night in the city near a lush and beautiful city square, a tropical delight filled with hedges, flowers, trees, brick walkways, food stands and a center courtyard with a fountain. Lively salsa and marimba music was playing from loudspeakers. And most startling to me after two years in Afghanistan was young couples everywhere, holding hands, strolling, and sitting on park benches and kissing and snuggling. I had a delicious Guatemalan dinner at a restaurant crowded with young travelers and spent a delightful evening with a young Chinese woman I met from Hong Kong.

The next day I caught a bus to Totonicapán driving along lush green mountain roads. The contrast with dry and dusty Afghanistan couldn't have been greater. On arriving at the town center, I enquired in the market about Pedro Marion. People immediately knew "Don Pedro" and told me he was up a main dirt road a distance out of town amongst the farms. Soon I was at the door of his small home and garden, encircled by walls. Marjie, later to become my sister-in-law, came to the door and said, "so you must be Toby." They had no word of my coming, and when Pete arrived late that evening on his small motorbike, he was totally surprised. We had a great reunion. Pete's work was establishing credit unions at the textile cooperatives of the region.

I spent a wonderful 10 days with them. It was the start of Mardi Gras, and across the road a wooden dance floor had been set up under a big tent. We heard marimba music from trumpets, saxophones, trombones, guitars, drums, singers, and dancing for days. We traveled around the province, one morning sharing "un octavo" (one-eighth of a bottle) of rum, an uplifting start to the day, again so unlike Afghanistan. We talked politics, and Pete was full of frustration and anger about the US supporting the United Fruit

My PCV brother Peter and Marjie Cummings with neighbors in Totónicapan (elev. 8,000 ft), Guatemala in 1974. He worked in textile cooperatives. A hugely different cultural environment from Afghanistan

177

Company which partnered with the dictators to control vast tracts of land needed to keep their monopoly banana business thriving.

We also visited Lake Atitlán, surrounded by towering volcanic peaks. There I met other Peace Corps Volunteers and ex-PCVs who had stayed in Guatemala to run businesses like trading, bars, and restaurants, and other young people of several nationalities who were working in international aid efforts for Guatemala. I was somewhat unsettled by the Guatemala experience as it was so open, friendly, and joyful, compared to conservative Afghanistan. A few years later, Pete and I had a brief debate over which country was less developed. Pete said they only had one source of water, the pipe and faucet outside the house that ran along the main road! I replied with mock astonishment, "You mean you had water in pipes?" Our dad laughed heartily, the debate finished.

My return to Afghanistan took me back to New York and then on to London where I saw the changing of the guard, Westminster Abbey, Parliament and Whitehall, Trafalgar Square, Piccadilly Circus. I was enthralled by Rex Harrison's electrifying performance in Pirandello's *Henry IV*. I visited Heidar's brother Rahman in South Wales. He was on a training assignment for government administrators hosted by the UK. His host family was dour, and not happy with his joining me at a nightclub and coming back late, waking them up on a work night. I spoke highly to him of the Afghans. He countered that in the UK, Afghans' status is like Pakistanis, even lower. He told of how he had been served food cooked in lard (pork fat, forbidden for Muslims). It didn't bother him, but smiled ironically, seeing it as disrespectful. He also opened my eyes to the fact that police respond to Afghans or people of color in the UK and America much differently than they do to white people like me in the better parts of town.

On my own one evening in a pub in Cardiff, I said hopefully to a pretty barmaid, "So you're English, huh?"

She snapped at me saying, "Not bloody likely. I'm Welsh." I realized my own ignorance, and that the Welsh were anything but fans of the English. In the B&B where I stayed the innkeeper said to me very pleasantly over conversation that the gin martini was America's only contribution to civilization. Slowly the insult soaked in, but as a typical Yank, I was happy with everything British. I felt that he did not have a lot of sympathy for Americans, which surprised me. In Afghanistan I didn't feel any prejudice but knew that the locals believed their religion and culture to be superior.

On a Wednesday I flew to Frankfurt, took a train to Bonn, and met Tom Vetterlein, the German American Field Service student who lived with my family in New York for school year 1962–63 and was like a brother to me. He was a dorm supervisor studying for his PhD at the University of Bonn. I hadn't been able to contact him and he wasn't there, so the first evening I spent with five Afghan students in the dorm. They played Afghan music, spoke Farsi, and made fun of Germans and all the ways they eat potatoes—they called Germany "*kachaluistan*" (potatoland). To Afghans the potato is a foreign and inferior vegetable. In Afghanistan they taunt foreigners by calling them "Mr. *Kachalu*". The story goes that years ago an Afghan studied oceanography in Turkey, a useless course for landlocked Afghanistan. When he returned, he had adopted strange western dress and habits, and was thereafter ridiculed as "Mr. *Kachalu*."

The next night we went to Tom's parents' home for his father's birthday dinner, and it was great to meet his parents and sisters. Friday was spent in the Koln (Cologne) Cathedral and the new Roman-German Museum, and Saturday in the Eifel Mountains seeing Mana Loch and Burg Elz and the Mosel Valley. Germany was stunning culturally: precise and clean, with middle-aged women in country towns sweeping spotless sidewalks. Later riding on a train, I lit a cigarette and a matronly fraulein immediately marched up to me pointing to a sign I couldn't read and said sharply "nicht rauchen!" (no smoking). I put it out immediately.

Stopping in Tehran again, Don Croll took me to a sumptuous pre-Nowroz (New Year's) celebration. I again enjoyed Persian life, drinking vodka and beer, and eating brains, kabob, liver and hearts, lamb's feet. It ended for me with a 4:30 a.m. flight to Kabul. I was itching to get back to Kabul.

Ah, Kabul! It was good to be home and I was ready for work to begin.

It was the week of *Nowroz*, the New Year's Day of Spring Equinox. Winter seemed over, with sunny skies. Aesthetically I missed not having seen any of the winter, but practically, it had been great. The weather was getting warm, though rainy, and the trees were budding and blossoming, beginning to show their summer cloaks of green. The birds were singing again, and midday was hot, sitting in a bus, or anywhere in the sun. I played some tennis and read about Britain's St. John Philby's explorations of the unknown "empty quarter" interior of the Arabian Peninsula in 1932 and 1936–37. I wondered if Philby had been seen in Britain as another Columbus or Marco Polo?

37. At the Faculty and Life in Kabul

It was the start of spring, and I was happy to be back in Kabul looking forward to the year ahead. The new year started with a bang. My new teaching assignments were three hours of Thermodynamics II and six hours of Chem lab, a challenging load. I had 29 students in Thermo and 2 sections of 23 students each in Chemistry I Laboratory. This load plus admin functions kept me busy.

The job was challenging. I was advised to write notes for thermodynamics on heat engines, power cycles, refrigeration, thermodynamics of fluid flow, etc., to aid the students who were using a difficult Naval Engineering School text. For each topic I prepared 10 to 15 pages of notes typed onto a stencil and then run through a mimeograph machine to make copies. The notes required diagrams and equations, such as how an engine cylinder works, or how the pressure vs. volume graph depicts how the combustion of fuel produces energy that is converted to work.

It was a laborious exercise to produce these notes but satisfying. For me, it was also a kind of cleansing, as I had to study again part of the curriculum of my last two years at Cornell. In Spring 1969 and 1970, there had been ongoing anti-Vietnam War demonstrations and strikes. Final exams were cancelled, most subjects were marked only by pass or fail grades, and many including me didn't work as hard as we should have. This was also a bone of contention with the faculty: the engineering professors said they respected the right to strike, but it should come with consequences. They were right, but the students "won," and we got our degrees without a full measure of academics! So in Afghanistan I had to dig deeply and learn the material well to teach effectively.

This work also had some amusing side effects. One night I had a dinner party at home for Afghan friends and was working late to finish a set of notes. I rushed home on my bike, reaching a few minutes after my first couple of guests had already arrived. We said warm hellos, but Heidar's brother Rahman looked at me with a strange look in his eyes and said, "You really must be working hard."

I excused myself to go to the bathroom and change out of my suit, and when I saw myself in the mirror, my face was covered with purple smudges from the mimeograph stencil that I'd been working on. I laughed!

In chem lab, I followed up Larry Bennett's fine laboratory manual with an inventory-ordering system so that the lab wouldn't stall in a year's time.

The students attended lectures, experimented in the lab, solved weekly problem sets, and took exams during the semester and at finals. By and large, they performed well, and some students were quite brilliant. It was enlightening but not surprising to have students smarter than their teacher. Most of the students were from Kabul and

Some of my chemistry students at Kabul University, who are amongst the top in Afghanistan

came from the best high schools. Some were children of important government figures and others had a foreign parent.

One day a rather shy student who was lighter skinned and more western than most approached me after class with questions. He said he was foreign and when I asked him from where, he said he was Palestinian. I must have had a troubled look on my face because he quickly said that Palestinians are simple and peaceful people and not terrorists. I realized that my American background had given me a biased view of that part of the Mideast, and that I needed to be more open-minded.

During one thermodynamics exam I caught an Indian student cheating. I took his exam paper and sent him from the room. Toward the end of the semester his parents invited me to a sumptuous family Indian dinner at their home to curry favor, pun intended. I accepted, but still held the student responsible, requiring him to do extra problem sets and sit an additional exam. In the end he passed. Heidar's nephew Zaman was also in the class and worried about his performance. One day at their home he sought my help. I judiciously offered suggestions for how to cope, and he bucked up straight away.

One of the biggest teaching loads was correcting problem sets and exams. I hadn't anticipated this, as professors in America always had teaching assistants to do this. It requires concentration to do it right and treat everyone fairly. I took the stacks of papers home to do them in peace and quiet without interruption. It always took many hours. Along the way I saw student creativity and learned how to improve exams and teaching.

My cook Mohamed Assif, distilling homemade arak liquor in front of the wood storage room at my Kabul house

One day several of us from the faculty were invited to visit the USSR engineering college known as the Polytechnic. We met the Russian dean who showed us around. There were questions on how we did things at the Faculty of Engineering and in the USA. He asked about computers, and I said that in the curriculum in America we had learned a Fortran-based programming language as first year students and used the computer to solve distillation problems in year three. The dean said that it wasn't possible to use the computer to solve distillation problems as it involved three equations and three unknowns. This surprised me as that is exactly why it's well suited for the purpose. There was some back and forth, but we dropped it. I wondered what the state of technology was in the USSR, and the qualifications of this dean.

Early in the year I had a still (a distillation apparatus) made for making moonshine, taking the design from the Encyclopedia Britannica in the PC library. I drew a picture of it and took it to the copper bazaar. The artisans there immediately knew it as a still for making rose water, a local cologne. I soon began making "white lightning" from raisins and solid, raw molasses, run through a meat grinder and fermented in the same way as the white wine in Baku Kham.

After fermentation, I would double distill the mash in a very large rice pot, with the still on top. Heated by a wood fire, alcohol vapor rose in a vertical pipe, hit a water-cooled dome, condensed and ran down to an annular (donut shaped) bowl with an outlet pipe to a spigot at the end. The dome had a closed upper section where cold water was siphoned in from buckets and then flowed to an outlet. All the parts were sealed with flour dough. The process was organic and homemade!

The product tasted pretty good and was quite powerful. I produced an Imperial quart of 95.6% liquor (the azeotrope for ethanol and water) for about 50 cents. A fifth of mediocre brandy from the local factory sold for $5 and a locally made product was $1.50. It was basically arak, common in the Mideast. Unfortunately, my efforts to make whiskey and rice wine produced only vinegar. With the arak I made "Cuba libres" like a rum and Coke. The Coca Cola was the most expensive ingredient, with a yellow sour orange for the garnish.

Social life in Kabul was much busier than it had been in isolated Kapisa. I frequently had dinner parties, Assif cooking Afghan or German food, and I serving my arak and store bought beer and wine. Guests included German DED friends, PCVs, faculty friends, USAID folks and other foreigners in Kabul. One night we had Dr. Kuis, the Yugoslavian UNESCO expert, along with his wife and daughter Sekitsa. We sat on the floor Afghan style and ate off the *sandali*. I had taped a National Geographic map of Yugoslavia to my wall which got a big surprise followed by a laugh from them when I said, "Of course I always have a map of Yugoslavia on my wall."

Living in Kabul I was able to play some tennis, and joined the American Club and played a few tournaments in the summer.

Frequent rains during spring weather kept down the dust and made for beautiful clouds, mountain vistas, and some brilliant green amongst all the brown. I tried to get outside more but was too often involved in indoor activities. Prior to joining the Peace Corps I would have guessed that going to Afghanistan would mean a simpler life. I learned that it did not!

June 14, 1974: letter to my parents from Ethan and Marion Svendsen, Mark's parents who had gotten to know my parents when they traveled through New York before their trip to Afghanistan:

> Here we are in this far-away land—so different from anything we have experienced heretofore. You were so right about the cultural shock! Sounds, sights, and smells which you can't adequately describe, as well as the warmth and friendliness of those we have met. Toby came to greet us the first night we were here, and the following evening invited us to his home for a delightful evening and delicious dinner. We were so happy to become acquainted with him and certainly understand Mark's friendship with him! Juris was also a guest that evening and we thoroughly enjoyed him as well.
>
> One evening we were guests at the home of an Afghan steward on the Ariana Airlines for a beautiful Afghan dinner followed by Afghan music and good fellowship.

184

Yesterday we drove to Ghazni and saw the museum, minarets, and shrines as well as the busy bazaar where it was almost impossible to walk for interested people who wanted to look at us strange people and our cameras etc. We had delicious kabob there. We drove home on a valley unimproved road, dusty & bumpy but tremendously interesting and a way to see the rice fields, the oxen and other animals, and the people at work. Today we went up to the old fort and saw & heard the cannon fired at noon. The view of the city was fantastic. Sunday we are looking forward to our trip to Bamiyan. Mark will drive us, & of course Carol will go too. We also plan a trip to Kapisa where Toby & Mark worked.

38. Tragedy in the Panjshir River

We Peace Corps volunteers had something of a pioneering spirit in those days, which was much assisted by our PC administrative support. We had good training and teachers, pay, and healthcare, with routine injections and vaccines given to us quarterly. The gamma globulin shots to protect us from hepatitis were really painful. At the same time, we were far away from anything that we had ever experienced before, and there was some danger in how we lived and what we did.

A knock on the door one evening brought Mark Svendsen into my house, and he told me that the day before, on May 31, Denise Blake fell into the Panjshir River in Golbahar, was swept away and drowned. She had been fishing with John at a spot where the river curved with a swift current, and there was a strong wind at their backs. She was sitting 10 yards upstream from John when their cook Iqbal shouted that she had fallen in. John jumped into the river and twice had a hand on her, but the water was swift, slippery and very cold (probably about 40°F), and Denise was well into the current and possibly unconscious. It appeared she may have fallen in head first and been knocked out. He was unable to hold on and save her. He managed to grab a large rock himself and was later rescued with a rope. Denise's body was recovered seven miles downstream. When John returned to the Sherkat with Denise's body, the scene was one of mass devastation and grief, with hundreds of girls and women on the street crying.

I was shattered by the loss of a girl as wonderful as Denise and heartbroken for John. I went to Dr. Johnson's house where John was staying and spent most of the night comforting and talking with him. He kept playing the tragedy over and over in his mind, telling of how he had her, but couldn't hold on. There was nothing I could do except grieve with him and mourn her loss. He was devastated and needed to go home, asking me and another friend to pack up his belongings and handle whatever needed to be done. He left Afghanistan two days later, on June 2nd.

Juris and I had a close call at the end of April when we joined Mark Svendsen and Dick Scott (from USAID) for mountain hiking. Dick parked at about 10,000 feet elevation behind Paghman, a famous village west of Kabul where the Royal Family used to vacation. We started to climb up the highest mountain of the southern tier of the Hindu Kush. Juris and I lagged behind, and unwittingly took a different fork in the path. Soon we saw that Mark and Dick were on a parallel, distant ridge. This high mountain had many ridges and valleys on the slopes rising from Paghman. We continued up a precipitous route of paths and rock cliffs, climbing from 7:45 a.m. to 2:30 p.m. with only a few short rest stops.

We reached about 15,000 feet elevation near the summit, were exhausted and took a breather. Just then black clouds and a blizzard blew in from the north, quickly limiting our visibility to maybe 40 yards. The rock formations became black, shiny, wet and slippery. We headed down immediately, but soon everything was white with snow. The terrain was steep and rocky, making footing difficult. Slipping and falling in some places could mean broken limbs. There were frequent forks in the barely recognizable snow-covered path, and a wrong turn could lead to cliffs and dead ends. Juris led the way, and his experience in the White Mountains of New Hampshire no doubt was an important advantage. We climbed down silently and very soberly for a full hour when again suddenly the wind changed, and we were once again in bright sunlight. The snow quickly melted, and the rocks dried over the next half hour.

We continued to descend, exhausted, and finally rendezvoused with Dick and Mark at about 7:30 p.m., just before dark at Dick's truck. We realized that we had been very under prepared, in shirtsleeves, Pendleton wool shirts, and with little water and only a few snacks. Mark and Dick said that they had decided to wait another few minutes and then go off to organize a search party. During the five-hour descent, we had been focused solely on taking extreme care with our footing and survival. We were drained, and our legs were shaky and knees sore. We had learned a hard lesson about preparation and separation from our group, but fortunately we lived to tell the tale.

39. Volunteer Living Allowance Study

For about a month in the summer of 1974 I was put on a committee appointed by Peace Corps Director John Guyer to review volunteer living allowances and living styles. The group included the Peace Corps finance manager Dave Chamberlain, volunteers Ted and Juanita Tumelaire, and me. We worked well together as a team. Dave knew all about the costs and budgets and the Tumelaires were likeable, easy to get along with, and perceptive. It was also necessary to have a woman on board.

Washington apparently had budget issues and asked for cost cuts, so a study was initiated to see if this was feasible. We interviewed many volunteers in Kabul and the provinces about rent, food and living costs and style, and concluded that volunteers would still be able to live reasonably if allowances were reduced. The results naturally were not popular. We on the committee were seen as agents of the staff, doing the dirty work for what would have already been decided. In part, that was true, but the facts did show that we were paid more than needed. We also learned that we were very well off compared to other Peace Corps countries. Afghanistan was one of only two of the 50-odd countries in which Peace Corps operated where the volunteers had higher salaries than the locals.

187

When doing the interviews, we saw volunteers with as much zeal as we had had upon arriving three years earlier, but we did notice some lifestyle changes. We had adhered to the advice given in 1971 that especially in the provinces having short hair and dressing conservatively would help us to gain respect with the locals. We supervisors were scientists and engineers and maybe more used to following orders. We dressed in used worsted wool suits from Germany from the used clothes bazaar, which imported full container loads of cleaned and pressed suits and all other kinds of clothing for sale. We paid $10 for each suit. The bazaar looked like a big warehouse in a department store.

In discussions during this study, we found a few of the newest volunteers were adamant that it was their right to keep their hair long and to wear jeans and parkas, and they naturally resented that their benefits might be cut. They also seemed to view Afghanistan more negatively and as a closed society, missing some of the thrill we had found in the exotic culture. We got some criticism for what we were doing, and we wondered if the ethos of some volunteers may have evolved over time, or if we were just the bad guys whose job it was to cut pay. But I also had to admit that my hair was now longer, in keeping with my colleagues at the University and the newly arriving PCVs.

After our results were in, the allowances for all were cut substantially, though I don't remember the numbers, maybe 20-30%? We all managed comfortably, nonetheless. As previously written, I had all the basics I needed for about a third of my monthly salary. After leaving the Peace Corps I learned from a pair of Malaysia volunteers who stayed with me in New York that their salaries had been around half of their colleagues and that they lived quite poor lives, with no servants and few luxuries. This was a part of their Peace Corps experience, and they were proud of having lived a much sparer experience. This was the same as the thinking of volunteers in Thailand that we had met when they traveled through Kabul at our start in 1971.

40. Studying Persian Literature

Part of my goal in joining the Peace Corps had been to learn about the culture of Afghanistan. At Kabul University I continued to study Persian literature for three or four hours a week with a former professor of literature at the Faculty of Letters, now at the Ministry of Foreign Affairs, introduced to me by a faculty member. He was an excellent teacher and abundantly knowledgeable; I absorbed what I could.

We mainly dealt with Sufic themes and some of Omar Khayyam, who wrote more approachable poetry than the likes of Hafiz, Mowlana Jalal-u-Din or Sayid Jamal u-Din. The Sufis were mystics in a heart-versus-brain and soul-versus-rationality struggle that dominated later periods of the golden Islamic Ages corresponding to the late European Middle Ages. The Sufis studied as a means of soul cleansing and improvement and followed elders in their growth and development towards God. They mocked the rationalists who followed the law and measured everything with logic.

Following are my translations of some classical Farsi poetry. The rhymes and sounds are lost, of course, and my translations are literal and neither artistic nor very good. Hopefully they will nonetheless convey some of the feel and meaning.

From Hafiz:

> Dark night and fearful waves and such frightening
>   whirlpools
> Where do they know our condition, the lightly loaded
>   on the shores?

This is perhaps my favorite two lines from Hafiz. It is a powerful metaphor for how the experience of sailing in an ocean storm cannot be understood by those people who are without burden and watching from the shore. This applies to much in life: how can those who watch know what we do?

We in the home of dear ones, what security and pleasure,
   as every moment
The caravan bell raises a clamor to fasten our loads

There is no rest or pleasure for those for whom duty calls.

People in Afghanistan enjoy fortune telling by seeing a *fal*, which is to blindly open a page of poetry: what is read is your fortune. This would often be the starting point for learning poetry from Heidar. We'd wonder about something, anything from whether to go to the movies or if his current girlfriend really loved him, and he would say, "Let's see a *fal*." He'd open a book, read the top lines, and draw a conclusion, or not.

Also from Hafiz:

A flower is dear, count its conversation as the spoils of
   victory
That it came to a garden from this road and will become
   that

This is interpreted allegorically: the flower can be a lover; the spoils of victory are something cherished; the garden is your relationship; this road may be life; "that" at the end means love, happiness or even death. So, the meaning could be "cherish the conversation of a person that came to you in life and will become a lover." Or it could be all about love of God. That's the beauty of these poems.

Chastisement and teaching from the wise is a sign,
I said my criticism and I will not repeat it

A flowery poem meaning "a word to the wise is sufficient."
From Omar Khayyam:

Now that the flower of your prosperity is fully laden,
Why is your hand unemployed of the goblet of wine?
Drink wine, as time is a perfidious enemy
And finding a day such as this is rare

Some say that wine represents religion or the love of God, others that wine is wine, and that Khayyam was always keen to enjoy and cherish life, love and friendship. So this means that now that you are who you are, why are you not enjoying life (or wine or God) because a fine day wasted will never return.

Of several thick notebooks filled with poetry and lessons, I unfortunately today can remember but little. This is another reason to appreciate Khayyam and seize the day, for it will not return.

41. Hike across Central Afghanistan from Samangan to Bamiyan

One of the greatest adventures of my time in country was a hike with three friends over 26 days in August 1974, across Central Afghanistan from Samangan to the high Hazarajat, Bandi Amir and Bamiyan. As the crow flies the distance was about 110 miles but hiking through valleys and over passes and mountains we covered over 200 miles, much of it along the ancient Silk Road. We experienced stunning and beautiful scenery, difficult climbing, scarce food, foot problems, water scarcity, and seeing the lives of nomads and villagers in wilderness far from cities. We also learned a lot about the nation.

I kept a diary and later wrote up details of the trip, covering only the first week. My diary notes were sparse and my memory even more so, but I've reconstructed our path and much of what we did along the way. Fortunately, I had US Air Force Operational Navigation Charts that my father had brought for me. A naval aviator during WWII, he knew how to get these. Heidar also gave me a government map of Afghanistan in Farsi. These maps were about four feet square and provided a lot of detail. Google Maps also was a big help, as I could drill down to the villages and sites that we passed through, with some of the current village names shown in the section headings in parentheses.

The map I prepared for this book reminds me of the old British military comment "big hands on small maps," used somewhat derisively by quartermaster officers when they prepared logistics

Map 5: Samangan (Aybak) to Bandi Amir

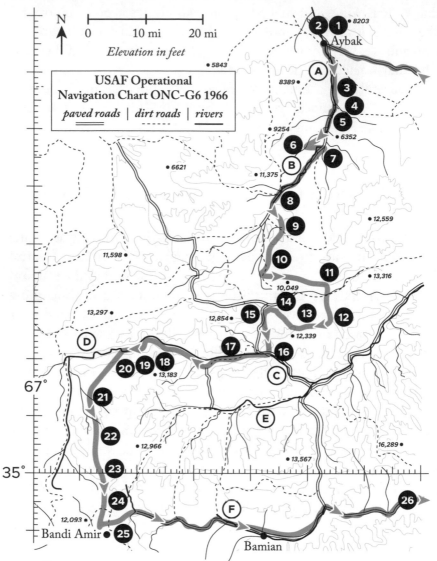

August Days

1,2. Aybak
3,4. Sar Bagh
5. Khurram Springs
6. Kwaja Buzrak
7. Khurram
8. Rui
9. Mui
10. Du Ob
11. Char Magz Sarai
12. Rui Sang
13. Do Ru
14, 15. Sorkh Shar Mountain
16. Kahmard
17. Ajar Lake
18-20. Ajar Park
21. Ob Nyack
22. Puddinatu
23. Siah Khawall
24. Khak Dow
25. Bandi Amir
26. Bamian to Kabul

Rivers

A. Samangan
B. Khurram
C. Kahmard
D. Ajar
E. Sayghan
F. Bamian

plans for generals. The small lines show little of the difficulties of moving through tough terrain. The Cast of Characters:

Abdullah Kakar (age 27), our leader and inspiration for the trip, and a fellow faculty member. Abdullah was the son of Dr. Keram-uDin Khan and Anahita Ratebzad. Dr. Keram-uDin was a well-known medical doctor who had held important medical posts in Afghanistan and at that time was Dean of the Faculty of Medicine in Jalalabad. Anahita was a famous progressive activist with a large following amongst the intelligentsia and youth, and political partner of Babrak Karmal, leader of the Parcham Party, the USSR affiliated Communists.

Abdullah had been an AFS student in North Carolina and a graduate of Stevens Institute in Electrical Engineering. He was an outdoorsman and athlete, and a patriot and lover of the motherland. In the summer of 1972, he had gone on a hunting and hiking trip with a group of Englishmen to the high Hindu Kush of the Panjshir, Nooristan, and Badakhshan, the gateway to the Wakhan Corridor bordering on Tajikistan, China and Kashmir, with mountains neighboring the Pamirs reach 24,000 feet in elevation, and extending east to the Himalayas. Abdullah was our guide and interpreter for which he was exceptionally well-suited, being a careful observer with a keen eye and a good memory, and a fine conversationalist who imaginatively found interest in everything. This trip was Abdullah's next step in his goal of hiking in all areas of Afghanistan.

Abdullah told us that American camping standards were far higher than Afghan living standards, which were indeed to learn.

Shah Wali (age 27), a longtime friend and school mate of Abdullah. He also was an outdoorsman, and party to numerous adventures, hikes, and hunts with Abdullah and others. A 1972 graduate of the Faculty of Literature, Kabul University, Shah Wali was a man of letters, a poet, a singer, dancer, an appreciator of all Afghan and Indian music. In short, he was of a refined Middle Eastern mold. His father was Abdul Jabbar Khan of Mazar-i-Sharif, a government civil servant and senior army officer, and a significant landowner in the Mazar-i-Sharif area. Shah Wali was one of eight sons from several mothers and had inherited the endless complications of large

Afghan families. He was currently in the Army, serving the one year required of university graduates.

Juris Zagarins (age 30), a Latvian American who, with his family, emigrated to the US from Latvia via Germany at the end of the Second World War. He studied engineering at Tufts and MIT and had extensively hiked the New England mountains and the shores of Massachusetts and Maine. He was a veteran climber of Mount Washington and a frequent visitor to Monhegan Island. He had an endless curiosity and always took long walks early in the morning whenever he travelled to a new city or country.

Toby Marion (age 24). My hiking experience was from family vacations and the Boy Scouts, first in southern California in the San Bernardino Mountains and High Sierras and later in West Mountain, New York. I had grown up with regular family camping trips in the Sierras, Mexico, Indian Country, and the famous National Parks that we are so lucky to enjoy in America.

Our plan was to meet with relatives and friends from Mazar-i-Sharif and Tashkurgan in the north in Aybak (modern day Samangan) by August 2 on the full moon. At least a week was to be spent in the Khurram valley hunting, fishing, and eating the delicious honeydew melons of the northern plain that were in season. Then we would continue along the Silk Route to Kahmard, Ajar and eventually Bandi Amir with the hopes of reaching Yakawlang and the Koh-i-Baba Mountains.

- August 1, Thursday, Kabul

We gathered our equipment—packs, sleeping bags, ground cloths, pots and pans, kerosene stove, rope, and medical supplies. Provisions included a pound of Indian tea, a kilo of sugar, three pounds of hard candy, four pounds of dried mulberries. That evening we bought our bus tickets, and I made a final distillation of three imperial quarts of white lightning, along with one purchased bottle of Stolichnaya vodka.

- August 2, Friday, Samangan (Aybak)

We rendezvoused at Abdullah's house and taxied to catch the 7 a.m. bus for Mazar. Abdullah had to stay behind to collect his boots that were still with the shoemaker being repaired. We were 15 minutes late and just barely caught the bus. It was filled to the brim and

194

included irate people who felt we should not have been allowed the extra grace, which was our deliverance as we had bought our tickets in advance. We lost 100 Afs on the deal, because the driver would not permit us to resell Abdullah's seat, even though he then did just that. In response, we squeezed together and left the seat between us unoccupied.

The familiar trip was beautiful: north through the fertile Kohi Daman (skirt of the mountain), the inspiring rise into the Salang Pass, the cold bite of the shadows at 12,000 feet on the north slopes of the Salang, and the descent into the North Country. It became hot and humid with rolling hills and flat expanse extending all the way to the Oxus River and beyond to the heartland of Central Asia. We lunched at Doshi eating *pilau*, yogurt, bread, and black tea. At 3 p.m. we arrived in Samangan, (today once again called by the ancient name Aybak) piled our bundles and packs onto a *gawdi* and headed into town. We stopped short of the main *chowk* to settle down at the Aybak Hotel. A shower and a drink helped to diminish the effect of the 95° F temperature. At 5 p.m. Abdullah walked in having retrieved his boot and caught several vehicles to get to the north.

The four hikers, from left: Abdullah Kakar, Toby Marion, Juris Zagarins, Shah Wali

195

Phone calls to Mazar and Tashkurgan failed to reach our other friends, and we then ate some delicious mutton and bread brought by Abdullah. Aybak is the capital of the Samangan province and had been a stopping place along the road to Kabul for thousands of years. The bazaar was bustling and famous for kebab and pilau, but since the new paved ring road was built about a mile outside of town, the traffic and prosperity on the main drag had decreased considerably. The town itself is laid out on orderly blocks with a central park at midtown, surrounded by the governor's office and government buildings, the large Friday Mosque and the boys' lycée a block west.

The main drag runs north and south, the connecting road from the Kabul to Mazar highway joining it at its southern end. At this intersection are restaurants which serve rice dishes, kebab, soups, bread, tea, yogurt, greens, sweets, and just about anything from the bazaar. The restaurants have some tables and chairs, both indoors and out, and knee-high carpeted platforms to sit on cross-legged. The Main Street is lined with shops made of cement (indicating a wealthy town), evergreen trees and open *jueys*. The shops number in the hundreds, where you can buy anything from Chinese scissors, Soviet vegetable oil, locally made rope to German pens, English razor blades, or American nylon twine. The town is situated in hills rising to the west, while the Tashkurgan river flows north through the outskirts on its journey to the Oxus.

We headed into town and for dinner ate soup and *naan* in the main samovar (restaurant or teahouse,) with a side dish of onions and tomatoes. After tea we bought and ate a melon and then, greeting a rising full moon, we followed the road up to Takhti Rustam, an archaeological site of an ancient Buddhist stupa. We lost our way and eventually cut across the plots of farms, through fallen walls, following along *jueys*, aiming for lights and tree clusters, and eventually finding the road near a cluster of *asias*—the flour mills described earlier. These *asias* are an Asian invention, with no connection to the English word Asia.

Upon rediscovering the road, we met a group of millers and they, after some difficulty, directed us to Takhti Rustam (throne, literally plank or platform of Rustam). They said these ancient ruins were the abode of evil spirits where you shouldn't go at night. They were from an ancient Buddhist monastery and stupa, part of a thriving community of the fourth and fifth centuries CE. Local custom has the impressive 80-foot diameter stone stupa raised upon a 30-foot-high stone dome and surrounded by a circumambulatory, as the seat of Rustam, the hero of the famous Shahnameh (the Persian Book of the Kings). The site is atop the first of the high foothills to the west of Aybak. We enjoyed the magnificent view that the ruins command of Aybak and the Samangan River Valley, the full moon flooding the plains and distant spurs of the Hindu Kush foothills to the east. We joked and thought of the morrow, our one-day delay now forgotten.

• August 3, Saturday, on Road to Sar Bagh

More phone calls to Tashkurgan in search of our friends were unanswered, so we trusted to the Afghan way and forgot clocks and telephones and headed for the bazaar. In our last time in a well-stocked market, we bought cloth, plastic bags, a watermelon, a large needle, four pounds of almonds, a large can of Russian vegetable oil, and Chinese toothpaste. We had boots repaired (five cents for reinforcement and re-sticking of a heel, and new toe patches) and reserved spots on a waz. A waz (means open) is a Russian flatbed truck the size of a Ford Econo-van and is open-topped with a removable tarpaulin for the roof.

In the early afternoon our friends arrived and included Ashraf (Shah Wali's half-brother) and his son Ashraf junior, his friend Sheraf, an eighth-grade relative named Nakhji and a family retainer. We collected our gear from the hotel and assembled near the road, awaiting departure, and struck up conversations with old timers who told us of fertile hunting grounds in the distant and barren mountains. Abdullah was collecting information to guide us along the Silk Route for two weeks and later for 10 days into the hinterlands of nomads and itinerant shepherds.

The moment for departure finally arrived, and the modest waz was loaded with about 30 people with bundles and packages of all sorts. We drove through town along wide streets lined with tall poplars and plane trees and headed south on the Khurram Valley road along the valley floor and up into the mountains. The Samangan River had eaten into the mountains forming precipitous cliffs of earth and rock in reds, browns, and yellows. The valley floor was studded with pockets of green cultivated land, poplar forests, clusters of houses and mills, and mosques. The road was frequently twisted and broken with deep gashes, forcing all of us to disembark and walk up steep inclines allowing the Russian workhorse truck to slowly climb in first gear.

Afghan drivers and their seconds (dirivar and *kilinar*, "cleaner", from English, who first introduced motor vehicles to India and the region during the Raj) keep these durable trucks on the roads for decades, for their value depreciates but little in a market where machinery value is paramount. Drivers earn their position beginning as early as age 12 in a 10-year apprenticeship, during which time they become skilled mechanics. They are well-paid and respected. Drivers can repair anything but a cracked engine block with their ancient toolkits and ingenuity. A famous minister's son once called himself a driver in his father's presence. This elicited a patient chuckle and a comment like, "My boy surrounds the steering wheel (eshteríng) and aims the vehicle and presumes to name himself amongst the maestros who are drivers," much to the embarrassment of the 20-year-old.

After a few hours of bumpy riding, the valley broadened and the mountains became more rolling, leading to remote peaks, with larger areas of cultivation on the sides of the river. We stopped at the farm of the Qaria Dar (qaria is village, and dar is a large house, meaning the regional leader who occupies the largest house and seat of authority) of the lower Sar Bagh area, where one of our party had arranged for us to be guests. After unloading all our paraphernalia onto the dusty road beside the low mud walls lining the road, we awaited the arrival of a greeting party. The valley was perhaps one-half mile wide here, cultivated in orderly plots of clover, alfalfa, wheat, and vegetables, with plots delineated by *jueys* and rows of tall poplars, *chinars*, and fruit (mulberry, pear, apple) and nut (walnut, pistachio, almond) trees.

It was a lush and orderly vista with an imposing backdrop of brown dusty mountains. A crude telephone wire strung on bent poplar poles along the road was the only sign of modernity. The *asias*, wells and *arads* (water wheels) were all ancient. An *arad* sits on top of a water well and is a large horizontal wheel from the center of which is a vertically suspended continuous chain of fixed buckets that drop down into the well, fill with water and at the top turn upside down, dumping the water into a *juey* which flows to the surrounding farmland. Asses or cows provide the power by walking in a circle, harnessed to the rotating wheel.

Soon half a dozen men emerged from the plots, and included Jamil Khan, the son of the Qaria Dar, who was away at the time. We were heartily welcomed and led by the group to a large square adobe platform bordered by a rounded curb, with a flowing *juey* on one side and catty-corner to another raised plot sleeping area. A very large *chinar* tree stood between the two plots, and rows of poplars led off into the adjacent cultivation.

By now the sun was setting, and the air was fresh and somewhat sharp, the dankness and heat of the Aybak plains now several thousand feet below us to the northeast. Large *kilims* (woven floor coverings) and pillows were brought to cover the seating platform and to back up against the curbing, and large brass trays of black and green tea, hard candies, and sugar-coated almonds followed to refresh us from our journey. A Japanese shortwave radio supplied music from Radio Kabul, and traditional exchanges of courtesy and respect led to talk of histories and hopes and ideas.

Jamil had finished high school in Kabul and completed his military service before taking a job with the USIS in Kabul, eventually returning to Sar Bagh to tend to his lands and raise a family. His deft compliments to the American people were welcoming while showing his preference for country life. Abdullah talked of our work at the university and of travels to America and the future of Afghanistan. An eternal positivist, Abdullah talked about how the good qualities of the Afghan peoples could be utilized in a non-aligned developmental struggle while not outstripping traditional values.

The absence of the Qaria Dar meant a more relaxed hospitality, and we were shortly joined by Jamil's maternal uncle (generally a friend and confidant to a young man, unlike the sterner paternal uncle) and several of his friends. Some Afghan tobacco and hashish was brought, and soon we were 15 men passing around loaded cigarettes and reveling in the beauty of the valley and the magnificence of the full moon, now arisen behind the mountains. The shadows thrown by the trees, and the forest and patterns all around us in the day-like-night of the full moon were breathtaking and inspiring.

We were all now thoroughly relaxed, and for Juris and me this was a novel experience—the Afghan equivalent of the American country tavern, beyond the vagaries of artificial conventions. Conversations broke into clusters, jokes and tales were told, cigarettes and *neswar* (a dizzying snuff taken under the tongue like chewing tobacco) freely shared, with tea the social lubricant. Jamil and Abdullah extolled the virtues of free, natural life far from cities with its electricity and machines controlling daily life.

After some time, heaping platters of delicious well-oiled rice were brought, and after ritual hand washing and breaking of bread, we ate the pilau with our hands. Nuggets of tender mutton were served by attentive hosts, and our side dishes of yogurt, cauliflower, tomato, and onion were kept full. We ate heartily, knowing that this feast was to be one of few in our trek across the mountains. After another washing, we held our open palms to the sky and said a blessing, then touched our faces in thanks and settled back to rest and await melons and grapes for digestion and to sweeten our palates.

Abdullah told of our plan to follow the Silk Route to Kahmard, with side excursions for hunting, and then head west to the central Hazarajat region and eventually south to the Bandi Amir. We would hunt for deer and quail in the days ahead and got advice on the trails and wild preserves to the west.

Eventually we again had tea, the fruit having settled and our stomachs ready for hot liquid. Fruit and tea are never taken at the same time, one hot and the other cold. Plans for the morrow were fishing, swimming, and building appetites for a fish fry at a neighbor's garden up the valley. We spread out our bed rolls and sleeping bags and slept beneath the brilliant moon.

• Sunday, August 4, Fishing, Sar Bagh

We arose early, relieved ourselves in the fields, and washed in the icy *jueys*. The day was sparkling and fresh, Kabul and the daily

200

exercises in thermodynamics and physics far from our minds. We drank hot, sweet milk, and then black tea and ate wheat bread with homemade butter and heavy cream, sugared and rich.

We fitted out for our fishing expedition with large nets of hand-woven rope and lead weights and packets of margi mahi (fish death), powdered lime and minerals that dazes fish. We trooped off to the river and found a deep bend where fish seek refuge in the banks and roots from overhanging trees. A party was dispatched upstream to powder the river, and within a half hour our first catches were thrown ashore by the waiting frogmen who deftly captured the sluggish, drugged whitefish floating down and burrowing themselves in the embankment. An hour's work proved very fruitful, and we headed upstream to a wide bend and sandbar. We stripped off our peran and tunban and waded into the cold water beneath the brilliant sun in our trunks, 10-cent purchases at the used clothes bazaar in Kabul.

We were exhilarated, and coaxed Jamil into joining us for a cocktail of moonshine and well water—the before-noon jolt of which added to our relaxation and enjoyment of the vertical, craggy cliffs so discordant with our verdant surroundings and the soaring, pure white clouds in the dazzling blue sky. Still fat from city life, we exercised on the sand and joked with our followers and onlookers— perhaps 20 all told. When the sun passed its zenith, we lolled for an hour, and then dressed and headed off to lunch.

A crackling fire now filled a stone-lined firepit on top of which was a large open cauldron loaded with vegetable and mutton oils. Two of our hosts had expertly decapitated and cleaned the morning's catch. The fish were coated with a batter of salt, spices and coarse flour and then fried, and we shortly fell to the delightful task of eating the sweet "milk fish" with bread and tea. There was plenty for all.

During the meal we received a neighbor and his obese baby boy, possibly the victim of a glandular disorder, whom we blessed but could not help. He told us news of the upcoming pistachio season, the appointment of a new governor of Samangan Province, the building of a new mosque, a recently returned *Haji* from Mecca, and new agricultural government programs for Sar Bagh proper.

After lunch we stopped a waz, telling the driver we needed to continue south to Sar Bagh in mid-afternoon. We collected our gear from Jamil's and thanked him for his hospitality and the great time we had with him and his friends. We were summoned by the waz and headed off. The road was smoother now, and in late afternoon we reached the larger town of Sar Bagh, with a bazaar of a few shops and a flood control area just before the town.

Spring flash floods are the rule in the Afghan terrain; the only defense is to build sturdy rock walls along the gullies running perpendicular to the roads. The walls funnel the floods to a flat spot in the road, which is well cared for, allowing the boulders and debris to flow over and past, leaving the road unscathed. Unfortunately, these last only a few years and require perpetual maintenance. Afghanistan is a hydrologist's haven for study of water and its distribution, circulation, and control and a nightmare as the eternal tale of drought and deluge wreak havoc.

After discussion with villagers, we were led to the nearby home of the local Director of Agriculture, who had just received a jeep load of Samangan Government Agricultural Inspectors and Officials, their drivers, and soldiers. The Director was a serious, middle-aged man of polite, but not imposing manner, who received us cordially, though we could easily guess that "the more the merrier" was not on the tip of his tongue. The government officials were young college graduates from Kabul, now stationed in Aybak, who eyed us both warily and with interest, for we represented several possibilities to them. We could be spies, or callous tourists, erosions to their expected pleasures of hospitality, or comrades in arms should we mix well socially. Fortunately, the latter prevailed, Abdullah ever the diplomat, and Juris and I the rare foreigners who knew the score and enjoyed Afghan company. Shah Wali was reserved, and his urbane and cordial manner instilled confidence and laid the groundwork for an evening's enjoyment.

In Afghanistan, social events are for men only and are refined affairs of conversation and repast, with music and storytelling in later evening hours. There are no movies, theaters, drinking or other diversions and a five-hour evening is most enjoyable when there are no debates or strong egos interfering with the egalitarian character of the gathering.

Because Afghans grow up in a traditional society with a lot of social interaction, they are good politicians, able to suppress feelings and prejudices to the good of the group. They see excessive book-reading or individuality as anti-social. Public discussion rarely pits two individuals head on, but rather provides a forum in which to agree as well as display discordant opinions, with consensus and cordiality as the goal. Two parties with different points of view direct their comments to listeners and not each other. It is rare for debates to turn to rudeness or loss of humor.

Westerners sometimes see this well-developed social sense as devious oriental character, when in fact our modern knowledge is sometimes acquired at the expense of the development of diplomatic or social skill. That's true especially for engineers like me! We learn these social skills at an older age, adapting to the real world. Our grandparents underwent this at 16, our parents at 20, and we are even later. In any case the process is simply learning to judge and deal with people with a minimum of friction.

Director of Agriculture's house construction in Sar Bagh

As I think about this in 2023, I recall that Juris introduced me to Marshall McLuhan, the Canadian philosopher who created the concept of "the medium is the message." He predicted that a result of the advent of television would be a global village, with more expression, less formality and the breaking down of barriers. This has proven to be true. For us, the way children are raised and how they speak to elders has changed dramatically from 1930 to 1960 to 1990 and onward. In some ways, we experienced an Afghan culture that was more like that of our parents in the 1920s.

We had a delicious *pilau* and soup dinner and learned about the agricultural plans for extension of the Sar Bagh Springs canals to bring more land under cultivation, the gradual introduction of steady supplies of fertilizer and agricultural agents for instruction in its proper use, and flood control to reduce the ravages on the local farms. The Afghan Fertilizer Company is a cooperative, a private enterprise venture aided by USAID, whose insistence upon its non-socialization is viewed by many locals as irrelevant and counterproductive.

The discussion was informative and lively and was followed by music from tabla (drums), a rabob (a traditional instrument somewhere between a guitar and a sitar) and a harmonium (an upright hand pumped accordion). Singing popular poems and dancing (men standing, moving to the beat of the music and clapping hands, singing) lasted late into the night. Before bed a local lad took us up onto a hill where his father was building a new home. We climbed to the flat roof and viewed another magnificent valley scene beneath the still full moon, the jagged rocky peaks melded with pocketed villages in the shadowy light. In the lunar calendar, a full moon is on the fourteenth night, and three days later the seventeenth night, it is still very bright.

• Monday, August 5, to Khurram springs and under *chinar* tree

We awoke early on Monday morning, 10 people sleeping on the floor of the newly built guest room of the Director of Agriculture. The room had adobe walls two-and-a-half feet thick, with one large multi-paned window.

The government agents were pleased to invite us to go with them to see the famed springs on the Khurram road, toward our destination. The agents were from Kohi Daman and were pleased that I knew and had worked in and liked the area—true to the local proverb "every man's homeland is Kashmir." The mountains of Kashmir which are today unstably shared by Pakistan and India are known as paradise, famed for their beauty, fertile earth, endless water supplies, and lush vegetation. Another related Dari saying is about the mother crow, who, when asked to choose the most beautiful baby animal, flies around the world seeing every animal, and ends up choosing the baby crow, a notoriously scrawny and ugly baby.

After breakfast, we went to the springs, the agents and Director of Agriculture discussing the irrigation schemes, sources of controversy amongst the locals, and need for improvements. The springs bubbled up inside small caves in the granite face of the mountains into a 40-yard-long dam of rock and cement, feeding three canals to the valley. This source was solidly built but downstream the canals could be damaged by spring floods. There were also questions about the fairness of the water rights system. We enjoyed the cold sparkling water and were told of the infinite depths of the springs. The locals at the springs were unsure as to whether Juris and I represented foreign capital or were just along for the ride.

We decided to go to Khurram while the officials continued their inspections, so we took photos, thanked the director and agents for their hospitality and offer of transportation, and bid adieu. They had been keen to have their pictures taken with us, as pictures are rare, and they hoped we might meet again. We arrived at Khurram before noon and thanked the driver and his soldier who dropped us and headed back down the valley.

The Khurram Valley is sandwiched between two massive spurs of the Hindu Kush running to the southwest and is cultivated along the Khurram River. Downstream it is over a mile wide rising to about one-half mile wide at its westernmost point. The road hugs the cliff of the mountains on the right (north) and passes through the bazaar of a handful of shops at the head of the valley. On the south side is a

20-foot drop-off to a mosque, a *chinar* tree 15 feet in diameter, and the yard and two-story house of a *Haji*, the main local landowner.

We unloaded our gear to the shade of the *chinar* tree next to a flowing stream from a spring in the mountains towering overhead. The entire area was about 40 yards square, with a three-foot retaining wall making a natural podium for this sanctuary.

We were a group of nine including two foreigners, quite a happening for the local villagers. Soon people were offering to sell us rice, meat, oil, vegetables, wheat, flour, eggs, milk, butter, and cheese, rent us horses or donkeys, and to serve as hunting guides. We carefully weighed the prices of goods and credibility of advice offered and were considering either traveling by vehicle southwest up the valley floor or hiking up even more steeply directly to the northwest. Passersby and the *Haji* advised us that hiking was best for hunting and further travel by vehicle unlikely once the pistachio harvest began.

A crucial factor was the imminent commencement of the pistachio harvest, to be declared by the Governor of Samangan. Most of the pistachio orchards are government owned, and orchard managers require migrant labor to pick the nuts. Laborers from poor localities in the mountains and rural areas begin to pour into Aybak from Puli Khumri and Tashkurgan. The population of Aybak swells by thousands each day, food and lodging becoming dear as local merchants become fat, until the Governor calls a stop to all traffic and orders the harvest to begin.

So, we bought a sack of vegetables and rice and got the name of a local *mirgun* (hunting guide) who would lead us to deer and quail. We hired two asses and a horse to carry our gear. We had a delicious lunch of fried scrambled eggs ranchero style with oil, onions, tomatoes, and peppers, cooked by Sheraf, who was already working on the evening's meal and demonstrating exceptional culinary skills. I was suffering from chills, so I napped, as did Shah Wali, while Juris took a walk and Abdullah dug deeper into the villagers. In late evening we feasted on pilau.,

• Tuesday, August 6, Khwaja Buzrak and Mulla Nazar

We arose to tea, and a late start at 9 a.m., our marching time for the remainder of the trip, never the early rise we talked about. The road dwindled to a path, and rose, fell, and twisted, never easy or flat, but also not plunging into gorges or surrounded by massive rock walls. We headed north and then west to a distant spring where shepherds brought herds of goats and sheep in their summer grazing in the high mountains. This spring was called Khoja Buzrak, where legend had it that the *Mulla Nazar* (priest with the gaze or eye, meaning bewitched or bad luck) was located. The surrounding peaks were wooded and reputed to have deer and wild animals. We washed and packed and girded our loins for travel after a short break for digestion.

Girding one's loins is the traditional phrase meaning readiness for travel with a sword, dagger or gun tucked in the belt for the open road. Traditional people will resist robbery before surrendering property and believe that thieves will attack only those they don't fear. Thus, a man travels armed and fearing none, trusting only to God. A related expression is "your strength in your loins," to indicate fearlessness and dissuade others from confrontation. Since time immemorial warriors have a well-padded waist secured by a broad *kamar band* (cummerbund, literally waist band, from Farsi) because if stabbed in the stomach, a slow and painful death will surely follow.

We headed further west toward distant peaks. Shortly after noon we entered a broad valley containing a stream, some cultivated land, and a temporary dwelling.

Our goal was in sight, so Abdullah and I pressed on and soon were close to the spring, the hub of three valleys fanning up from our 9,000feet to peaks of 14,000 feet elevation. As we neared the spring, we surprised a flock of a hundred quail. Realizing that Juris and Shah Wali were several hundred yards behind us with our shotgun, our dinners, breakfasts, and lunches flew away, and we cursed our lack of preparation.

After hiking most of the day, we had a simple dinner of bread and tea, and slept wearily.

- Wednesday, August 7, to Khurram (Kalowr va Dah Sil), Haji Abdul Razaq

We hiked from the Khoja Buzrak spring to Khurram covering difficult landscape and making but little progress for all the up and down and switchbacks. At the end of the day, we stayed in a garden in the home of the local dignitary *Haji* Abdul Razaq. Reports coming from Aybak told us that the pistachio time was in full swing and that there were no vehicles going our way. We had a chicken dinner, quite the treat, and spent the night.

• Thursday, August 8, Rui (Khalak)

We rented a horse to carry our loads and headed to the village of Rui. We learned of a battle over water with the upstream village of Mui, who were refusing to release water for them. The Rui women had to walk all day to the closest well, collect a goatskin sack of water and carry it on their backs all the way home. We came face-to-face with what drought means to a remote, preindustrial population. There is no plan B, no way to get water when the streams and *jueys* run dry. The people in this village were Hazara.

That afternoon an elder was brought to us with a wound in his forearm, a hole an inch-and-a-half in diameter, and a half-inch deep, exposing dry, red flesh. This wound had not healed in several months, and they asked if we had any medicine to heal him. We had neither the knowledge nor the medicine to help. However, Abdullah said some soothing words, and we offered a prayer for the man. This was another realization of what life can be like for injured people far from civilization with no medical help available. We spent the night in the house of a local *Haji*.

• Friday, August 9, Mui (Mohu)

We rented another horse driven by an old man and headed towards Du Ob via Mui. The hiking continued to be strenuous, and we were happy to have the horse carrying our packs. In Mui we slept in the local school, made of mud and with open windows.

The Tatar, or Turkomen, of Du Ob were the first minority ethnic population, other than Hazara, that we saw. Their heights and complexions varied, though they tended to be tall and rather light skinned with brown hair and blue, hazel and even light brown eyes. Their accents were clipped, with vowels like Tajiks, for example "i" for "u." They were hard mountain folk who expressed little use for cities or governments, unless they provide money (capital investment) for education and health services without meddling or cost to them. We heard stories of yesteryears, like the proud headmaster who defied a corrupt (bribe seeking) Kabul inspector in support of one of his students.

• Saturday, August 10 , above Du Ob Rui

We arrived in Du Ob along the river front and determined to spend this day resting. Juris and Abdullah were off to the market for supplies. When they returned, they brought news that they had heard that President Nixon had resigned. We shared a toast, and I also won a bet of a kebab dinner, though I don't recall from whom.

In the afternoon, the Commandant sahib (means sir) called on us, and we sensed his concern about our group including two foreigners hiking in the wilderness and unprotected. We were worried that our trip might be cut short. However, that evening Abdullah paid a call on the Commandant at his residence, spent several hours with him and gained his confidence, so he gave us permission to continue on our trip. I wondered if Abdullah had used the prominence of his father or mother to instill confidence in the Commandant that we were safe to continue our journey.

Trekking thru mountains with pack horses between Char Magz Sarai and Rui Sang

- Sunday, August 11, Char Maghz Sarai

In the morning, we had a delicious breakfast of eggs cooked in yellow oil, sweet milk, and *naan*. We spent the day hiking to Char Maghz Sarai (means walnut compound). Char maghz literally means four brains, the shapes that shelled walnuts have, two brains in each half. The day's hike was very long, at first fairly flat and then rising towards Kara Kotal (kotal means pass.) I had become somewhat lame as I wasn't able to break in the fine Abercrombie and Fitch hiking boots I brought from America and that were too small for me. I'd tried to replace them in the used bazaar before the trip without luck. I had blisters and strained feet and had to hike on the flattened heels with the laces loosened, like slippers. Shah Wali laughed about my feet in a supportive way and coaxed me into sharing the last of my hard candy, which I had carefully husbanded while he had greedily eaten his days earlier. He should have had an academy award for his performance about how I had no choice but to share, regardless of the past.

That evening we stayed in the yard of a man named Ghulam Mohamed and ate a light dinner of tea and bread.

- Monday, August 12, Rui Sang

In the morning, we hiked a short distance through the Kotal Pass just west of a 13,000-foot mountain and through a rocky canyon to the village of Rui Sang. Abdullah went into the village to make some telephone calls. When he returned, we made a hunting plan that was shelved, and we decided to rest there for the day.

We slept under a large *chinar* tree.

- Tuesday, August 13, Du Ru

We carried on hiking through striking gorges along the river, with soaring mountains to our right and rocky overhangs above our trail. On the way to Du Ru village, we went swimming in the Kahmard River, which meant soap and water, and was a beautiful way to get clean in the refreshing, cold water. We organized some villagers to fish for us in the river, and then we had a fish fry followed by melon eating. The melons were sweet and luscious. In the afternoon we rented donkeys and headed for Du Ru.

On the way some villagers were excited to show us a fawn in a pen with a flock of sheep. The mother doe had been killed by a hunter, and her tiny fawn was then put in a pen with the sheep. It became domesticated as a sheep, docile when grazing and behaving naturally like a sheep in the group. It was a fascinating sight. In the evening we met with Haji Shikari (means hunter), who was to be our *mirgun*, and made our hunting plan. We slept in the open air.

• Wednesday, August 14, Sorkh Shar

We hiked to the north into the high mountains to reach the best hunting grounds. We arrived in a region called Sorkh Shar (red city) because the cliff faces were colored red from the exposed oxidized iron ore. There was a small village there and we slept in the mosque. In places like this, mosques are just one-room buildings, with four walls and no domes or minarets, and few if any windows. They're like humble churches in remote areas at home, nothing fancy.

• Thursday, August 15, Sorkh Shar, hunting day

Eleven of us with the *mirgun* and his aide rose at 4 a.m. and headed west, to spend the day hunting. We followed the river to a spring filling a large trough for animals. Nearby was a cave under the overhang of a huge boulder. We made a camp in this oft-used spot to leave our packs while we headed further up the mountain to hunt.

Swimming and washing in the Khurram River near Du Ru, like paradise as we were tired, sore and dirty.

Our *mirgun* was tall and thin, with a gaunt expression and short white hair. He was a sparse conversationalist who led us along the steep and zig-zagging path through the boulders up the mountains. We could barely distinguish shadow from pitfall as we went. We hiked doggedly, though tiring quickly alongside our guide and pack animal attendants and reached the summit within two hours. To the west and north were mountains deceptively smooth and pleasant beneath the clear night sky in which a waning moon still robbed the stars of their brilliance.

We followed a well beaten path into *lalmy*, dry (not irrigated) cultivation of wheat, and to where shepherds and nomads passed. Vast tracts of land in central Afghanistan are dry cultivated and bear produce in years with wet weather. This cultivation is a gamble for the rich and a hope for the poor, and a constant factor in Afghanistan's agriculture. After five hours hiking, we arrived at the farmer's tent and bedded down, the worst of the march behind us. The air was clear, and the hard, clumped earth beneath us a welcome bed in our first trek into the wastelands.

Suspended trail close to cave where we camped near Sorkh Shar

We then followed the ridge which led into the high forest, a mountain sparsely dotted with short twisted Asian oak and evergreen trees. The rapidly rising ridge had many precipices and gullies, so we climbed with difficulty. The *mirgun* had headed west, and we thought that the probability of finding deer was slim. However, the *mirgun* and Ashraf did see six does and shot at them, never hitting any. Abdullah saw them also but would not shoot at a female deer.

We used the climb as training and pursued the ever-receding mountain. Juris hiked up to the east side and Shah Wali and I climbed to the south side of the mountain. By late afternoon the three-pronged valleys had become four ridges dwarfed by an opposing mountain range in the north with another looming mountain to the west. Our distant campsite where we'd left our packs was a dot, and we watched an eagle circling overhead. We felt alone on the earth, the desolateness and sound of the gentle wind with no forest sounds accentuated how small we felt. We sat for an hour in wonderment upon a great flat stone on the ridge, a temporary victory for hikers, flanked by oaks of eerie and convoluted shapes. We had an exceptional view. Further

On Sorkh Shar: Juris on left with Toby and Shah Wali from right, with hunter and aide, viewing the Kahmard River valley

213

south was Koh Fuladi (Steel Mountain), Ajar Valley, Kahmard and Paein Bagh villages.

In the late afternoon we hiked back down to our camp and at nighttime we had a dinner of quail with wheat and barley *naan*. It was a very basic meal of only protein and carbohydrates. We slept tucked into the rocks in the cave exhausted after a very long day.

• Friday, August 16, Paein Bagh, Kahmard

In the morning we hunted near the campsite for quail and managed to shoot two. We left at 11 a.m. and headed down the valley to the village of Paein Bagh and on to Kahmard, a larger village less than a mile further west. We again slept under a *chinar*.

In the village there was a local disturbance, a row over women. These can be very dangerous. We were aware that there are three subjects Afghans are taught never to discuss, the three "Zs": zar, zan and zamin, which mean gold, women, and land.

Our friends Ashraf and Sheraf had come along for the deer hunting. As that was now over, they and the rest of their group were to head back to Mazar-i-Sharif the next day. We bid them and the *mirgun* farewell and for the remainder of the trip we were a foursome: Abdullah, Shah Wali, Juris and me.

• Saturday, August 17, Ajar Lake and Marsh

We had a short hike of less than 10 miles along the marshy river in the direction of the Ajar Valley. There we met a foreigner named Tim McNeill, working in a "government-related activity." We set up camp under some trees on soft grass surrounded by wide, flat, wet, grassy marshlands. We enjoyed arak and water, and smoked, letting out some of the tension and tiredness from days of hiking in very difficult terrain. We slept deeply in what seemed like a fairytale environment after days of rocks, cliffs and steep mountains.

In the morning I awoke to discover that there were three or four large dead bullfrogs in my sleeping bag with me. They had discovered a warm cave-like place to crawl into overnight, and sometime in the night I had rolled over, killing them. It was a bit disgusting, the guts spilling out of several, and Shah Wali laughed hysterically. He mockingly joked that I had slept with *murdar*, which is dead or rotten meat that has not been slaughtered properly and is forbidden.

214

A bunch of local village children came to talk with us, small boys and girls. They were very excited to see *khorijis,* whom they had rarely seen. They were delighted to find that we spoke Farsi and played with us and asked us a lot of questions. They were rugged, ragged, brimming with energy and cute as hell. They ran around and laughed and squealed and cheered us up a lot.

In the afternoon we hiked further up the riverside to Ajar Park, where there was a government farm. We set up a comfortable campsite, collected wood, built cooking fires and made dinner with the *naan,* veggies and meat we had bought in Karmard.

• Sunday, August 18, Ajar Park

In the morning we met and talked with the German manager of the government farm. Germany provided aid and the management of the farm. We made plans to meet the next day with the Germans. We planned to spend three nights in Ajar Park, and we felt relaxed and able to gain strength and sleep soundly on comfortable land. That night we had a very late dinner.

Ajar Park: the lush and green marshes where we spent several days resting after many days of difficult hiking in the arid mountains

215

- Monday, August 19, Ajar Park

The next day we spent preparing for an evening cocktail party with the Germans. We gathered wood, prepared a spot for our party, and chose a good place for our camp for the next two nights.

- Tuesday, August 20, Ajar Park

We had decided to have a dinner together with the Germans, so after buying local provisions we spent this day cooking, eating, drinking, and basking. We had dinner with Heir Meier, the leader of the group.

We now were on the eve of the final leg of our journey. Bandi Amir as the crow flies was maybe 35 miles to the south. However, with mountains and valleys, the distance was easily double that. During the last week, we had traveled along the northern side of the east-west mountains that were the watershed separating rivers flowing to the north from the Hindu Kush, eventually to the Oxus River. After climbing over the mountains on the way to Bandi Amir, we would be in the watershed that flows south and then east, the Bamiyan, Ghorband and Kabul Rivers ultimately into the mighty Indus River between Peshawar and Rawalpindi in Pakistan. The land in this high region was very dry, with very sparse vegetation.

- Wednesday, August 21, Ob Nyack

In the morning we headed south out of the Ajar village and up the hills, where we had been told to go. The land was now rolling hills, flatter than before and as we reached the top, we met a man coming our way. Abdullah stopped him and talked with him for some minutes. He told us that the trail was regularly used by shepherds and *koochis*, and we had only to follow the mostly straight path—there were no turnoffs to be taken or missed. He said that if we walked all day, by evening we would come to a spring.

Up until this day we had been following rivers and creeks, climbing up and out of canyons and over mountains. Huge mountains had always loomed in the distance and to our sides, and we were never far from water. However, now it felt like we were literally on top of the world, at 11,000 or 12,000 feet elevation, and for the first time I felt fear. It was hot and there were no trees, the only vegetation being shrubs here and there amidst rocky and dusty soil as far as the eye could see. In the far distance in all directions loomed even larger mountains reaching to 14,000 to 16,000 feet elevation.

Water was our main concern. We each had a large canteen, but that was all. The sun was hot, the sky cloudless, and it was starkly obvious that we would need to find water by nightfall. This was our unspoken fear. Off we headed, walking all day, drinking sparingly, and enjoying sucking on the few pieces of hard candy that we had left. We munched on some *naan* for our midday meal. We probably covered around 15 miles.

Sure enough, as the light was beginning to wane, we heard what sounded like the faint distant sound of a waterfall. What music it was to us! Within a half hour the trail descended into a sharp valley, a gash in the mountains at the bottom of an escarpment. We walked down hundreds of feet to a sandy area and from the right came the roar of a spring from the vertical rock cliff on the north. We climbed up to a large pool, water gushing from a gash in the rock. It overflowed at one end and disappeared into the earth. We were silently overjoyed with relief, splashed our hot faces with the cold water, filled our canteens and tea kettles and went back down to the sandy canyon floor. To the south the canyon extended for hundreds of yards between soaring cliffs straight up on either side.

We made a camp and collected shrubs and bits of wood. It's amazing how, in the middle of nowhere with seemingly no vegetation, there are shrubs and plants all around, and it's easy to collect large amounts of firewood. Obviously, shepherds and nomads came through here regularly, as there was dung about from sheep and cows. We built a healthy fire, boiled water, made tea, and ate a dinner of *naan* and dried meat followed by tea and bits of rock candy. We drank some arak and smoked and then went to bed in our sleeping bags. Overhead between the cliff walls was a narrow strip of sky, brilliantly lit by stars.

We awoke well rested and enjoyed tea and bread again. By now we all had lost quite a bit of weight, having large meals only from time to time, mostly eating what we could buy and carry.

• Thursday, August 22, Puddinatu

We broke camp and headed for the village of Puddinatu, about

15 miles further south. Not just its name was exotic, the place was, too. It was a small Hazara village stuck on top of the world, with mud houses half underground and clustered like a tiny city. People came out to meet us and were very friendly. Somewhat starved, we happily bought from them 34 eggs, a large brick of just churned butter and many barley (naani jow) breads. At this elevation, wheat will not ripen, so the people grow and eat the hardier barley. The villagers cooked the largest omelet that we had ever seen using butter in a three-foot diameter frying pan like a flat wok. The four of us devoured it with the bread and tea with great relish.

We talked with the villagers, one of whom told us of serving in the army and seeing Kabul and other parts of the nation. A few proudly showed us their watches and short-wave radios. We spent the night in the local mosque, again simply four mud walls, with woven *kilims* covering the floor.

• Friday, August 23, Siah Khawall

In the morning we rented a donkey to carry our loads—the only one they could provide was heavily pregnant. The donkey driver who owned her said it would be no problem, she was a good worker. I was not convinced of this but there was nothing to be said. Sure enough, within an hour, the driver told us that she was not doing well and would not be able to make it. So, he turned back, and we shouldered our packs feeling not at all good about it as the day's hike ahead again was long and we were all weary. We headed through the mountains slowly sloping downwards through switchbacks and ravines.

By the end of the day, we reached an area that was open and grassy, cold and marshy, but glorious. We made our camp and gathered up a big pile of dried cowpat (dung). These readily burned, and soon we had hot tea to drink and bread for dinner with some jerky, dried meat locally called londi, that we'd bought in Puddinatu.

• Saturday, August 24, Khak Dow

In the morning we had eggs also from Puddinatu, bread and tea for breakfast. Nearby a *koochi* caravan of about a hundred camels was arriving and setting up camp. After some time, several of the men came over to talk with us. We learned that they were eight large families. They invited us to join them for dinner that evening, but we

Puddinatu Village: Shah Wali, Abdullah and Toby with welcoming people who made us a terrific breakfast with 34 eggs. Note the dried cowpat fuel stacked on the roof.

declined expressing our thanks for their generosity, telling them that we had a schedule to meet and needed to carry on to Bandi Amir. I wonder what that dinner might have been like—the only time I was ever invited by *koochis*, whom I also had never met or spent time with.

Our hike this day was close to twenty miles, and we came to a Hazara village called Khak Dow. The houses were made of tiny rooms built into the earth—similar to Puddinatu—with almost no windows to be seen. Here too there was only barley bread available. The villagers told us that the mal (wealth or property) that they tended belonged mostly to Pashtuns, and sometimes Tajiks or Tatars. They were referring to the sheep, donkeys and cows they cared for, earning a benefit like share cropping.

In the morning we watched barley bread being made and baked, and butter churned. The bread dough was formed into flat pointed shapes and then slapped onto the upper walls in the tandoor to bake. The butter was churned by a woman pressing and rolling a sealed goatskin filled with milk and cream for hours.

• Sunday, August 25, Bandi Amir

Our last day of hiking was less than 10 miles, mostly gently sloping downwards with switchbacks. We were approaching suburbia! When we joined the straight and flat road heading south, we met other travelers talking of trade, business, and hunting. Cars, trucks and buses began passing us occasionally in both directions.

Soon the brilliant blue lakes of Bandi Amir at 9,500 feet elevation came into view, a stunning and welcome sight after so many days in the high mountains surrounded by rock, cliffs, dust, and earth. The lakes were formed by naturally deposited carbonates that built up and grew high walls over centuries. They are fed by rivers flowing from the north and west and are one of Afghanistan's most famous tourist attractions for their natural beauty. We shared a drink on the lake and then went to the town for cheap meals and a cold night spent in a local boarding house.

• Monday, August 26, return to Kabul

In the morning, we opted for a fast jeep ride, then a waz for the

West of Puddinatu: Abdullah and Shah Wali with the pregnant donkey, showing the feeling of being on top of the world in dry terrain heading towards Bandi Amir in the final days of the trip.

Shepherd in the high Hazarajat tending *mal*, the livestock of wealthy farmers.

40 miles to Bamiyan, and then a taxi to Kabul. The trip through the mountains traveling east from Bamiyan was spectacular, passing through tight passes and soaring mountains, following the Bamiyan and Ghorband Rivers. Reaching the Kohistan plain, we turned south and soon were back in Kabul.

When we got home, we went our own ways, with plans to meet again soon, after developing our films and getting our feet back on the ground. My weight was down to about 150 pounds, what I was when graduating from high school, and I was quite thin.

For months afterward when Juris and I would be at a party, we would discover the other sitting quietly in a corner with a large plate of food, slowly and meticulously chewing and savoring every bite of fine Afghan fare: lamb, rice, chicken, *naan*, vegetables, yogurt, fruit. I recall such nights specifically at Heidar's home with many friends, local and foreign. Being on a forced diet for most of 26 days had left a lasting psychological impression and gave me a tiny glimpse of what famine might be like.

We learned a lot about Afghanistan during this hike. We saw the network of government services including agricultural extension agents, government farms and the provincial ownership and regulation of water distribution, fertilizer and the pistachio industry. The provinces had governors and commandants responsible for public safety, with a limited number of telephones at key locations. We met people even in the most remote locations that had served in the military and seen the nation far and wide. We recognized that we were lucky to be in a country that was peaceful and respected authority, previously the monarchy and now the Republic. Unfortunately, we could not know that the coup d'etat of the previous year had set in motion changes driven by idealogues, revolutionaries and the USSR that would lead to national disaster.

The last day of our hike with Abdullah in front of the famous Bandi Amir, lakes of the king

42. Keeping the Fast, Ramadan, 1974

The first day of the holy month of Ramadan fell on the day before the start of the new university term. Lethargy began setting in, along with closed or sleepy bazaars. I decided to keep the fast to experience how it would affect me and my ability to work. During Ramadan the work schedule was shortened, leaving afternoons free for relaxing at home, sitting under trees, on rooftops and in parks.

Fasting by the religious includes much prayer and time spent with family, mullahs and neighbors. Islam requires Muslims to pray five times a day, though in practice this is rare. But during Ramadan, many do pray more often. My fasting was not the proper custom, being simply not eating or drinking from daylight to sunset. At night I would party and drink as normal and spent most of the month hanging out with Heidar and other friends. I didn't mean to be sacrilegious or insulting to Muslims, I simply carried on with how I lived, while experiencing the effects of the fast.

The experience was illuminating. At first it was difficult. Iftar, literally breakfast, is at sundown. In the first few days I was anxious as the time approached and then ate too much too quickly. As the days pass, you discover that it feels much better to eat and drink less and less. Saar is the last meal before sunrise, taken in the dark and quiet hours of the morning and which gets you ready for the day ahead. Again, it felt best to take but a little food and drink at that time. Although I'd planned to fast only for a few days, after the first week I decided that to really experience Ramadan, it would be better to continue for the full month. It was restful and I spent more time thinking, and contemplating and sleeping while working less, and with less worry about "taking care of business."

When the month ends, there are big celebrations and the return to normal routines. I found that I felt healthier and more relaxed, ready to get back to work and the rat race for another year. The experience made a strong case in my mind for a sustained annual timeout for renewal and spirituality and helped me to understand why many religions have fasting and meditation as core elements. It also made sense of the French custom of August being a month of holiday. My stomach also had slimmed down a little.

Jewish Yom Kippur and Christian Lent have fasting as religious duty. But the modern world has left many of these customs behind. I never grew up with fasting but see it now as another tool for renewal and self-reflection. Unfortunately, I doubt it will come back as a regular custom in our ever-busier culture.

As a good Muslim, Assif always kept the fast. Just before Ramadan began, he had an infected tooth which was extracted by a local dentist, which must have been very difficult. Pain killers were not used, the tooth was simply yanked out. That evening he was in great pain and asked me if he could have some *dawa*, medicine. I didn't get what he meant, so he asked if he could have some of my arak, explaining that Muslims are allowed to take medicine for pain, and that this is not the same as drinking *sharab* or alcohol, forbidden by Islam. So, I made him two strong Cuba libres, which knocked him out and he slept it off. He was much better in the morning.

I found myself getting close to the end of my time in Afghanistan and making observations about history. From my diary:

> Oct 25. Have been reading a lot of Persian lately—now is a time when reading and conversation are constructive—I would enjoy staying here longer. Hope the US can be instrumental in achieving a permanent peace settlement in the Mideast. I wager that if the US fails in the peace efforts, history will see a decline of American influence or the prelude to another major war.

43. Final Term at the Faculty

For my last term, I taught manufacturing process topics and Chemistry II lectures, laboratory, and recitations. The chemistry load came about suddenly because the two colleagues who taught chemistry left unexpectedly for further study in the US and Beirut. I was given Chem II lecture to be joined with an older full professor as a lab instructor. Unfortunately, this professor was absent for four-and-a-half of the first seven weeks, so I was saddled with three hours of lecture, eight hours of recitation, and 12 hours of laboratory plus supervision, grading, and all that teaching entails. It was tough, but the lab technician was very helpful, which lightened the load.

For Manufacturing Processes, I prepared notes and process flow diagrams for plastics and polymer manufacturing, cellulose acetate, rubbers, glass and nylon manufacturing, natural gas processing, petroleum refining and more. These were compiled from my chemical engineering texts that my parents had brought to me. This work was neither original nor difficult, but I had fun trying to make the topics as understandable as possible, particularly in an economy where, but for some natural gas production in the far north, none of this industry yet existed. I also realized that my own experience in these industries was limited to less than one year in three temporary jobs at Cyanamid, Texaco and Union Carbide, so the work was useful to me too.

Midway through the term, the Ministry of Mines asked if the Faculty of Engineering could analyze coal samples from the north. The dean pointed out that apparatus for this was available and asked if I could do this, then assigned it to me. Our lab technician also helped. The procedure calls for the use of an autoclave (an oven), to heat a known weight of the coal sample at a high temperature for a fixed period of time. The carbon in the sample is oxidized (burned off), exiting as vapors, and the weight of what remains is then measured. From this the carbon content percentage and calorific value of the coal can be calculated. The sample we measured was high value, 85 or 90% anthracite, or coal with relatively pure carbon that burns well at high temperature with little smoke. We then wrote up the report and sent the results to the ministry.

A few weeks later, I received a call from a senior ministry person who asked what we had done and what the results meant. We spent about a half hour on the phone, and I explained the steps in the analysis, the calculations and what it meant, and he asked many questions. At the end he asked me my name and I told him. He said, "No, what is your name?" I told him again. He repeated saying something like, "No, what is your name?" I explained that I was an American Peace Corps Volunteer and had been in Afghanistan for three years. He hadn't realized that I was not an Afghan and could not believe it at first. I was, of course, happy and considered this my final Farsi exam. At my exit from Peace Corps a few months later the tester from Princeton Testing Service rated me as 4+ out of 5, which is native speaker. I quietly filed that away, wishing I could have done the test over the phone.

One day, at the time we did the coal analysis, I was sitting in the back of the faculty library located next to the lab. I was behind the stacks working at a desk. I heard the door open and the lab tech and one of the janitors entered carrying on a conversation. They were talking politics. The tech said how good it was that there had been a coup d'etat in Afghanistan and that the country was now closer to the USSR. They said that America had lost the Vietnam War, was in turmoil with drug and discipline problems and declining as a power, and the Soviets had strong discipline, were rising internationally and would be the leading power in the future. The tech asserted that this was great, and in future the Muslims would be able to drive Israel out of Palestine and restore Muslim order in the Middle East. About this time, I packed up my books and walked out of the stacks and past them to the door of the library. He looked up very surprised to see me and his face showed that he knew I had heard all that was said.

It was one of the few times that I was to hear unvarnished opinions from locals. It also made me realize even more strongly how important it was to secure a lasting and just peace for the Israelis and Palestinians.

44. Visit of Secretary of State Henry Kissinger, November 1, 1974

On November 1, US Secretary of State Henry Kissinger visited Kabul to meet with the Ministry of Foreign Affairs and President Daoud. I don't know whose idea it was to invite Peace Corps Volunteers to meet with him but give credit both to Secretary Kissinger and US Ambassador Eliot for this thoughtful invitation to meet him on the front steps of the Embassy in the open air. This was in an era when there were few security issues for such a meeting.

The backdrop was that most of us PCVs were distrustful of Kissinger because he was a supporter of the Vietnam War and had been negotiating to end the war for years without success. Nixon had recently resigned, and Kissinger was then serving President Ford. We asked questions about the Vietnam War, and he made comments regarding the administration's peace efforts and the "Vietnamization" of the war effort, as American fighting troops had been largely withdrawn at that time. I felt that his comments were knowledgeable and specific, but also diplomatic, meaning that he didn't tell us anything that we couldn't read in the newspapers. I was also overawed to an extent by his commanding presence and appreciated that we had been given this opportunity.

Somewhat naïvely, we volunteers also believed we really understood Afghanistan, and that those in their suits working for organizations like the CIA stuck out like sore thumbs and were of dubious value, lacking local knowledge. We caricatured them as "spies in trench coats."

Kissinger was visiting Afghanistan as the first senior American Government official following the Afghan Coup d'etat in July 1973, 16 months prior. His meeting was important for the two countries to communicate directly and understand each other's positions during the ongoing Cold War. The minutes of the meeting of Kissinger, Ambassador Eliot and staff with Mohammed Naim, Foreign Policy Adviser to President Daoud, Waheed Abdullah, Deputy Minister of Foreign Affairs and Samad Ghaus, Director General of the Department of Political Affairs, MFA are available in State Department records online. ("Memorandum of Conversation...")

Quoted below are excerpts from that meeting:

> **Naim:** ... The first item is relations between Afghanistan and the United States ... Because of the politics prevailing in the region, sometimes a misunderstanding might have occurred in our relations, but it is always our wish to remove the misunderstandings and have really close and friendly relations with you ... we always have been of the opinion that the presence of the United States was needed.
>
> ... I wish now to inform the Secretary of Afghanistan of foreign policy in the region.

... Our relations in the region, with our western neighbor Iran, are extremely close and cordial ...

... Another country of great importance in the region is India. We have very close relations, and the closeness of views leads us to think we can expand this closeness and bring friendship closer.

With our northern neighbor [USSR], which is at the same time a great power, we have a very close relationship, and over the years, we have built friendly relations ... they have assisted us on many projects in Afghanistan, and over the years they have learned and we have learned that our close cooperation does not mean any ideological interference in our country.

Our other neighbor is China. With China we can say our relations are correct ...

Now, with your permission, I'll say a few words about the darker side.

... We don't speak of the past but of the future. In the last months, Pakistan brought accusations to Afghanistan which are absolutely false. One of the first accusations is they claim we are working for the disintegration and breakup of Pakistan. We are categorically rejecting this claim. We in no way expect or foresee or wish the disintegration of Pakistan, and we cannot do anything in this regard.

... the pressure being brought there on Pushtunistan and Baluchistan cannot leave Afghanistan indifferent ... We should not forget these two regions were part and parcel of Afghanistan and were severed by colonialism from their motherland. ... we don't have any territorial claims on Pakistan and we don't want the disintegration of that country. If on one hand the Government of Pakistan accords rights according to the Constitution to these people and with the other hand takes them away, we can't be indifferent.

Secretary Kissinger was being very active in his peacekeeping role lately throughout the world, and also achieved successes. We hope his trip here will also be successful to help find an understanding between Afghanistan and Pakistan to find a solution to this problem.

Kissinger: No one ever asks me to deal with problems that are less than a thousand years old. [Laughter]…

I appreciate your presentation very much …

First of all, the United States's interest in Afghanistan is its independence and sovereignty. We have no interest in any dominant or exclusive or unique position … we consider it absolutely natural that you have good relations with your northern neighbor … we have good relations with your northern neighbor …

We also understand why you would want some American presence here, and we are willing to cooperate with this …

We know if Afghanistan is part of a nonaligned grouping … Afghanistan has not been particularly bothersome in this respect, and I say this to every nonaligned leader. So you can bear in mind that we don't welcome the nonaligned to vote against every American position. Although I say this isn't directed at Afghanistan …

Naim: … The aim of the present Afghanistan Government, and the wish, is to reestablish democracy in a way that is appropriate and suitable for the Afghani people … our friend Pakistan, which has established a so-called democratic constitution, saw fit to draw laws to curtail the right of the parties to function democratically … we are not satisfied with the existence and prolongation of the present set-up …

Kissinger: That is very interesting, and we'll be watching with great interest.

On your foreign policy points, I have already commented on your relations with your northern neighbor. And we think that is appropriate, and we have no concern. After all, you have some record in maintaining your independence. I don't think from my reading of Afghanistan's history that you've specialized in submission. And therefore we consider it a natural policy.

With respect to the People's Republic of China, as you know, we have good relations with both China and the Soviet Union ...

We welcome if you improve your relations with the People's Republic of China, but, again, it's your affair. They were very concerned when your Chief of State came into office, because they expressed this to us. They thought you would conduct an extension of Soviet policy ...

Incidentally, that is true of Iran too. The Shah was in Washington when, or shortly after, it happened. There were questions on his mind.

With India, we really have no comment.

Now with respect to Pakistan. I'm not absolutely clear what you want from Pakistan. I think a territorial change is impossible, at least without war ... if the United States can do something to be of some assistance, we'll be glad to consider it ...

Naim: The Pakistanis always accuse us of interfering in their internal affairs. But I can tell you here, we have never done it and have no intention to. But we have documents, proof, that twice they interfered in our internal affairs They are counterfeiting millions of Afghanis, our national currency, and distributing them here. This is immoral and inconsistent with international relations.

So I hope you will trust what we have said.

... If Pakistan succeeds in solving this problem and secures the rights of Pushtunistan and Baluchistan within a reasonable and satisfactory manner, there will be no problems, and we can foresee good relations between Pakistan and Afghanistan.

Kissinger: I agree, it is a very natural relationship. Could you give our Ambassador some suggestions about what you see as a normal relationship?

Eliot: some specific ideas, and with respect to which Baluchis and which Pushtuns.

Naim: Whatever the present Constitution of Pakistan says, which is not being implemented. It's a matter of its own constitution. If they did it, we would have no quarrel.

Ghaus: Just the other day, all the other political parties were outlawed.

Kissinger: I'm very sympathetic to that. It's probably our only solution in America, to outlaw the Democratic Party. If we can't do that, we can start with the press. [Laughter]

Naim: … They created the situation where they lost Bangladesh.

Kissinger: No question.

Naim: They're creating the same conditions now.

Kissinger: Really?

Abdullah: The key to solving the problem is not here but in Islamabad. The ball is theirs.

Kissinger: That's what they told me to tell you—that it is in Kabul [Laughter]

Naim: It should be something real, not fake.

Kissinger: We'll look into it.

Following this meeting, Secretary Kissinger requested a short tour of Kabul and then met with President Daoud. From the Secretary's telex dated on the same day to the President's Deputy Assistant for National Security Affairs (Scowcroft) (14. Telegram HAKTO 76..."), he states:

> This is a fascinating country and a stalwart people whose geographic location has made them probably the world's oldest and most successful practitioners of non-alignment. Afghan hospitality is also legendary and that was richly evident today in the warmth of their reception, including a command performance of Buzkashi, a tribal sport of incredibly rough but able horsemanship that itself suggests why these people have managed so well in maintaining their independence.

Kissinger also says that President Daoud is sensitive that the US might see him as a Russian stooge and Kissinger made it clear that we attached high importance to Afghan independence. President Daoud also wants a continued American presence. Kissinger goes on to say:

> … we supported Pakistan's integrity and strongly hoped a process could be found to resolve this peacefully. I said that if at any time we could be helpful in achieving this we would consider that and see what we could do.
>
> I intend to raise this problem with the Shah when I see him tonight, since he has recently attempted a mediatory role. He has good relations with both Daoud and Bhutto and seems to me a logical candidate to be involved to ensure that this issue is kept manageable until time and history resolve some of the emotions. The fundamental problem is that the Afghans, despite their insistence

that they respect Pakistan's territorial integrity, never accepted as legally or ethnically valid the boundary imposed during the British period and incorporating minority ethnic groups that they believe should be part of Afghanistan, or at least should have had that option.

I do not believe this situation risks hostilities in the foreseeable future, but it feeds Bhutto's preoccupation about an Indian-Soviet-Afghan conspiracy against Pakistan, provides a source for would-be troublemakers to exploit, and is one more element complicating the process of bringing stability to South Asia.

My observation today is that Kissinger's meetings were aimed at achieving mutual understanding between our two governments and obviously broader and deeper than we young PCVs were aware of. He and the Department of State at that time were dealing with the alignments of the USSR, Iran, Afghanistan, Pakistan, India, and China, who also at that time had a political rift with the USSR. Understanding and working to resolve threats to regional stability amongst these countries was a high priority.

Kissinger's short five-hour visit to Afghanistan seems focused and useful for both sides, even if progress could not be made. One could also see how the US/Pakistan alliance clearly predominated over the US/Afghanistan relationship—a situation unchanged to today.

As an aside, when I started work in New York in 1975, one day I saw Dr. Kissinger walking along Madison Avenue at 48th street close to my office. Starstruck, I followed him for a block. I wish I had had the courage to have spoken with him. It could have proved interesting, and at worst he might have politely dismissed me.

With the recent passing of Kissinger at age 100, we are reminded of his life spent in diplomacy rooted in the concept of realpolitik, which seeks the balancing of practical rather than ideological considerations between states and alliances. The US has historically claimed to put democracy and freedom as its highest ideals, but the reality is that our sense of realpolitik has often put more weight on power and good economics for our country. Examples abound where we have supported dictators for the sake of our business interests and alliances. Kissinger, in the view of many, bears a heavy responsibility for military actions and civilian deaths over many decades.

It can be argued that the security and safety of America have not been improved by our wars and military actions following the Second World War. Often, we have made enemies and alienated countries and societies with our aggressiveness.

The argument that we highly value human life is also questionable, as collateral damage has been widespread, and we have engaged in wars where we sent our own people to fight where the enemy is not clearly defined and is sometimes backed by the very people whom we support, such as in Afghanistan in the 21st century: more on this at the end of this book. In Vietnam we coined such phrases as, "We had to destroy the village in order to save it," and sent soldiers up hills in deadly fights to gain territory only to bring them down shortly afterwards, relinquishing the territory gained at the expense of human lives.

45. Finishing up in Kabul and Heading Home, 1975

Work at the Faculty was coming to an orderly end, with the term ending in January 1975. Students were all graded and passed and details submitted to the department. Dean Zewari asked me to make a report on the status of the chemistry courses. The first item was that a second professor was necessary, as I had found that all teaching and lab work was too large a load for one professor. I also recommended that a sanitary engineering technician be promoted to be a standby technician to the existing tech in the lab, to ensure one is always available when there is absenteeism. I submitted a lab schedule and organization proposal and brought attention to the plans for a research lab and the need to deploy quite a lot of new equipment that was still in its original packaging. Lastly, I noted hopefully that additional AID funding might be available.

Based on discussions with the deans, I was also asked to write up academic needs for chemistry research at the university for analyses, providing advice and commentary on chemistry problems to the government. The specialties we identified were agricultural, chemical engineer, chemist, geologist, nutritionist, pharmacologist, and petroleum engineer. We agreed that an agriculturalist, a geologist and a chem engineer would fit this bill, and that pharmacology might best be left to the medical faculty.

My last assignment was to write recommendations to the Peace Corps Director of Programs, Abdul Matin, on follow-up to my role at Kabul University. I described the structure of the Faculty of Engineering, my work there for three semesters and the positive environment. My conclusion was that it would be a good job for a PCV, and that they would be well received. Given that instruction is in English, they could start immediately and language learning and becoming familiar with local culture could follow as a personal responsibility. My recommendation was that it was a rewarding job for a young American engineer.

The head of the US Engineering Team from Stevens Tech, Richard Gibson, was kind enough to write a very good letter of recommendation for me and I used this in writing job search letters to Standard Oil of California, Aramco, Caltex Petroleum and Union Carbide about job prospects and visiting their Mideast operations in early 1975. At the same time, I was yet undecided about what I wanted to do next and was also considering business school or studying Middle Eastern languages, which I decided could come later or be an avocation.

Heidar was now back from Tehran, and very generously spent days with me in the carpet bazaar across from the *jeshun* grounds and national football stadium. After visits to many shops and much haggling, I bought two very fine large carpets for around $2,000 to bring home. The price of a new VW Beetle had gone from $2,000 to $3,000 during my Peace Corps years and investing in carpets seemed to me a better alternative. I've had those carpets on my floors now for almost 50 years.

One of the days on my own in the bazaar, I ended up desperate for a bathroom, and had to duck into a darkened half-finished shell of a two-story shop house that had been abandoned and obviously had been used for the same purpose by many others. Along came a small boy who proceeded to watch me squatting to relieve myself and to taunt me with, "Hey, Mr. *Kachalu.*" I was embarrassed and furious and shouted insults at him. He was unfazed and remained amused. I had thought I was some kind of respected foreigner, but apparently not.

Next was to tie up loose ends and dismantle my household in Kabul. It was still winter and snowing, with some days sunny and warmer than freezing. I gave Assif a big bonus, and when it came to my household goods from furniture to kitchen equipment, he was interested in all of it. So, we played an elaborate game of bargaining over the items, and he used a good part of the bonus to buy nearly everything. Parting with Assif was tough, as I had spent more time with him over my three years than with anybody else. He was true and hardworking, and we wished one another well and said we hoped we'd be together again in future.

I gave my arak still and Sony tape recorder and music tapes to Heidar's nephew Zaman. Then I arranged to ship a large metal crate of carpets, small marble boxes, wooden bowls, local sweets and various souvenirs and clothing overland through the USSR to New York.

My correspondence at that time to brother Pedro in Guatemala today looks like a revolutionary manifesto, and not at all like someone who would soon join the international oil industry. C'est la vie. We talked of reservations about returning to the States. We called fraudulent the "free press," "democracy," and "liberty" programmed into our American heads by a "feudal oligarchy," like the regimes of other countries, but with pomp in proportion to US wealth. But I also mocked myself, calling out that my thinking was neither new nor enlightening. I wrote that our parents doubtless accepted all this ages before and would find our narrative amusing. When older, I wondered what it meant for the WW II generation to fight a desperate and dreadful war away from home for four or five years, only able to embark on civilian life at a much older age. They had perspectives beyond what we could know.

I took a final trip in Afghanistan on January 22 to Kunar and Nooristan in the northeast with Afghan Government and USAID Rural Development Department personnel, including Heidar and

David Garner, a friend over the years. The purpose was to inspect completed projects that used gabions, wire cages filled with rock, to make retaining walls on roads in the high mountains. This was an inexpensive way to protect the roads, which have many switchbacks and steep mountain overhangs often washed out by rain and melting snow, making it difficult to keep the villages at higher elevations from becoming isolated.

We headed to Jalalabad, turned north into Kunar province along the Kunar River. The land was a mix of green and barrenness, filled with farms and villages. At Chagh Sarai we turned to the west, then north, and rose rapidly from 9,000 to 15,000 feet elevation and with mountains rising to 17,000 and 18,000 feet on either side, and even higher in the distance. Poplar trees like those in the Colorado Rockies appeared on both sides, though sparse, unlike in North America.

This region was known as Kafiristan, "land of *kafirs*," with an animist religion until 1895 when it was converted to Islam and was renamed Nuristan, "land of light." The houses were made of wood and clung to steep mountains, the air fresh and oxygen thin. Some of the people were red headed with light eyes, some even blue. It is said that they include descendants of Alexander the Great who conquered lands through here on the way to India.

We inspected work groups and finished gabion emplacements, and then hiked several thousand feet on a narrow trail up a steep snow-covered mountain to meet a village leader and have a meal. The stacked and interconnected wooden homes, clinging to sheer mountains, with children playing in the snow and gaping at us, was a completely new vision of Afghanistan. On the way down, a government representative from our group said he was cold and asked to borrow my cashmere scarf, a Christmas present from my parents. I said yes, and when we arrived back at the car, he said he lost it on the trail. I went up the mountain looking for it and then gave up, realizing, not happily, that this obviously had become my gift to him.

This excursion reminded me of meeting an older USAID woman who had been on assignment in Nepal when the Apollo 11 astronauts had landed on the moon. She told us how excited she had been and rushed to tell one of the farmers nearby. He was not at all stirred, and said yes, he knew that. It turns out that the day before he had for the first time seen a helicopter, as it rose and disappeared over the mountain … apparently he then imagined it had gone to the moon. Amazing.

Returning to Kabul, I had only to say final farewells and depart. My first stop was the faculty and professors I'd worked with for three semesters. The deans and American professors thanked me for working with them and were complimentary of my efforts and interested in what I would be doing next. I told them how much I enjoyed working with them and all the faculty, and said I wasn't sure but was interested to stay overseas and would be interviewing with companies in Iran and the Persian Gulf.

My last visit in Kabul was to Heidar's home. It was difficult saying goodbye to this most gracious family and home away from home. When departing, Heidar's mother, Shirin Jan, asked me to leave from

Locally made wooden bridge on Kunar River on the way to Nuristan

the back kitchen door, where she held a Quran over my head and said a prayer for my safety.

I left Kabul on February 15 at 7 a.m. by bus for Herat, Mashhad, and Tehran. As I rode on the ring road from Kabul southwest to Kandahar and then northwest, I contemplated how I knew the country and would miss it, even though much of this nearly 700-mile ride was through Pasthtun territory in the south where I didn't speak the language and had spent little time. My Farsi experience had given me an understanding of the elite of the country, Kapisa, and much of the north, but not of the Pashtuns, the majority who controlled the country. It has been only now reviewing the history and writing this book that I have truly begun to appreciate the complexity of this ancient crossroads of Central Asia.

I spent a night in Herat, and then crossed the border into Mashhad, Iran.

My Afghan experience was over.

The soaring Hindu Kush mountains in Nuristan with stacks of hay leftover from recent wheat and barley harvests

V

Modern History

Crossroads Again

46. President Daoud to the Soviet-Inspired Coups of 1978–79 and the Democratic Republic of Afghanistan

The July 1973 coup d'etat had brought Daoud Khan to power again, a result of Soviet efforts and the growing strength of the Parcham and Khalq factions of the communist PDPA. Contributing factors included King Zahir Shah blocking full implementation of the legislatures stipulated in the new constitution, the severe drought of 1971–72, and a struggling economy. Afghanistan was again in a new Great Game, with the USSR and opposing US alliances in the region. President Daoud lobbied hard that America should not view his presidency and Afghanistan as a Russian stooge.

His government started writing another new constitution, liberalizing trade, allowing women freedom for education and public life and from wearing the veil, and reaching out to other Islamic regimes in the region. However, Afghanistan began to stagnate economically and Daoud's rule became more conservative in economic policy. He turned to appointing cronies to key positions, and in reaction to his modernizing moves, massive demonstrations and violence ensued.

The PDPA factions reacted by coming together again and planning another coup d'etat for October 1978. However, Daoud Khan, in response to the unrest, jailed Karmal and Taraki and so the Khalq faction under American-educated Hafizullah Amin brought the date forward. A bloody coup d'etat known as the Saur Revolution was executed in April 1978 creating the Democratic Republic of Afghanistan. Prior to surrender to the rebels who had surrounded the palace with tanks and troops, Daoud's last words were, "It is my mistake" (Assifi, p. 146.) During his reign he had favored certain officers with training, exceptional opportunities and promotions to high rank who turned out to be revolutionaries.

On day two of the coup, "President Daoud, and two ministers … altogether about 40 unarmed people, old and young, women and children," including most of his family, were machine gunned in the Presidential Palace. (Assifi, p. 152.) Tawab Assifi, a cabinet member who was Minister of Mines and Industry, was captured in the coup and spent two years in prison, beaten and tortured and in constant fear of execution. He describes the suffering and resilience, saying,

> The people of Kabul had made up their minds to fight this regime and the Soviet military forces. This result corroborated the observations I had made in Pul-i-Charkhi [prison]: this was the reason that a large number of people were brought into that place for torture and execution every day and night. I learned from this that Afghans may be poor and backward, but they are truly endowed with national bravery and spiritual strength! (Assifi, p. 279-80)

Mr. Assifi had been the head of engineering and chief engineer at the American sponsored Helmand Valley project in the late 1960s in southwest Afghanistan and in 1972 was appointed president of the Rural Development Department of Afghanistan. He had high praise for American advisors David Garner of USAID, a friend whom I'd met through Heidar, and Lou Mitchell, our first Peace Corps Director.

During this reign of terror, the father of Heidar's brother-in-law Aman (and whose brother Zaman was my student at the faculty) was taken away one night and never seen again. He had been a respected Shia mullah. The Soviet-inspired revolutionaries were trying to subdue the country through imprisonment and executions.

A Revolutionary Council was established and Khalq leader Nur Mohammad Taraki elected president, prime minister, and secretary-general of the new government. Parcham leader Babrak Karmal and Khalq member Hafizullah Amin were elected deputy prime ministers.

In 1978, Adolph Dubs was appointed United States Ambassador to Afghanistan following the coup d'état. On February 14, 1979 (the same day that Iranian militants attacked the US Embassy in Tehran, Iran), he was kidnapped by militants and taken to the Kabul Serena Hotel. The US urged negotiation, but the Afghan authorities, with Soviet advice, stormed the hotel and Ambassador Dubs was killed.

The US was not permitted to investigate and the identity and aims of the abductors have never been determined. The US then cut humanitarian aid, all military support and reduced the embassy to a skeleton staff headed by only a chargé d'affaires. Shortly thereafter the Peace Corps was pulled out of Afghanistan and has never returned.

Intra-party fighting continued to increase and in March of 1979 Amin took over as prime minister and positions were shuffled. Taraki was then invited to Moscow and told by Brezhnev to get rid of Amin. In mid-September in Kabul, when a planned confrontation between Taraki and Amin went wrong, a gun battle broke out and Amin mobilized a force to control the presidential palace, and Taraki was removed from his post as secretary general. On 10 October, Taraki was strangled at his home, and it was announced that he had "died of his illness." (Ewan, p. 200). Thereafter assassination squads began the killing of Khalqis, while Amin was said to have a vision of revolution based on terror.

Now in power, Amin implemented a Marxist–Leninist agenda, including socialist land reform, banning the veil, women's rights, shaving men's beards, closing mosques and embracing atheism, and moving even closer to the USSR for modernization. Anahita Ratebzad (my colleague and friend Abdullah's mother) was a member of the Revolutionary Council and established many reforms for women. Parcham leaders were sidelined, some sent into exile as ambassadors. Parcham leader Babrak, one of the 1973 coup planners and Anahita's political partner, went into hiding in Prague and later was sent to Moscow.

The revolutionary actions of the government were highly unpopular with most Afghans, and widespread unrest broke out across the country. In December, the USSR, fearing that Amin might shift alliances to the West (Ewan, p. 202), planned a full-scale invasion. Battalions of infantry and armored units were positioned in Bagram air base, Kabul airport and surrounding the capital, and for several days soldiers, tanks, personnel carriers and other heavy equipment were airlifted from the USSR to Kabul. On December 24, Parcham party leader Babrak Karmal announced a coup d'etat on Kabul Radio, actually broadcast from Termaz in the USSR, and became prime minister. Amin was assassinated. The next day two Soviet motorized divisions crossed the Soviet-built bridge over the Oxus River. The total Soviet forces in Afghanistan were estimated to be from 60,000 to100,000.

Creating international outrage, the Soviets "… failed totally to conceal the truth … that they had unilaterally sent troops into an independent, non-aligned Islamic country, killed its president and installed a puppet regime." (Ewans, p. 205.) At the time, the US was distracted by the American diplomatic hostages being held in Iran, and there was no significant reaction by the international community. Thus began the era of direct communist rule that was to last for 12 years, until 1992.

47. Resistance to the Communist Democratic Republic of Afghanistan to the Fall of Najibullah in 1992

Initially it was believed that Afghanistan would be unable to oppose the might of the USSR; however, as it became clear that the Afghans would not submit, the US and Saudis, as well as Pakistan and others, began providing financial assistance and weapons to Afghan freedom fighters. The resistance was led by Mujaheddin, meaning those who fight jihad, holy war against infidels. Young men from Pakistan and other mostly Arabic speaking Muslim countries in the region also joined the fight. Some said that the Mujaheddin welcomed support from the US as a largely Christian country over the godless communists of the USSR. According to US law, American support had to be funneled through Pakistan's Inter-Services Intelligence (ISI) organization.

Support was distributed to the seven resistance parties recognized by the Pakistani government:

> **Mahaz-i-Milli Islami** (National Islamic Front of Afghanistan), a pro-royalist and pro-western group headed by Pir Sayed Ahmad Gailani, also a leader of Sufism
> **Jamiat Islami Afghanistan** (Islamic Society of Afghanistan), headed by Professor Burhanuddin Rabbani,

with ties to the Muslim Brotherhood and Commander Ahmad Shah Massoud in the Panjshir Valley

Jabba-i-Islami Afghanistan (National Front for the Rescue of Afghanistan), a pro-royalist group headed by Professor Sibgatullah Mojadidi

Harakat-i-Inqilab-i-Islami (Movement for the Islamic Revolution of Afghanistan), headed by Maulawi Mohammad Nabi Mohammadi, an influential theologian and member of Parliament

Hezb-i-Islami Khalis (Islamic Party, Khali faction), headed by Maulawi Mohammad Younos Khalis, a respected Pashtun mullah and university lecturer

Hezbi-i-Islami Hekhmatyar (Islamic Party, Hekhmatyar faction), headed by Gulbuddin Hekhmatyar, an Islamic extremist and highly controversial figure who attacked Soviet and Communist units

Ittihad-i-Islami Baraye Azadi Afghanistan (Islamic Union for the Liberation of Afghanistan), headed by Abdul Rasul Sayyaf, member of the Muslim Brotherhood funded by Saudi sources and closely associated with Wahhabis and Salafis

(Assifi, p. 336)

These resistance groups represented the diversity of Afghanistan: its language and ethnic groups; Sunni and Shia Muslims; and all regions. However, they were never able to unite, which hindered and delayed their success, and is perhaps a hangover from centuries of strife in Afghanistan.

In attempting to subdue the rebellion, the communist Democratic Republic imprisoned large numbers of opponents, bombed villages, tortured enemies, and booby trapped the countryside. A UN Human Rights Commission document in 1985 reported that the Mujaheddin had the support of the vast majority of the population.

This support, along with the rugged and brutal geography of the country, set the terms of engagement with the Soviets decisively in favor of the resistance. In 1984, American-supplied hand-held stinger missiles began knocking out fighter jets and helicopters, taking away the Soviet and Afghan air supremacy and the tide began to turn against the government and Soviet ability to suppress the insurrection.

Since 1982, the Soviet KGB (intelligence service) viewed Karmal as a liability, being passive, vacillating, lazy and a heavy drinker. (Ewans, p. 229) In 1986 the Soviets, unhappy with government policy and the ongoing insurrection, replaced Karmal with Mohammad Najibullah, head of the secret service, KhAD. In 1987 the Republic of Afghanistan was declared, with a new constitution.

Soviet casualties continued to mount, and when it became clear that they were in a quagmire, the regime lost support at home. In 1985 Gorbachev had come to power in the USSR and given the Afghan project one year to turn around. In November 1986 the Soviet leadership concluded that they had lost the battle for the Afghan people. International negotiations followed, culminating in the Geneva Accords of April 1988, leading to the withdrawal of all Soviet forces by early 1989.

Some believe that the Afghan fiasco was one of the catalysts for the collapse of the Soviet Union. In his memoirs Gorbachev called the Afghanistan war a "hopeless military adventure" that had "brought shame on our nation." (Ewans, p. 236)

With Soviet support and the disunity of the resistance, Najibullah managed to stay in power until he was ousted in April 1992, when the advances of Dostum and Massoud from the north and Hekhmatyar from the south forced him to step down.

For Afghanistan, the Soviet invasion and occupation were a disaster. Estimates of Afghans killed range from 600,000 to two million, while creating five to six million refugees, mostly in Pakistan, and in Iran. An estimated 15,000 Soviet soldiers were killed and 37,000 wounded. (Ewans, p. 235)

48. Civil War to the Islamic Emirate of Afghanistan and 911

What followed the fall of Najibullah was chaos and civil war. The nation had suffered thousands of imprisonments and executions at the hands of Soviet inspired revolutionaries, who were steeped in bookish "scientific socialism" and had seen themselves as the wave of the future for Afghanistan like the Russian Revolutionaries who overthrew the tsar in 1917. But a twentieth century proletariat did not exist in deeply religious and largely rural Afghanistan and the people were also not interested in the ideology of the communists. The USSR indeed had failed shamefully in its attempt to make Afghanistan a communist client state.

The Saudis from the late 1970s began contributing large amounts of funding to establish religious schools, madrassas, mainly in Pakistan. In 1994, Mullah Mohammad Omar, a Mujaheddin fighter against the USSR, began a movement known as the Taliban (meaning student). The madrasas began turning out conservative religious Muslims seeking to reestablish Muslim power. They often became recruits to the Taliban mostly from Pakistan Pashtun tribal areas and Kandahar. In my time in Afghanistan, these madrassas were unknown, and today are viewed by many Afghans as outsiders.

What was noticeably lacking was support from the United States, who had lost interest after the Soviets were defeated. This was a significant failing on the part of the US, which had played an important role supporting the Mujaheddin in defeating the Soviet occupation and might have contributed to a better outcome for Afghanistan. It became clear that the US support for the resistance in the 1980s had been mainly about opposing the USSR, with little interest in the development and modernization of Afghanistan. Much later my friend Heidar asked me not to mention to him the name of Bill Clinton, whom he otherwise would have supported, because he had not said the word Afghanistan during his eight years of presidency.

A UN-recognized interim government was established in Kabul in 1992 by the Peshawar Accord proclaiming the Islamic State of Afghanistan, first led by Sibghatuallah Mojaddedi and then by minority Tajik professor Burhanuddin Rabbani. However, control could only be maintained in Kabul and some major cities, with large areas of the countryside left to lawlessness and rule by warlords and the resistance groups.

The Taliban Mujaheddin grew rapidly and began to win political control of the cities and provinces throughout the country, including the minority Shia in Herat in 1995 and multi-ethnic Kabul in 1996. After taking Kabul, the Mujaheddin renamed the nation the Islamic Emirate of Afghanistan, under the leadership of Mullah Omar. Also in 1996, Ahmad Shah Massoud, the Tajik Panjshiri commander, and Abdul Rashid Dostum, an Uzbek from the north, established the United Front (Northern Alliance) opposing the new Emirate. However, the Taliban in 1998 defeated Dostum and captured minority Uzbek Mazar-i-Sharif in the north leaving only Massoud in opposition, based in Panjshir. From then until 2001, Massoud continued developing a constitutional government, establishing women's rights, and training national police and United Front armed forces to maintain the peace and protect the populace in parts of the north.

In 1996 when Kabul fell, the Taliban captured Najibullah who had been hiding in the UN compound for four years since his fall. He and his brother were executed, and their bodies strung up in Kabul to be seen by the public.

Al Qaeda (meaning the base) was formed in 1988 by Osama bin Laden with Mujaheddin veterans of the war against the Soviet Union. Its goal was to unite Muslims in a new Caliphate to wage global jihad against apostate Muslims such as Saudi Arabia, long supported by America and western powers, as well as Israel whom they viewed as having illegally captured Palestine. Al Qaeda had grown in the Mideast and northeast Africa under leadership that included bin Laden. The mostly unsuccessful bombing of the New York World Trade Center in 1993 and the devastating East Africa US Embassy bombings in 1998 had shown the intent and capability of Al Qaeda. With the approval of Mullah Omar, Osama set up a training camp in Afghanistan, and "from 1996 to 2001 the Al Qaeda of Osama Bin Laden and Ayman al-Zawahiri became a state within the Taliban state." [Wikipedia.]

The Taliban could not take complete control of Afghanistan with Massoud's Northern Alliance still not defeated. On September 9, 2001, Al Qaeda succeeded in assassinating Massoud by a suicide bomber posing as an interviewer with a video camera packed with explosives. Two days later the 911 attack happened, the New York World Trade Center was destroyed, and the Pentagon badly damaged by Al Qaeda.

49. Overthrow of the Taliban in 2001, US and NATO and the Islamic Republic of Afghanistan to the Return of the Taliban and the Islamic Emirate in 2021

Following the 911 attack, Mullah Omar refused the American demand to hand over bin Laden, and the US and the UK coordinated with the Northern Alliance, attacking and bombing the Taliban in Kabul, Al Qaeda's training camps near Kandahar, and Mazar-i-Sharif. The Islamic Emirate government quickly folded, and many of their fighters retreated across the long porous border with Pakistan. This included the Haqqani tribe of Pashtuns centered in Waziristan in northwest Pakistan close to the Khyber Pass, and where Osama bin Laden was later apprehended and killed in 2011.

A new Afghan interim government was formed in 2002 with the selection of Hamid Karzai, a khan from a politically active family of the Popalzai Durrani Pashtuns from Kandahar, as president. An International Security Assistance Force was established by the UN Security Council.

Whitlock in *The Afghanistan Papers* questions the decision to consolidate power in the hands of a president, resembling Washington. In *Lessons Learned* interviews by the US Government post-2021, it was found that

> … numerous US and European officials admitted that the decision to put so much power in the hands of one man was a disastrous miscalculation. The rigid system conflicted with the Afghan tradition, typified by a mix of decentralized authority and tribal customs … In hindsight the worst decision was to centralize power.

Richard Boucher, the former State Department chief spokesman said,

> We did not know what we were doing ... The only time this country has worked properly was when it was a floating pool of tribes and warlords presided over by someone who had a certain eminence who was able to centralize them to the extent that they didn't fight each other too much. (Whitlock, p. 37-38)

A *Loya Jirga* of regional elders approved a new constitution which was ratified in 2004, and in October, Karzai won an overwhelming popular vote to be elected president of the Islamic Republic of Afghanistan in the first national election in their history. People in Kabul and the major cities welcomed the new regime and a return to a more modern life: men once again were allowed to shave and women to discard the veil, and progress began in modernizing the government, education, healthcare, and the economy.

I spent a parents' weekend in January 2002 with my son Guy and about 10 of his classmates who were living together and working at the Stanford Hopkins Marine Station in Monterey, California. One of the students was David Wolfowitz, son of Paul Wolfowitz, the Deputy Secretary of Defense. Paul was a fellow Cornell grad said to be a renowned intellect, and who was friendly and very welcoming. But I was stunned that we were at the beginning of Afghanistan nation-building with a large military commitment, yet when I told him that I'd been a Peace Corps Volunteer there for over three years and knew the country intimately, he showed no interest, and the subject did not come up again over the course of three days. It seemed to me that this likely reflected closed thinking in the Defense Department. Or perhaps it was just "loose lips sink ships."

So began 20 years of nation building with American, NATO and UN support. We were supporting Farsi speaking Pashtun and ethnic minority leaders, many of whom in the 1990s had opposed the conservative Pashtun Taliban Mujaheddin who were the major force fighting the Soviets in the 1980s. Our job was to build up the

Afghan armed forces and police, as well as government and civil institutions. However, the resources employed were mainly military and less of what is needed for nation building: peaceful government and institutional development, grass roots economic support, business development and consensus building. Karzai was to remain president of the Islamic Republic of Afghanistan until 2014.

In the early years and after Karzai had won this historic democratic presidential election, the US and NATO partners had the balance of power. According to *The Afghanistan Papers*, the coalition partners right from 2001 in the Bush administration "… squandered multiple opportunities to reach out to the Taliban when the United States and its allies held maximum leverage." (Whitlock, p. 264) Some speculate that had the US and coalition reached out to the Taliban when they were weak, a better solution to national government may have been found. This failure to communicate with the Taliban continued in the Obama administration.

The US and NATO assumed military responsibility for the international forces and began training the Afghan national armed forces. The Taliban began growing its support and they increasingly engaged in anti-government terrorist acts including bombings and massacres. Their goal was to destabilize the Republic. By 2008, the US recognized the need for a political settlement with the Taliban, and under the new Obama administration held meetings with the UN in 2009 in Dubai and with some 70 nations and organizations in 2010 in London. But the Taliban refused to make any deals if foreign forces remained in Afghanistan.

The Obama administration said it would reach out to the Taliban but limited this to low-level fighters excluding Taliban commanders and mullahs, whom they labeled as irreconcilables. They saw a process of bringing the foot soldiers over to the government and being able to isolate and target the leaders. Marine Gen. James Mattis said, "We're going to have to break them, irreconcilable from reconcilable … if they'll work with the government and work within the constitution, then there's going to be a home for them." Whitlock goes on to say, "US military officials showed little understanding about what motivated the Taliban to fight." This got it terribly wrong.

In time despite the local population despising the brutal tactics of the Taliban, "shared ethnicity, religious beliefs and tribal allegiances" prevailed in favor of the Taliban.

In *Directorate S* by Steve Coll, in "a stark, impolitic, even shocking summary of the American position in Afghanistan," Major General Mike Flynn (who was convicted of a felony in 2017 and pardoned by Trump in 2022) provides a summary regarding the guerrilla war by the Taliban against the Republic and the ISAF from a paper he coauthored in 2010 as part of an assessment of the American war effort (Coll, p. 391):

> Eight years into the war in Afghanistan, the US intelligence community is only marginally relevant to the overall strategy. Having focused the overwhelming majority of its collection efforts and analytical brainpower on insurgent groups, the vast intelligence apparatus is unable to answer fundamental questions about the environment in which US and allied forces operate and the people they seek to persuade. Ignorant of local economics and landowners, hazy about who the power brokers are and how they might be influenced, incurious about the correlations between various development projects and the levels of cooperation among villagers … US intelligence officers and analysts can do little but shrug in response to high level decision-makers seeking knowledge, analysis and information they need to wage a successful counterinsurgency.

To me this read like an assessment we volunteers could have written in our Peace Corps days of the lack of on the ground knowledge of US embassy and government players. Today I recognize the validity of our grassroots know-how but that the statement also shows naïvete and hubris.

Karzai was also advising Brigadier General Stanley McChrystal (leader of the US Central Command force in Kabul distinct from NATO) to reduce Afghan casualties in the war. McChrystal introduced strong rules of engagement to minimize casualties, undoubtedly not favored by soldiers on the ground whose lives were at risk. He famously said, "We're going to lose this fucking war if we don't stop killing civilians." (Coll, p. 395)

At a briefing to Karzai of the war assessment given by McChrystal, CIA Chief Vogle in Peshawar, Pakistan, and US Ambassador to Afghanistan Karl Eikenberry, Karzai disagreed with our description of the strategy. He said:

> You call this an insurgency; this is not an insurgency. An insurgency, as I understand the meaning, suggests there are citizens of a country who are fighting against their government because they think the government is illegitimate. Now, we are a conservative, simple Muslim people. If they are fighting against an illegitimate government, then who are you, the United States? You are propping up an illegitimate government. No. There is no insurgency. There is a problem of international terrorism. We are allies in a battle against international terrorism.

According to Coll:

> Karzai believed, like many other Afghans, that the true story of the war—the essential problem—was not his own legitimacy but the mysterious unwillingness of the United States to challenge ISI and Pakistan … He didn't seem sure that the Taliban and other fellow Afghans his security forces fought were truly enemies; they were merely misguided hired hands of Pakistan. (Coll, p. 397)

In 2009, "Eikenberry warned that Pakistan will remain the single greatest source of Afghan instability so long as the border sanctuaries remain." (Coll, p. 152)

American military support for Afghanistan by law had to be delivered through the Pakistani ISI. This was a formula almost impossible for success, with two major flaws. First, a great portion of the support never reached Afghanistan, being retained (stolen) by the Pakistani military or by middlemen. Second, more than half of all Pashtuns lived in Pakistan, which the Taliban used as a safe haven, crossing into Afghanistan to fight and retreating into Pakistan for safety.

Coll quotes McChrystal's assessment with the key "convoluted" sentence: "While the existence of safe havens in Pakistan does not guarantee ISAF failure, Afghanistan does require Pakistani cooperation." (Coll, p. 397) Ambassador Eikenberry pointed out the best choice for deploying more troops would be "in the 'Federally Administered Tribal Areas' inside Pakistan."

Karzai countered:

> ... that's exactly the point. You're fighting a second-best strategy. You're fighting Taliban foot soldiers in Afghanistan and destabilizing the country. You can't play the game of saying Pakistan is your ally and telling me in private that they're not.

The CIA and the American Ambassador agreed that to defeat the Taliban, they would need to eliminate the sanctuary in Pakistan. But this did not happen, and Karzai disagreed with the American war strategy but kept them at bay and preserved his power by meeting with embassy, CIA and military separately. In essence the Americans were unable to gain information and control over the Taliban leaders and the Pakistan-based political and military strategy.

Coll finally writes that "Pakistani generals had been lying to American counterparts about their support for the Taliban since the movement's birth in 1994. It was evidently a hard habit to break." (Coll, p. 400)

Population data for Afghanistan has always been uncertain. Ethnic data indicates Pashtuns in Afghanistan and Pakistan were around 5 million and more than 11 million in the 1970s rising to 18 and 38 million Pashtuns in 2023. Against these odds, defeating the Pashtun Taliban inside Afghanistan was untenable.

In my view, sending our troops into danger for nearly 20 years while at the same time having an ally that was playing both sides was indefensible, worse than a Catch 22.

Meanwhile the Taliban was growing in control around the country, and the local folk were being "kicked like rocks" by both the Taliban and the American forces. But given their druthers, they preferred the Taliban. From Wikipedia:

> After the killing of bin Laden in 2011 many prominent Afghan figures began being assassinated ... border skirmishes intensified and many large-scale attacks by the Pakistan-based Haqqani network took place across Afghanistan ...

In 2009 in a disputed election Karzai retained the presidency, and Obama announced that forces in Afghanistan would be reduced by the end of the year. The US also wanted the Afghan government to take over the fight allowing US forces to leave. However, the US demanded Karzai accept an agreement allowing a small US force to remain to fight Al Qaeda and to immunize them from prosecution under Afghan law. Karzai refused, and this was signed only in 2014 when the Pashtun Ashraf Ghani was elected president of the Islamic Republic.

The effort at US troop reduction foundered. Troop levels in fact rose with a surge between 2009 and 2011. In 2011 NATO and Afghan forces launched an attack against the Pashtun Haqqanis in southeastern Afghanistan. As time went on, fratricidal attacks on Americans by members of the Afghan armed forces rose, becoming no longer isolated, and adding to the ongoing terrorist and guerrilla attacks. The quality of Afghan army recruits also deteriorated, and corruption grew, with local leaders able to make money from the coalition military in numerous ways. The Afghan police forces were no better; one unnamed US military officer estimated that one-third of local police recruits were drug addicts or Taliban.

In 2014 American educated President Ghani began initiatives to expand international trade, build manufacturing and modernize the nation. But his election was heavily contested, not unlike what had happened in 2009, and the nation was not yet unified.

In 2016, the Islamic State, the fast-growing terrorist network in Iraq and Syria, expanded into Afghanistan and Pakistan. American military officials estimated that they had several thousand fighters. The war had become more complicated, and the

> US military put the Taliban into a new category … not necessarily the enemy. Obama administration officials had concluded that the only way to end the war and to stabilize Afghanistan was for the Afghan government to negotiate a peace deal with the Taliban." (Whitlock, p. 235)

During that year, Army General John Campbell, commander of US and NATO forces, testified to the Senate Armed Forces Committee that "our country has made the decision that we are not at war with the Taliban." The Taliban however thought and acted otherwise, continuing to attack and seize control of parts of the country. Campbell's successor Army Gen. John Nicholson Jr. one month later testified in response to a question of whether we were winning or losing the war that "I believe we're in a stalemate." (Whitlock, p. 236-7)

At the beginning of the Trump administration, the President reversed his promise to get out and began to send more troops and expand military operations, while declaring inaccurately that we were not again nation-building. He agreed with the military to a careful review of the war strategy before action. However, in special briefings with the top military brass, Trump called it a "loser war," trashed Nicholson saying, "I don't think he knows how to win," and later told *Washington Post* journalists that he wanted to win and that they were "a bunch of dopes and babies." His administration and the military attempted to reduce the visibility of the war and suppress statistics, but the recruiting and war efforts of the Taliban continued to strengthen.

The Trump administration then began negotiations with the Taliban and sought finally to end the American role in Afghanistan.

In February 2020, the United States and the Taliban reached a deal, known as the Doha Agreement, under which the United States agreed to withdraw all US forces from Afghanistan by May 2021, and to release 5,000 imprisoned Taliban. The Taliban refused to negotiate with the government of Afghanistan, who were thus left out of these negotiations, and to which the US acquiesced. The Trump administration also made no plans for this agreed withdrawal.

Vice President Biden had been the only inner circle member to oppose the surge in 2010–11 in the Obama administration, and he had been right that the effort was unwinnable. Given the lack of planning and that the Afghan government wasn't part of the Doha Agreement, the new Biden administration in 2021 postponed the withdrawal for a few months, then ordered it in August. Contrary to intelligence estimates that the Afghanistan government armed forces could withstand the Taliban initially for up to years and then up to months, the Islamic Republic of Afghanistan and Kabul fell to the Taliban peacefully and in days.

President Ghani fled to Tajikistan, and the country has been under the Taliban ever since. I have heard stories from Afghans in America that they know of people in government who spirited off millions of dollars to buy properties abroad, truth or rumor?

The new regime promptly declared itself once again to be the Islamic Emirate of Afghanistan and is yet to be recognized by the US and other western governments. The Islamic Emirate's US dollar bank assets were frozen overseas, and foreign aid hobbled. In addition, the economy soon collapsed, extreme conservatism was reintroduced, requiring women to wear the veil, and barring them from work and public activity. Women's schools and university attendance largely shutdown and men were no longer allowed to shave their beards. Many have fled the country which increasingly lacks human resources with the necessary expertise and administrative ability. Two years on, only time will tell how the Taliban-led Islamic Emirate of Afghanistan will fare.

One of the most difficult realizations about the US nation-building efforts and 20 years of war is that many of the mistakes of the past were repeated. *The Afghanistan Papers* was so named because of the similarity of the effort to *The Pentagon Papers* during the Vietnam War. The *Washington Post* obtained documents from the Special Inspector General for Afghanistan Reconstruction (SIGAR) after lawsuits under the Freedom of Information Act. From these documents and more than 1,000 interviews of people who played a direct role in the US war in Afghanistan as well as hundreds of Defense Department memos (Whitlock p. 283), author Craig Whitlock wrote a compelling history of how the US had no effective strategy for the war, failed in many initiatives and how the Bush, Obama and Trump administrations and the military had sugar-coated, lied and misled the public for 20 years with positive news stories and predictions of success.

Apparently, President Joe Biden is the only president who stood up to the reality and pulled the US out of Afghanistan.

50. What Happened and Where Afghanistan Stands Today

My view is that Afghanistan has long struggled with the Pashto and Farsi language split, regional ethnic differences and the competition of international powers over its land, perpetuating the long and tragic history of being a violent political crossroads, the cockpit of Central Asia.

Over the last 40 years, I often felt that the news lacked understanding of the complexity of the Afghanistan situation. In writing this memoir, I realized that I needed to study a lot more of the history, that it is more complicated and nuanced than I knew.

The people of Afghanistan will not be dominated but they are open to cooperation and assistance. If a strategy were developed to build consensus and to work cooperatively with them, then the Afghans would likely be able to make real progress. The idea that they are backward, and incapable of progressing is misinformed. No people or nation likes being told what to do, but Afghanistan is especially resistant to this. They believe that Islam is the right path, and to be successful with them, this must be appreciated, along with an understanding that their sovereignty has been repeatedly challenged by foreign powers.

Steve Coll's brilliant books *Ghost Wars* covering from 1979 to just before 911 in 2001 and *Directorate S*, from then until 2018, show this clearly. Unfortunately, these books focus on the abundant range of American activities, with little intelligence on the Afghanistan nation and how it works, or the internal workings of Pakistan. America engaged huge resources during these 40 years, including diplomatic, military, intelligence, presidential administrations, congressional, political, profit-seeking contractors, and private. The main issues in Afghanistan were seen and studied by them, but the actions led by America ended up being a free-for-all with many institutional players and different points of view, and no leadership synthesizing a unified and coherent strategy. In a sense, they were all extras in an as-yet unwritten play.

Craig Whitlock's outstanding book *The Afghanistan Papers* documents this tragedy, and how the public was repeatedly misled and often lied to by people and events during the Bush, Obama and Trump administrations. This book also reveals a profound lack of understanding of Afghanistan and its culture and history. A simple example is how a US army major who was a civil-affairs leader commented that in one region, villagers were so isolated they had to marry their first cousins (Whitlock, p. 74), not knowing that to Afghan Muslims, this is the ideal marriage.

Another example relates to how American officials often thought the Afghans incapable. Yet US efforts to stop the growing of opium poppies and the drug trade were a dismal failure, while repeatedly being reported as successes. Alternative agricultural projects mostly were failures, and often backfired. Yet Air Force Maj, Matthew Brown commented that "these guys have a history of smuggling and growing drugs that's second to none … our smugglers would probably be able to learn … from these guys …" And later, "… they've got the capacity to provide the entire world's worth of opium." (Whitlock, p. 255).

Regarding the Taliban, Staff Sgt. Bickford, who was severely injured in an ambush in 2006, in an oral history interview said,

We said that we defeated the Taliban, but they were always in Pakistan and regrouping and planning and now they're back stronger than they have ever been. Anytime that they did an assault or an ambush it was well-organized, and they knew what they were doing … These are very smart people, and they're the enemy but they deserve tons of respect and they should never, never, never be underestimated. (Whitlock, p. 100)

I do not doubt the sincerity, skill and efforts of our administrations and departments of state and defense, but I do question their approaches. It has been reported by the AP that the US spent $2 trillion on the Afghanistan and Iraq wars, and that in Afghanistan there were 6,300 American service member and contractor deaths, and 165,000 deaths of Afghan military and police, civilians, Taliban, aid workers and others. USAFacts.org reported that 70% of the total foreign aid to Afghanistan in the 20-year period was military spending. In my view military spending is neither the most important part of foreign aid, nor the most effective, but it seems this is the one activity where the US is most capable. It is also profitable. Various Chinese people have said to me in this century that the US needs these wars because they sell a lot of weapons, which I hope is false, but nonetheless stings.

Coll, in *Directorate S*, in discussing Karzai's personal relationships crucial to his retaining power in 2009, commented that he "renewed private channels to the CIA and the Pentagon, legendarily the true centers of American power." (Coll, p. 387) In the US, politicians make wars and the military execute them. Unfortunately, politicians rarely admit mistakes and the military rarely say that they cannot achieve an objective they have been given. This can be a tragic combination.

America in nation-building attempted to impose a top down democratically elected republican form of government with a strong executive on a country with a long history of a multi-tribal and multi-ethnic collective form of government. Pashtuns in Afghanistan were destined to prevail. Taliban were the strongest of the Pashtuns. Madrasas in Pakistan turned out large numbers of Pashtun religious zealots who became Taliban with safe harbor in Pakistan. The US military alliance with Pakistan, compounded by it having nuclear weapons, was of greater importance to the US than fighting the Taliban, and thus the US military was not able stop Pakistan and ISI from supporting the Taliban, which might have been impossible anyway, given the successful independence of the ethnic Afghans for centuries.

Foreign ISIS radicals joined and fought for Islamic government. Conservative Islam has long opposed modern social progress. The Afghans believe that throughout history the West has been an aggressor and will always choose Muslim government over foreign intervention. And finally, the US mistakenly ignored Afghanistan during the crucial decade after the fall of the USSR in 1991 and did not attempt to negotiate with all parties after 911.

My Baku Kham roommate Mark Svendsen whose opinions I deeply appreciate offered this comment on the end of America's 20 years in Afghanistan: "It was a fool's errand anyway to expect that infidels could prevail in a battle of ideology, retribution, and tribal affiliation."

Putting all these elements together, perhaps a unified American strategy in Afghanistan was not possible, and the chance of success in regime change and nation building was minimal. But we certainly did not go about it the right way. That requires diplomacy, effective communication, understanding and peaceful development work. It can only be delivered with aid and support on the ground and not focused on political domination or military solutions. America has strong capabilities in governing and administration, construction, road building, water treatment, medicine, education, the arts, manufacturing, business, and finance, and it is a shame not to lead with these. Many have pointed to the irony that we lost the Vietnam War but are winning the peace.

A final note, the West is very concerned with the Islamic Emirate's denial of women's rights. But objectively, in America women's rights are fairly recent and even today there are disagreements over women's pay, employment and healthcare. So, is it realistic to expect a much older, more conservative, and economically backward and rural society like Afghanistan to change rapidly to be more like our modern world? In Afghanistan today there is much local support for women's rights, and I would like to believe that change and real progress can and will be made in future years.

51. Looking Forward

The Afghanistan that I lived in from 1971–1975 was peaceful, and the people were proud, friendly, and worldly wise, yet living in some ways like in the Middle Ages. They were almost entirely Muslims who lived peacefully with small minorities of Christians, Jews and Hindus. Most did not support American policies in South Africa, Vietnam and Palestine and Israel, even as they respected America. The Afghan people, however, were gracious to all foreigners working there, accepted our offers of aid, and believed that modernization was essential for their national development. Women were being educated and assuming public roles, which was accepted in most of the country.

My hope for Afghanistan is that the US and western nations will engage with the Islamic government there, and that compromises and greater understanding will contribute to progress on the road to modernization. It will not be easy and will require hard work to understand one another and build bridges in thinking. The Taliban believe we are the invaders spreading terror, with no business in their country, though this is not a view shared by all. We believe that the Taliban are backward and imposing their will with little regard for the wishes of all the people.

The current loggerheads between the West and Afghanistan under the Taliban highlights the need for peace in the Middle East, not a rosy picture today. The American invasion of Iraq was a mistake. The countries who knew the most about Iraq strongly advised against it. This included France and, more friendly at the time, Russia. We were ignorant and naïve, and failed to have a political plan of what to do after the initial military success. Much of the world believed that we did it only for the oil.

The Iraq War inflamed the Shia Sunni split, a bitter struggle for over 1,400 years, and set the Mideast on fire. This empowered the current Shia Iran religious regime (said to be a minority!) and created an east-to-west wall of support from Iran across majority Shia Iraq, Alawite and Shia-controlled Syria, backed by Russia and the Iran-supported Hezbollah in Lebanon. This put Saudi Arabia and the Arabian Peninsula nations governed by Sunni Muslims but with significant Shia populations, at great risk, and dependent for survival upon US military support. It also also led to creating over four million Iraqi refugees of which only 6,000 have been accepted for resettling in the United States (Center for American Progress). It is a clear example of how bad policy can backfire and achieve opposite effects of that desired. It was also the first big international war of the 21st century that we had no business starting.

The latest 2023 Gaza Israel War is a great tragedy and makes it clear that the most important task today for the Mideast is to make peace, no matter how difficult. Ironically and tragically, people on both sides of the Palestine/Israel conflict say, "How do you make peace with people who refuse to accept your right to exist?" The answer is yes, this is the challenge. There will be a price, but in the end, it will be less than continued failure to make peace.

When this happens, it may also contribute positively and significantly to resolving the problems that face Afghanistan.

Afterword

In February 1975, the Iranian border guards and customs people in Mashhad were dressed in modern uniforms, smartly groomed and spoke confidently about the Iranian American alliance. On the way to Tehran, I travelled on paved roads through electrified towns and cities made of concrete buildings, and through orderly agricultural lands.

My plan was to interview American companies in Iran and Bahrain for future job prospects and enjoy Iran for a last time before heading home.

The economic situation in Iran was difficult. The first oil crisis of 1974, when international oil prices rose from around $2 to $12/barrel, resulted in a tsunami of dollars flowing to the Middle East creating huge inflation, fueling growth and also causing local suffering. The Shah had predicted that by the year 2000 there would be five great countries in the world: US, USSR, Great Britain, Germany, and Iran. Massive industrial projects were underway employing the very capable Iranian people, including plants to make steel, automobiles, plastics, helicopter manufacturing, and more.

One company in Isfahan was Polyacryl, a Du Pont plastics joint venture, whom I interviewed. Also in Isfahan, Bell Helicopters was building a helicopter plant staffed by American employees who, on short notice, had been given a choice of being laid off or going to Isfahan. Many came reluctantly. Practically overnight, American high school students were in the streets, some on motorcycles, some making out on park benches. Foreign companies had bid up house rents so much that young Iranians couldn't afford them. Iranians were not happy, adding to religious disapproval of the Shah's European style behavior with banquets serving wine, an unveiled Empress Farah in glamorous gowns, and Iran's alliance with the US and Israel. In time these deep cultural conflicts and economic woes built to the point that all political sides came together and overthrew the Shah in 1979, not imagining how the new regime would turn out.

From Isfahan I headed south to Bandar Abbas on the Persian Gulf and took a ferry trip with Don Croll and Heidar to the island of Qeshm. This was a wonderful excursion after years in land-locked Afghanistan. Hilly, dry, and brown, Qeshm, on the beautiful turquoise Persian Gulf, was dotted with oases and towns, with a culture of seamanship and fishing and terrific seafood.

From Qeshm I flew to Bahrain for a two-day interview with the Bahrain Petroleum Company Bapco. I was intrigued by the cosmopolitan local culture, a balanced mix of Persian and Arab, Sunni and Shia, and including subcontinentals from Pakistan and India. Bahrain had been a British Protectorate until 1971 and was instilled with British order, law, and tolerance. On my last day the wharf superintendent got me a job as second pumpman on the American tanker *SS San Antonio* loading jet fuel destined for NATO in France. The next day I put to sea.

After 34 days, we entered the Bay of Biscay and docked in Donges, France. I had learned a great deal and earned $1,195 wages (a lot of money back then!) and studied navigation and the southern hemisphere stars. We had sailed around Africa and run into a Beaufort Scale 10 storm in the Madagascar Channel, plowing through massive seas of up to 40 feet. Luckily, I was one of only two crew who did not get seasick. During the trip King Faisal of Saudi Arabia was assassinated, and I saw that the world was continuing to change. Disembarking at Donges, I caught a train to Paris, and after some touring flew home.

Director Guyer of Peace Corps told me before I left Kabul that Denise Blake's parents were still upset about the circumstances of her death, that they hadn't had enough information and were thinking of taking legal action. He asked if I could help. During the ocean voyage to France, I wrote a fifteen-page letter describing our friendship and how the tragedy had occurred, trying to soothe their still immense grief. Denise was a lovely girl, John and Denise were a unique and happy couple, John somewhat eccentric, and I could understand how difficult it was for them. They wrote to me months later with thanks, and I was relieved that the effort had been successful.

265

Back in the States, I interviewed potential employers in New York and Washington DC, from the State Department, the Asia Society, and the Ford Foundation, as well as in industry. At the State Department I'd need to take the foreign service exam and go thru a lengthy process to be employed, while at the foundations there were only vague possibilities of jobs. I soon had several industry offers using my professional qualifications and accepted a position with Caltex Petroleum Corporation, owner of Bapco, who offered the opportunity to promptly go to Bahrain. I decided to join the oil industry because Peace Corps had transformed me. I wanted to return to the international life, and oil was one of the biggest and most solid of industries.

Living in Manhattan on E 59th St. in 1975 was terrific. It was a liberated decade, and I enjoyed the social life and the theater, museums, movies, clubs, restaurants, exhibitions, and tourist sites of New York. I also had many visitors, not from my popularity (duh!) but because it's great to have a place to stay in the Big Apple, and I was happy to accommodate. Visitors included Peace Corps volunteers from Afghanistan and Malaysia, Werner from Germany, Iranians, and old friends from California and upstate New York. I bought a motorcycle and parked it between a Mercedes and a Rolls Royce in a basement garage a few blocks north. It was super to tour the city at night or ride to Long Island or Westchester. My California friends were disgusted with "dirty, smelly" New York City, at a time when the city was facing bankruptcy and suffering garbage collection strikes.

I was surprised when I returned how I no longer saw skin color, which in Afghanistan varies from light to very dark, and is never an issue. An African American PCV from Atlanta visited me one weekend in Baku Kham and the villagers asked if he was African, only out of curiosity. It's an act of faith in Islam that all people are equal before Allah. Our definition of African Americans as anyone with some African blood had become both inaccurate and sadly often ridiculous. It also reminded me of a Farsi saying that people of mixed race are du nejada, or two races, a meaning of strength, as opposed to the English pejorative of half-breed.

Life in Afghanistan had changed me in other ways, too. I was aware of how much we had of everything, and how much more expensive things were. Also, I was inclined to bargain and had a hilarious experience in Boston with an old high school buddy when I tried to bargain in a liquor store on the price of a bottle of gin. My friend roared with laughter when the shopkeeper ridiculed me and said not here and, yeah, he knew all about it having traveled in Afghanistan on the hippie trail when he was younger. More importantly I realized that culture is defining for everyone, and that we all grow up thinking that how we live and do things is the right way, when in fact, there are many different approaches and ways of life around the globe.

Heidar's brothers Asghar and Daoud and nephew Babuk stayed with me one night en route to San Francisco. The next morning I took them to the Irving Trust Bank in my office building to cash their money. They (and I) were astounded at the midtown NY skyscrapers, unlike anywhere else. I also connected with Zarghuna, Juris and Cathy Stephens. Zarghuna finished her Vermont study, returned to Kabul and after several years married a USIS leader in Kabul and eventually had a daughter and settled in the States. Juris soon married Robin Varnum, and they settled in Massachusetts where they had children and he taught engineering and she English. She has written two terrific books, one on her Peace Corps experience.

Ehsan Lavipour visited from Iran with a batch of copper pots, heading west. Heidar and I visited Billy Frank in Pittsburgh. It was an exuberant time. I got together with Don Croll in the city and my parents' home, and one weekend we went apple picking at his family's orchard in Poughkeepsie. Cathy Stephens studied at Wellesley and then returned to England, ending up working for the British Council. We later met in London and stayed with her. Caltex sent me to Texas for Bapco business. There, at Texas A&M, I saw John Blake a couple of times. It was great seeing him. He had remarried but was still grieving his Afghanistan tragedy.

Heidar and Anne returned to America, and we partied in DC, New York (the City, Mamaroneck and her home in Cazenovia upstate), and New England. They married shortly after I left for Bahrain in September 1976. Most of Heidar's family emigrated to the States in the 1970s, centering around Washington DC and northern California. We have stayed in touch with Heidar and Anne through the years, our children knowing each other from a young age. They visited us in Hong Kong and other places that we lived.

I arrived in Bahrain in September 1976 where development, as in Iran, was exploding, with large numbers of young English-speaking workers from UK, US, Canada, Ireland, Australia, New Zealand, South Africa, and elsewhere in jobs ranging from oil and construction to finance, teaching and the airline industry. Within months I met Eileen Sandford, from Wales of English stock, who was running an English infant school (ages four to seven) that she and another woman had started when the local British infant school had closed. We were married within a year. She took my last name, and friends asked her why she didn't keep her maiden name, a popular convention at the time. She said, "I come from a country with a woman Queen, a woman Prime Minister, and I started my own business in an Arab country. I don't need my maiden name to be who I am, and it'll be more convenient to take my husband's name." On home leave we went camping with Heidar and Anne and Juris and Robin in the White Mountains of New Hampshire.

By 1979 the Shah was gone, and overnight things changed in the Middle East. Where the western women had worn bikinis on the beach and local women rarely came, the locals now went to the beach in numbers and wore swim costumes like my grandmother wore in 1900: full-length flowing dresses covering neck to feet. People were proud, Islam was on the rise and foreigners adopted a lower profile.

That year we visited lifelong family friend Professor Tom Pigford (who co-authored the first textbook of nuclear chemical engineering and had shared a lab at MIT with my dad in 1949–52) and his family in Berkeley. He asked if the Soviet invasion of Afghanistan would be successful. I said that the Afghans were very tough and would never give up. Years later he said I had predicted the Soviet failure, which I had forgotten. And had I? I had also predicted another major war if Mideast peace was not achieved. This was true with multiple intifadas beginning in 1987, the rise of Al Qaeda in the 1990s leading to the Beirut and East Africa bombings and the 911 attack, and now the 2023 Gaza Israel War.

In 1980 Iraq invaded Iran, which led to years of death and destruction. Don Croll decided it was time to leave Tehran. He went to the airport and met the Islamic revolutionary military general in charge. Speaking perfect Farsi he showed his US passport and long-expired Imperial Iranian visa and said, "I think it's time for me to go," asking if he might be allowed to leave. The general told him to come back the next day at four o'clock and he would put him on the Air France flight to Paris, "but don't bring much luggage and don't fail to come." The old rule of "we don't have problems with the American people, only with their government" held true.

After his tour as Ambassador to Afghanistan, Ted Eliot became Dean of the Fletcher School of Diplomacy at Tufts University (my grandad's alma mater from 1904). In 1984 I called Ambassador Eliot seeking career advice, and he was most helpful. I also remember he'd called me into his office in Kabul my last summer to diplomatically rap me on the knuckles for poor behavior one day on the tennis court at the AID Club. I thanked him; he was a man of many distinctions. Eileen and I had lunch with him in 2008 in Santa Rosa. He'd retired to the Sonoma Hills, and I sought advice about my Hong Kong wine import company. He passed in 2019 after a distinguished career.

I saw Marty Kumorek in New York and DC. Sadly, he had not adjusted well from his important role in Afghanistan and died from ill health in the early 2000s. From Robin Varnum I learned only recently that Larry Bennett perished in the Pan Am Lockerbie bombing in 1988, a tragic shame for a fine person and family. I recently spoke with Bill Barlak, who settled in the Bay Area, and finally have reconnected with him. He has published a book of Afghan stories that is currently out of print.

During our nation-building years, Heidar had contracts with US government agencies in Afghanistan. He and my brother Pete had become friends in Washington DC in the late '70s. Pete worked for the World Council of Credit Unions, later in Madison, WI. Heidar brought him into projects in Afghanistan to develop credit unions, and he had several extended stays in Kabul in the early 2000s.

Initially he was thrilled with the vibrancy and ethos of the people and urged me to join him on a visit, but I reluctantly decided not to vacation in a war zone. Regrettably, on his final mission to Kabul, he discovered that the manager had stolen the money, and the credit union had become insolvent. He was infuriated and washed his hands of Afghanistan. Sadly, Heidar died of dementia in 2018, and Pete and I celebrated his life in Virginia with Anne, his extended family and his many friends.

A few years ago, Naim Hakimi, a student of mine at Kabul University, found me on Facebook and we've met and stayed in touch since then. He had an American mother and is well connected with the educated and upper echelons in Kabul. Funnily, he was only a few years younger than I, though the age gap in 1974 had seemed larger. Juris, Naim, and I as well as others have been trying to locate Abdullah Kakar, but he's retired from teaching at Washington State University, and we've been unable to trace him. Mark Svendsen became a professor of hydrology and water engineering and ended up in Washington State, also marrying a former PCV in Afghanistan. In the last year I've contacted Charlie Ferrell, a retired Minneapolis real estate law partner, and Tom Schillinger, retired from his construction and painting business in Pittsburgh. Both have interesting insights about our time in Afghanistan, though after 50 years, we all suffer from loss of memories.

Eileen and I spent most of our adult lives overseas, with Caltex in Bahrain, Australia, Japan, Thailand and Hong Kong, along with New York and Dallas. Our last posting was Hong Kong, where I retired from Caltex in 1999. We stayed until 2015. I managed two consulting companies, and then in 2004 founded a still-operating wine import business. We retired to California in 2016. Our son and daughter grew up attending multiple schools and have successfully found their own paths in life, he in tech and she in law. They have terrific spouses and have blessed us with four grandchildren.

A final irony is that from the time I joined Caltex in Manhattan in 1975, there are those who thought I was in the CIA. I was asked this, even recently, and heard the whispers many times. I visited various countries, often travelled to meetings, and had a supposedly exotic past. The rules when we joined were that nobody who has been in the Peace Corps can ever have anything to do with the CIA. Knowing what we know today, I suppose stuff can happen, but I never had anything to do with the CIA.

Remembering my service, I would like to see national service reintroduced for all American men and women, with institutional choices ranging from the Armed Forces to the Peace Corps, the Coast Guard, the Public Health Service, VISTA, Americorps, Teach for America, and more. It would help all young people, build and improve our nation and bring us closer together.

I also believe that my Peace Corps Afghanistan experience achieved all my objectives and more. I saw the world, learned Farsi and lived in and celebrated the Afghan culture, did my best at two interesting and often challenging teaching jobs and contributed to America's peaceful role in the world, benefiting Afghanistan. Like most volunteers, I also got a lot more out of the experience than I gave and had a lot of fun!

--Tiburon, California, December 2023

Statue "Let us beat swords into plowshares" donated by the USSR in 1959 to the UN, in front of the General Assembly Building in Manhattan, with the Chrysler Building behind. An ironic theme considering the USSR invasion of Afghanistan and subsequent bloody attempts at social revolution

Acknowledgments

Thanks go to lifelong friends Clark Sorensen, anthropology professor at the University of Washington, and Marc Pickard, television journalist and anchor in Atlanta, who reviewed my draft and gave me vision and ideas. My wife Eileen also offered many helpful edits and thoughts. Robin Varnum's fine PC memoir spirited me to get going and her husband Juris Zagarins shared insights and a large collection of photographs over the decades.

Thank you to Anne Masterson Nowrouz, Mark Svendsen and Asghar Nowrouz for helpful inputs. Tony Agnello, whom I knew in Kabul and is today president of Friends of Afghanistan, also added to my understanding. Charlie Ferrell and Tom Schillinger brought memories and Mark Luce shared experiences and writings from his work with the Defense Department during the US and NATO time in Afghanistan.

I will always remember and deeply appreciate now-departed close friends Heidar Nowrouz, Don Croll and Marty Kumorek, my mentors and teachers for years.

I also remember with fondness and appreciation Shirin Jan, Abdullah Kakar, Shah Wali, Deans Zewari and Pashtoon, Ghulam Rasool Kohestani, Hamid Ghazzanfar, Sayid Qamar uDin, Mohamed Saeid Khan, Bart Harvey, Lou Mitchell, Dr. Dean Johnson, John Guyer, Mohamed Assif Khan, Zarghuna Qaderi, John Blake and his departed first wife Denise, Ted and Juanita Tumelaire, Abdul Matin, Mohammed Yasir, Dave Chamberlain and Jaya Dixit.

Robyn Harrison has been my faithful editor and layout designer always with good ideas, clear editing, and quick response. Jason Enterline did a brilliant job of preparing the maps. Thank you also to the Peace Corps Writers organization and Marian Haley Beil, who provide a terrific pro bono service to help us PCVs write our books.

I have gained immeasurably in the past year from reading Ghost Wars and Directorate S by Steve Coll, The Afghanistan Papers by Craig Whitlock, My Three Lives on Earth by Tawab Assifi, and Afghanistan by Martin Ewans. This book is not a history, but I've tried to tell the history as I experienced and learned it, and hope that my work has added to our collective knowledge.

For all errors, I apologize and take responsibility.

Glossary

adam	person in Farsi
Afghanis	the Afghan unit of currency, 90 Afs/$ in 1971
arad	water wheel
asia	water driven flour mill
bacha	boy
bamani khoda	goodbye, literally entrust to God
bolesht	pillow
bukhari	boiler, literally a wood stove
burria	straw mat
buzkashi	goat pulling, Afghan polo played on horse back
chadri	full length Afghan veil
chai khanah	tea house
chaprostie	janitor or caretaker
charagh	lantern
charpoi	four feet, a wooden bed with mattress on rope
char zanu	four knees, sitting cross legged
chinar	plane tree
chowk	intersection
dawa	medicine
dewana khoriji	crazy foreigner
Eid	religious holiday
enshallah	if God wills
fal	fortune, seen in words of poetry
gawdi	two-wheeled cart pulled by a horse
Haj	Muslim pilgrimage to Mecca, one of five pillars of Islam
Haji	a person who has gone on the Haj
halal	food or action permissible in to Islam
haram	food or action forbidden in to Islam
Hindu Kush	Hindu killer, the high mountains of central Afghanistan

iftar	breakfast, the afternoon meal that breaks the fast
jeshun	the holy month of Ramadan, also a celebration
juey	open stream that distributes water
kachalu	potato
kafir	a non-believer in Islam, an infidel
kamar band	waist band
karakul	the soft and curly fleece of an Asian sheep
karoi	a dish of lamb kebab, eggs, tomatoes, onions and herbs
kashook	spoon
khak	earth or dust
khak bod	dust wind, a dust storm
khana	house or home
khanook khordi	cold eaten, meaning to become cold
khar	donkey or ass
Khoda	God
Khoda hafiz	God keep (you), meaning goodbye
khoriji	outsiders, meaning foreigners
kilim	a wool, short nap woven floor covering
kilinar	cleaner, the assistant to a driver
koh	mountain, becomes Kohi in the name of the range
Kohi Baba	granddad mountains
Kohi Daman	mountain skirt, the plain northeast of Kabul
Kohistan	mountain land
Kohistani	mountain people
koochi	nomad, mostly Pashtuns traveling on camels
lalmy	unirrigated, dry farmed land
Loya jirga	grand council, a meeting of elders
lycée	high school, from French
mirgun	hunting guide
mudir	director
mullah	Muslim preacher
murdar	unclean, rotten

naan	Afghan unleavened bread, whole wheat and barley
naqal	to transfer, cheating on a test by giving answers to another
neswar	Afghan snuff, green powder of tobacco and white lime
Nowroz	literally new day, New Year, the first day of spring
panjah	fork
Pashtun	an ethnic Afghan or Pakhtoon or Pathan
PCV	Peace Corps Volunteer
PDPA	People's Democratic Party of Afghanistan
pilau	rice pilaf
qabuli pilau	a rice dish with raisins, sliced carrots and almonds
RPCV	Returned Peace Corps Volunteer
sandali	coffee table heated by hot coals, covered with a quilt
shamal	north
shamali	a northerner
sharab	alcohol or liquor
talkhon	food made of ground walnuts and dried mulberries
tawildar	caretaker or janitor
tushak	mattress, fluffed cotton in a cotton cover
WT	world traveler, euphemism for hippy

Bibliography

"14. Telegram HAKTO 76 From Secretary of State Kissinger to the President's Deputy Assistant for National Security Affairs" (Scowcroft). Washington, November 1, 1974, 1300Z.

Assifi, Tawab. (2015) *My Three Lives on Earth: The Life Story of an Afghan American*. Bloomington, IN: Author House.

Babur, Zahiruddin Muhammad, translated by Annette Beveridge. (1922) *The Babur-nama in English*. London: Luzac and Co.

Coll, Steve. (2004) *Ghost Wars: the Secret History of the CIA, Afghanistan and Bin Laden, from the Soviet Invasion to September 10, 2001*. New York: Penguin Press.

Coll, Steve. (2018) *Directorate S: the CIA and America's Secret Wars in Afghanistan and Pakistan*. New York: Penguin Press.

Dupree, Nancy Hatch. (1967) *The Road to Balkh*. Kabul: The Afghan Tourist Organization.

Dupree, Nancy Hatch. (1971) *An Historical Guide to Afghanistan*. Kabul: Afghan Tourist Organization.

Elphinstone, Mountstuart. (1839) *An Account of the Kingdom of Caubul, and its Dependencies, in Persia, Tartary, and India*. London: Richard Bentley.

Elwell Sutton. (1963) *Elementary Persian Grammar*. London: Cambridge University Press.

Ewans, Martin. (2002) *Afghanistan: A Short History of Its People and Politics*. New York: Harper Collins.

Frye, Richard N. (1963) *The Heritage of Persia*. Cleveland, OH: The World Publishing Company.

Glubb, John Bagot. (1970) *The Life and Times of Muhammad*. London: Hodder and Stoughton.

Hitti, Philip. (1970) *Islam: A Way of Life*. South Bend, IN: Regnery/ Gateway.

Hodson, Peregrine. (1968) *Under a Sickle Moon: A Journey Through Afghanistan*. New York: The Atlantic Monthly Press.

Irwin, Frances Hopkins and Irwin, Will A. (2014) *The Early Years of Peace Corps in Afghanistan: a Promising Time.* Oakland, CA: A Peace Corps Writers Book.

Klass, Rosanne. (1964) *Land of the High Flags: A Travel Memoir of Afghanistan.* New York: Random House.

Konishi, Masatoshi. (1969) *This Beautiful World,* Vol. 7: Afghanistan. Palo Alto, CA: Kodansha International Ltd.

Levi, Peter. (1972) *The Light Garden of the Angel King: Journeys in Afghanistan.* Indianapolis/New York: The Bobbs-Merrill Company, Inc.

Macrory, Patrick. (1966) *Signal Catastrophe: The Story of the Disastrous Retreat from Kabul, 1842.* London: Hodder and Stoughton.

Matheson, Sylvia A. (1973) *Persia, An Archaeolgical Guide.* Noyes Press

Matheson, Sylvia. (1961) *Time Off to Dig: Archaeology and Adventure in Remote Afghanistan.* London: Odhams Press Limited.

"Memorandum of Conversation, Kabul, November 1, 1974, 10:10–11:30." Office of the Historian, Department of State, Foreign Relations of the United States, 1969–1976, Volume E–8, Documents on South Asia, 1973–1976, 15.

Sachar, Howard M. (1969) *The Emergence of the Middle East: 1914–1925.* New York: Alfred A. Knopf.

Sale, Florentia. (1843) *A Journal of the First Afghan War.* Hamden, Connecticut: Archon Books.

Varnum, Robin. (2021) *Afghanistan at a Time of Peace.* Oakland, CA: Peace Corps Writers.

Whitlock, Craig. (2021) *The Afghanistan Papers: A Secret History of the War.* New York: Simon & Schuster.

About the Author

   Guy Toby Marion, known as Toby, is pictured here with his wife Eileen in San Francisco in 2021. They currently live in Tiburon, California, having spent most of their working life together from 1977 to 2015 living in Bahrain, Australia, New York, Dallas, Japan, Thailand, and Hong Kong. Toby worked in a multinational oil company, two consulting companies and his own wine distributorship in Hong Kong. He has a BS in Engineering from Cornell, MS in Chemical Engineering Practice from MIT and a Graduate Diploma in Business Administration from the University of Sydney. He has enjoyed studying languages and in retirement plays tennis and sails, while enjoying family. Eileen is an avid quilter, a terrific Granny and a homemaker and advisor par excellence.

Toby can be contacted at   tobymarion.kabul@gmail.com.
This is his first book.

Made in United States
Troutdale, OR
02/22/2024

17884444R00157